DREAMTIME
AND
DREAMWORK

This *New Consciousness Reader*
is part of a new series of original
and classic writing by renowned experts on
leading-edge concepts in personal development,
psychology, spiritual growth, and healing.

Other books in this series include:

Healers on Healing
EDITED BY RICHARD CARLSON, PH.D., AND BENJAMIN SHIELD

Reclaiming the Inner Child
EDITED BY JEREMIAH ABRAMS

Spiritual Emergency
EDITED BY STANISLAV GROF, M.D., AND CHRISTINA GROF

To be a Woman
EDITED BY CONNIE ZWEIG

What Survives?
EDITED BY GARY DOORE, PH.D.

Also by Stanley Krippner:

Song of the Siren: A Parapsychological Odyssey

*Dreamworking: How to Use
Your Dreams for Creative Problem-Solving*
WITH JOSEPH DILLARD

Healing States
WITH ALBERTO VILLOLDO

The Realms of Healing
WITH ALBERTO VILLOLDO

Dream Telepathy: Experiments in Nocturnal ESP
WITH MONTAGUE ULLMAN AND ALAN VAUGHAN

*Personal Mythology:
The Psychology of Your Evolving Self*
WITH DAVID FEINSTEIN

DREAMTIME
AND
DREAMWORK

Decoding the Language of the Night

EDITED BY

STANLEY KRIPPNER, PH.D.

JEREMY P. TARCHER, INC.
Los Angeles

Library of Congress Cataloging-in-Publication Data

Dreamtime and dreamwork : decoding the language of the night / edited
   by Stanley Krippner.
      p. cm.
   Includes bibliographical references.
   ISBN 0-87477-594-9 (pbk.) : $12.95
      1. Dreams. 2. Symbolism (Psychology) I. Krippner, Stanley.
1932—   .   90-40390
BF1091.D77 1990   CIP
154.6 '3—dc20

Jeremy P. Tarcher, Inc.
5858 Wilshire Blvd., Suite 200
Los Angeles, CA 90036

Distributed by St. Martin's Press, New York

Manufactured in the United States of America
10   9   8   7   6   5   4   3   2

For

Dr. Robert L. Van de Castle

dreamworker extraordinaire

Contents

PART VI
FRONTIERS IN DREAMWORK

Acknowledgments

I would like to thank the contributors to this book for their creativity, diligence, and patience during the conceptualization and revision of their chapters. I would also like to express my gratitude to Connie Zweig, our editor at Jeremy P. Tarcher, Inc. Her shrewd judgment and hard work were evident from the book's origins to its publication.

Stanley Krippner

Preface

Consciousness researchers, psychotherapists, and neuroscientists have used several major vehicles to explore the vast reaches of the human mind—meditation, hypnosis, drugs, biofeedback, free association, and even brain imaging devices. But in many ways, dreams have been the most useful. Despite their bizarre narratives and puzzling imagery, dream reports are fairly easy to obtain from anyone in a sleep laboratory or through dream diaries.

The night's first period of dreaming generally begins 90 minutes after you fall asleep. The neurons at the base of your skull start to fire a random barrage of high-voltage impulses that unleash a cascade of potent chemicals pouring into your forebrain. There, your visual and motor centers are stimulated, triggering memories that are presented and combined in original, vivid, and often baffling ways. Immediately, your brain's mind creates a story that will make sense of these fragments, either providing a script that has waited patiently for the material that would allow it to surface or producing a narrative on the spot that matches—as best it can—the images and activities that have been kindled.

Sometimes these stories reflect basic problems in living with which you have wrestled for years; at other times they reflect the events of the past few days or hours, some trivial, some consequential. And in still other instances, as far as we know, the mind's search for meaning produces what seems to be little more than a jumble of disparate pictures and events. This process of tale-telling and story-making is remarkably similar to what transpires when you use language while awake. Dreams can be thought of as a language of the night.

Some tribal groups spoke of the "dreamtime"—a sacred or heroic era from the past that can only rarely be obtained in the present. Dreamtime can be evoked through nighttime dreams, through daytime visions, and through rituals involving storytelling, singing, dancing, and painting. In this book, we will use the term to refer to the thoughts, feelings, and images that are arranged into narrative form while we are asleep. But it is important to recall that its use by native people is broader, referring to more concepts and experiences than those found in nighttime dream content.

The mental and emotional processes involved in dreamtime are similar in many ways to the thoughts and feelings experienced during wakefulness. People who were asked to make up a dream while awake produced accounts that judges could not discriminate from written reports of their nighttime dreams.[1]

When you record your dreams, you write a report that typically connects a series of action-oriented images that are usually visual. Many scientists (including myself) believe that these reports can help you to understand your behavior, experiences, and intentions. Many psychotherapists are convinced that their clients will benefit from an understanding of their dreams because, on reflection, dream activities appear to be metaphors for our waking concerns. And it is often helpful to find a metaphorical image or activity for a personal problem.

Some writers, artists, and other creative people have made deliberate use of their dream narratives and images in their work. An even larger number of individuals have claimed that their scientific, technological, athletic, or artistic breakthroughs resulted from dreams that were serendipitously recalled. For example, Harriet Tubman claimed that her dreams helped her to locate the routes for the "underground railroad" that rescued hundreds of slaves in the years before the Civil War. Jack Nicklaus discovered a golf swing in a dream that brought him out of a slump. Elizabeth Rauscher, a physicist, told me about solving some difficult equations in a dream and showed me the scientific journal in which her results were published. Leo Katz, a visionary artist, showed me paintings that originally took form in his dreams.

I first began to record my dreams when I was in high school, but my interest was dampened when one of my university professors reported that dreaming in color was a symptom of schizophrenia. About the same time, investigators at the University of Chicago had discovered that dreams are naturally occurring phenomena that take place periodically during the night, usually during stages of rapid eye movement (REM) sleep.[2] Soon afterward, it was observed that most dreams contain color,[3] although color is easily forgotten and often omitted from dream reports.

A dozen years later, I became director of a dream laboratory at Maimonides Medical Center in Brooklyn. We conducted the first study of dream diaries kept by pre-operative male transsexuals. We found that their dreams resembled neither the typical male nor the typical female dream of that decade, but fell someplace in between. For example, the participants had as many dreams about outdoor streets as the average woman, but far more than the average man. The dream content reflected their concerns during wakefulness and suggested a continuum between dreaming life and waking life.[4]

We also conducted one of the first studies of pregnant women's dreams, observing an unusually high number of references to architecture, small animals, and family members. Dreams about family members should not be unexpected at a time when the dreamer's family is a frequent concern. But what secrets did architecture and animals hold? The small animals might have been symbols for the fetus, while the buildings might have represented the pregnancy itself—"building" the baby inside the mother's womb.[5]

Our laboratory was best known for studies that investigated unusual or anomalous communication during dreamtime, such as telepathy. Our basic research procedure was to fasten electrodes to the head of a subject, take him or her to a soundproof room, then randomly select a sealed, opaque envelope containing a colorful art print. A psychologist would then take the envelope to a distant room, open it, and study the print while the laboratory subject (in bed and asleep) attempted to incorporate material from the art print into his or her dreams without ever seeing it.[6] Upon completion of a series of experiments, outside judges compared the typed dream reports with the total collection of art prints, attempting to identify the print used on the night of each experiment. We obtained statistically significant results about two out of three times, with odds against chance so great that coincidence was unlikely. For these experimental studies, the results were considered to be anomalous because there was no obvious, logical way to explain the correspondences between the dream reports and the art prints. For example, one subject dreamed about going to Madison Square Garden to buy tickets to a boxing match. On that same night, the psychologist in a distant room was focusing his attention on a painting of a boxing match!

Such prominent dream researchers as David Foulkes, Gordon Globus, Calvin Hall, and Robert Van de Castle attempted to replicate our findings.[7] Because the replication rate from other laboratories was inconsistent, we did not claim to have conclusively demonstrated that communication in dreams can sometimes transcend space and time; however, we did open a promising line of investigation.[8]

Next, I reviewed the entire body of research data, focusing on the first night that each subject in a telepathy experiment had visited our laboratory. A colleague and I matched the results of these nights with data collected at weather stations, discovering that the subjects' telepathy was higher during calm nights with little sunspot activity than during nights marked by electrical storms and high sunspot activity. These results indicate a potentially predictable pattern in such events and an association with the environment that may lead to a natural explanation of anomalous events.[9]

After a decade of laboratory work, I joined the faculty of Saybrook Institute, a graduate school in San Francisco that gives a high priority to the study of human consciousness. Many of our students have used dreamtime and dreamwork as the topic for their doctoral dissertations, among them Patricia Maybruck, who contributed a chapter on pregnancy and dreams to this volume. In addition to my academic work at Saybrook, I co-lead a dream group with a friend who is a psychotherapist. I also attend a leaderless dream group to share and discuss my own dreams.

During the span of time in which I have worked with dreams, I have met most of the pioneering dreamworkers who share their knowledge with the readers of this book. The authors of these chapters, who work in several different countries, represent a variety of disciplines and a range of orientations. Many of them have contributed to *The Dream Network Journal* (P.O. Box 1321, Port Townsend, WA 98368), a periodical that reports current dreamwork developments. An educational group that deserves special mention is the Dream Educators Network (P.O. Box 788, Cooperstown, NY 11326).

Three of the authors (Gayle Delaney, Ernest Hartmann, and Jayne I. Gackenbach) are past presidents of the Association for the Study of Dreams (P.O. Box 3121, Falls Church, VA 22043). This group of professional and non-professional dreamworkers and dreamers boasted over 500 members at the time of its sixth annual convention in London and even more when it met in Chicago in 1990.

This book is dedicated to another former president of the association, Robert Van de Castle, who has developed content analysis methods by which he has studied cross-cultural and age differences as well as dreams of psychiatric patients and of women during their menstrual cycles and pregnancies, Van de Castle also has studied anomalous dreams both as a researcher and as a subject.[10]

Dreamtime and Dreamwork marks a growing recognition that dreams are no longer the exclusive province of the shaman, the priest, or the psychoanalyst. There is an emerging awareness, in both the public and professional world, that dreamtime and its products properly belong to the dreamer.

I

Current Trends in Dreamwork

A dream which is not understood is like a letter which is not opened.
TALMUD

We have learned from dreamwork that there is often a sharp contrast between the significance of the dream to the dreamer and the significance of the dream for the social context in which the dream occurs.[1] The first chapter of this book is a provocative description of the spiritual dimension of dreams by Louis Savary, a spiritual counselor and former Jesuit priest. The next chapter gives a vivid account of the "grassroots" dream movement written by Deborah Hillman, an anthropologist. Our exploration of cutting-edge approaches in dreamworking concludes with a superb rendition by David Feinstein, a psychotherapist, of how dreams can be used to help dreamers identify their personal myths and decide whether they want to keep them.

These authors discuss three different approaches to dreamworking. But like the other dreamworkers represented in this volume, they all see the value of recording and working with the language of the night. I am in agreement with psychotherapist Rollo May who takes the position that "we can often get a more accurate and meaningful picture of the significant changes in the patient's life from the symbols and myths he creates and then molds and re-creates in his dream existence than we can from what he says."[2]

Since 1980, David Feinstein and I have conducted workshops in various parts of the world in which we elicit personal myths from people's dreams.[3] For me, myths are imaginative statements or stories that address important concerns and issues and that have direct consequences for people's behavior. There are cultural, ethnic, institutional, family, and personal myths, among others. Rather than being judged as "true" or "false," myths can be evaluated

3

as functional or dysfunctional in regard to growth, development, and the attaining of goals set by a group or an individual.

Dreams appear to synthesize the dreamer's existing mythic structures with the information gleaned by life experience. Personal myths seem to develop in a manner that is parallel to the way dreams develop because they are related to the brain's propensity for language, imagery, and story-telling. These are the raw materials for myth, and I believe that dreams play an active role in the ongoing revision of the dreamer's personal mythology.[4]

After listening to my workshop participants use dreams to discover their personal myths, I tabulated the themes that appeared most frequently. Curiously, these themes appeared in pairs of polar opposites, often within the same dream. Some dreams—and personal myths—centered around achievement, while others focused on failure. Many dreams contained stories of nurturance, while others centered on deprivation. Other polarities were creation and destruction, completion and fragmentation, affirmation and cynicism, acceptance and rejection, empowerment and debilitation, reconciliation and alienation, wisdom and ignorance, loyalty and betrayal, intimacy and separation, questing and passivity, and death and rebirth.

One of my students at Saybrook, Michael Pieracci, wrote his doctoral dissertation on the topic of mythic themes in stories people told about their psychotherapy experiences. When he applied my list of mythic themes to these stories, he found that, of twenty stories, eleven contained the questing theme and none contained its opposite, the passivity theme. Thus, we might say that for many clients, the psychotherapeutic process resembles the "Hero's Journey" that psychoanalyst Carl Jung felt best described the psychotherapy experience.[5] However, the themes of wisdom, acceptance, nurturance, and intimacy also appeared frequently. Two of these themes, questing and wisdom, are concerned with *achieving* something, while the other three involve *receiving* something.

Based on this analysis, Pieracci concluded that Jung was only half right. The Hero's Journey is a major theme in psychotherapy experiences, but it does not predominate. The Search for Relationship, in one form or another, is an alternative theme for psychotherapy clients. Sometimes the two themes are combined. One of Pieracci's clients told a story in which he was "just in search of someone to understand me," and he concluded by stating, "I'll always search for love; it's part of my blood."[6]

One of my workshop participants demonstrated the polarities of intimacy and separation in his dreams as well as in his personal life. Jeff, a successful writer who appeared to be leading a fulfilling life, found himself unable to achieve closeness. He returned home one evening, having just ended a relationship with a woman who seemed desirable in every way. Not knowing why he had acted so irrationally, and despairing that he would ever be capable of a long-lasting relationship, he fell asleep. A few hours later, he awoke with a start. Jeff had dreamed that he had entered the basement of a house. Hearing a muffled sound, he walked to the corner of the room where his attention was drawn to a plastic bag. In the bag, he recognized his own face; it was screaming loudly, the voice all but inaudible because of the covering plastic container.

Jeff was able to dismiss this dream, but it recurred over the next few months in one form or another. He made an appointment with a psychologist, who began to discuss his early relationships with women. As an adult, Jeff had paid little attention to memories of his childhood. His recollections were unpleasant, because his father was rarely at home and his alcoholic mother had subjected him to various types of physical abuse.

One day, while working with his psychotherapist, Jeff recalled his mother walking around in a drunken stupor, complaining about his whimpering and crying. In her frustration, she attempted to place a plastic bag over Jeff's head to muffle the sounds. Jeff summoned all of his strength to push away the bag to prevent suffocation and ran away until his mother became sober. From that time on, he never allowed his mother to hear his whimpers or see his tears for fear that she would again try to suffocate him.

Upon reflection, Jeff realized that his behavior had been directed by the following personal myth: "Don't let women see you cry or you will be suffocated." This sentence expressed a myth of considerable proportions, one that had become embedded at deep levels of his psyche (symbolized by the basement in his dream). It mirrored cultural myths in which Medusa and Kali figures kill young men who show any sign of tenderness, compassion, or weakness, and it effectively kept Jeff from sharing his intimate feelings with the women he dated.

The breakup of Jeff's most recent love affair had demonstrated the dysfunctional aspects of this personal myth. His psychotherapist effectively used this incident as an impetus for change and a new myth eventually evolved: "Crying can be liberating, even though it needs to be shared selectively." Eventually, Jeff was able to obtain satisfaction in his relationships with women. In fact, his overall quality of life improved significantly as he modified his defensiveness and became open to sharing thoughts and feelings.[7]

Jeff's story serves as a preview of this section, which discusses the value of using dreams to explore a sense of community, life's spiritual dimensions, and our personal myths. To cite Rollo May, "Dreaming has some connection with man's distinctive capacity for transcendence, *i.e.*, his capacity to break through the immediate objective limits of existence and bring together into one dramatic union diverse dimensions of experience."[8]

Louis M. Savary

Dreams for Personal and Spiritual Growth

From earliest recorded history, people have observed their dreams and found in them a source of meaning, wisdom, and guidance. Through the centuries, the dream was presumed to be a spiritual event, a gift of God or a gift from some source beyond the ordinary. And, in all major religions and most minor ones, of both East and West, dreamwork was an accepted spiritual practice. In many religious and spiritual traditions—from the most primitive to the most civilized cultures—the dream was viewed as a holistic event, an experience reflecting the wholeness of the individual. Sometimes, as in biblical and shamanic traditions, the dream was viewed as benefitting not only the individual dreamer, but also the entire community to which the dream belonged.[1]

In contrast, among Christians the practice of dreamwork has been discouraged for the past centuries by the official Church, probably because, in the Church's eyes, dream interpretation has turned from a spiritual activity into a superstitious one. By the fifth century, it seemed many Christians were no longer using dreamwork to develop their moral and spiritual growth, but rather to predict their fortunes and further their material goals. As one person put it, "Many Christians were no longer interested in the God-life, but only in the 'good' life." Even so, dreamwork continued to be practiced throughout those centuries by holy Christian men and women, many of whom were canonized as saints by the Roman Catholic Church. Now, in the present generation, the practice of dreamwork is again finding a place in Christian spirituality as it had throughout the first five centuries of the nascent Christian Church.[2]

SPIRITUALITY AND CONCIOUSNESS

I define spirituality as "a way of being, acting in light of ultimate values." According to this definition, all persons, by virtue of their nature as spiritual, value-seeking beings, have a potential spirituality. Their ultimate values may be conscious or outside of awareness, healthy or destructive. In turn, the spirituality that is built upon those values may be clear or confused, simple or complex. Part of my work as a "technician" of the spiritual path is helping people bring their spirituality to light.

I have learned through my experience that dreams can help you clarify and live up to your ultimate values. Clarifying and living up to those values is a major part of the process of becoming conscious.

Consciousness is a very important term in spirituality, but not one whose definition is universally agreed upon. For some, consciousness refers to awareness, perceptions, thoughts, and feelings; for others, it implies intention and will. Strephon Kaplan Williams, with whom I wrote *Dreams and Spiritual Growth*,[3] gave a simple and clear definition of the term: "Consciousness is awareness PLUS appropriate action." According to this definition, an insight never becomes truly conscious until you somehow put it into action in your daily life.

Spiritual practices, such as meditation or dreamwork, serve as ways of tapping into your inner resources, so that insights from these resources may be brought back and integrated into your ordinary life choices. I believe that spiritual practice is primarily a matter of consciousness, as defined above, and that a spiritual practice is complete only when the insights and gifts it releases are being incarnated in your life. Spirituality almost always involves values and choices being made in everyday activity.

For example, a forty-year-old woman named Marie dreamed that she had given birth to twins. Though one of the infants was well-loved and healthy, the other had been forgotten. Not only was the forgotten child hungry and angry but its head had also, somehow, become completely encased in a seamless golden metal mask.

This dream did not make any decisions or choices for Marie. Rather, based on the data revealed by the dream and her dreamwork, she made choices about nurturing parts of her life that had been forgotten and masked over. On one level, most dreams metaphorically reveal what is going on in your life and portray a current situation in a fresh light, from which you can grow spiritually. In spiritual practice, the waking ego becomes conscious by raising insight to the level of action. When using dreams and dreamwork as an authentic spiritual practice, there is no substitute for ego-reflection and choicemaking.

In almost all traditions, the purpose of bringing the discipline of spiritual practice into your life is to live more in line with your goals and higher life-purposes. The call to a full and whole life is often experienced during the moments of spiritual practice with striking clarity. During dreamwork, Marie realized that the angry cry of the forgotten and hungry child in her dream was a clear call to live her life more fully and wholly, as well as an indication that she had the inner strength to do what was required. From the standpoint of spiritual growth, the purpose of dreamwork, as with other spiritual practices, is to tap into the deepest resources of your self in order to bring up hidden potentials and integrate them into your waking life, that is, bring them into consciousness.

SOME PREMISES OF DREAMS AND SPIRITUALITY

Here are a few of the premises, or assumptions, about dreams and spirituality that I hold. Many of you also may study dreams from other perspectives. As a psychologist, a physician, a neurologist, or other practitioner, you may not hold some of these premises; it is not unusual in science even to hold some contradictory positions. For example, two psychotherapists may hold contradictory premises about the function of emotions, yet both may be successful in helping people. Or two physicists may hold contradictory assumptions about the physical universe, yet both may create valid mathematical equations to describe physical reality. As long as people listen to each other, I believe they can undoubtedly learn from one another. As a technician of the spiritual realm, I focus on the spiritual aspects of dreams and dreamwork.

The dream is usually presented symbolically and/or in the language of metaphor. In some ways, your dreams may speak a universal language, and therefore they belong not only to you but to the larger community. Others may find wisdom for themselves in your dream. Many people who have heard Marie tell her dream of the golden mask have been able to acknowledge that they, too, have gone through life wearing masks. Metaphor is the dominant language of spirituality. Dreams provide holistic data in metaphoric form for the choices and decisions that the waking ego—the choice-making part of the personality—will be called upon to make.

The dream is, among other things, a spiritual event. Many have called the dream "the voice of the soul." Your dream presents symbolically the options available to you—and others—at the level of the human spirit. During her dream, Marie discovered her resourcefulness by telephoning a goldsmith, who agreed to come and remove the mask. As a result of dreamwork, she decided to work with a therapist to help her remove the emotional masks she wore in daily life.

The dream can provide healing and wholeness. It is, in part, the dream's purpose to put you in touch with your ultimate values. It can get you involved in your own development and growth. Marie realized that the golden mask would need to be removed before she could become a whole person. Others, too, have found wisdom and healing insights for themselves from her dream.

The dream releases energy or insight. It is possible for you to bring the dream's insights into waking life and integrate them into the choices you make at the conscious level. Sometimes, the waking ego's ranking of ultimate values is dysfunctional or conflictual. When this happens, the deepest self, in dreams, is likely to reveal the problem. For example, upon reflection, Marie began to recognize her own anger at being forced by her family to live behind a mask for most of her adult life, and she realized she wanted to begin living in an emotionally honest way.

The dream allows your waking ego to establish a relationship with your deepest self. From the spiritual technician's perspective, dreamwork offers a way for building and using a line of communication between the waking ego and the deepest inner self. For Carl Jung, this self is the center and integrator of all life experiences, conscious and unconscious. Establishing a relationship between the waking ego and the inner self is perhaps your most important spiritual task in bringing yourself to spiritual maturity.

In light of spiritual growth, the dream is more powerful when viewed as a question rather than as an answer. A question invites growth in any relationship much more effectively than a command, especially in the ego–self relationship. Questions evoke consciousness. Marie discovered that her golden mask posed many questions: "How did I forget this other child I had? How did the golden mask get put on the child? Do I sometimes find my mask valuable to me? What professionals would help me take it off?"

The dream is incomplete without dreamwork. In spirituality, the dream is the gift; dreamwork is what we do with it. Like a gift, the dream is meant to be opened, used, and cherished. Since a dream often speaks a universal language and triggers insights in others beside the dreamer, I believe the richness of its gifts may sometimes be more fully recognized when dreamwork is done with a partner or in a small dreamwork group. Nevertheless, it remains the dreamer's task to realize the dream's healing insight.

In pursuit of spiritual growth, the purpose of dreams and dreamwork is to bring you to higher levels of consciousness—that is, to awareness plus appropriate action. Marie found that her mask dream was of such profound depth and meaning that for the next ten years she continued to profit from dreamwork on it. She discovered she had been wearing layers of masks, and as one layer was taken off, another was discovered beneath it.

Dreamwork provides a way to channel the energy and insights of the dream into daily life. For Sigmund Freud, dreams were the royal road to the unconscious. The unconscious realm was a boiling cauldron of energy, and dreams led to this energy source. For Freud's disciple Carl Jung, dreams used symbols to reveal different kinds of energies in the unconscious realm that were available to us in waking life. Jung called these energy sources archetypes. For Jung, archetypes were bundles of energy, like the myriad strands of electrical wire bundled together in a power cable carrying energy from one place to another. Dreams and dreamwork can be used to release these spiritual energies. Whenever Marie worked on her golden-mask dream, she found energy to make everyday choices that helped her put aside the mask.

In the Western tradition, spiritual energies are called virtues. (*Virtus* is the Latin work for energy.) In the Eastern traditions, these energies are associated with spiritual energy centers called *chakras.* Major spiritual energies include creativity, the transmitting of life, self-awareness, courage, forgiveness, empathy, willpower, wisdom, meaning, discernment, unity, vision, and cosmic perspectives.

DREAM TASKS

Many approaches to dreams simply help you find meaning in them; so that once you have discovered what your dream is all about, the problem is considered solved and the process is over. Perhaps in certain approaches to the dream, it is enough to stop there. But in spiritual practice, which involves the way you live and act in light of your ultimate values, the purpose of the dream and dreamwork is consciousness: awareness plus appropriate action.

For this reason, the final step in dreamwork is to turn the energy and insight of the dream into choices and actions. At this stage, it is up to the waking ego, after reflecting on the energy and insight of the dream, to make choices for living and acting in the world. The easiest and most effective way of doing this is to create a list of possible dream tasks that could be accomplished to keep the energy of the dream alive, then to choose some of these tasks and actually carry them out.

Why actually carry them out? If you don't use the energy released in the dream, it will slip back into the unconscious and no longer be as readily available. How many of us have had insights about our lives that we recognized as important, intended to do something about them, but never turned those insights into concrete tasks? Consequently, our lives were never changed. The great insight soon became merely a vague memory, taking up a forgotten line or two in our personal journal. Marie kept her golden-mask dream alive by returning to it periodically over a period of years.

Furthermore, the accomplishment of such tasks keeps the energy of the dream alive and growing. The more Marie used her gift, the more that energy became available to her. This principle is true in all domains of life: the more you exercise your muscles, the stronger they become and the more energy they make available to you. The more you discipline yourself to keep the dream energy alive, the more access you have to it. If your dream reveals to you that you have the courage to face an important issue in your life, create a set of tasks to keep that energy alive and exercise that courage. In doing so, you will develop courage to face not only that particular issue but future issues as well.

There are three different kinds of dream tasks that you can use to keep the energy of the dream alive.[4] The first are *Dreamwork Tasks,* techniques to clarify and nurture the energy revealed by the dream or by a symbol within it. Dreamwork tasks might include reflecting on dream symbols, having a dialogue with a dream figure, bringing an unfinished dream to resolution, and using artwork to concretize a dream image. For example, Marie conducted dialogues with her dream figures—the mask itself, the good baby, the forgotten baby, and the goldsmith—and all of them had wisdom for her. She also researched the meaning of "mask" and "persona" in the writings of Jung.

The second kind of dream tasks are *Personality Tasks.* These are *inner activities* that you, your dreamwork partner, or someone acting as a spiritual technician (such as a member of the clergy, a spiritual director, or a shaman) might suggest to keep the dream energy alive. Personality tasks might involve you in making a list of the ways you are like or unlike a certain dream figure, jotting down what positive things might happen if you were to incorporate dream energy into your daily life, or practicing some reflection or personal discipline that keeps you connected with the dream energy, such as marking down every time you affirm yourself. Marie made lists of the places in society where she still wore her golden mask and of the diminishments to her life the mask had caused. She even attended a mask-making workshop.

The third set of dream tasks are *Outer Life Tasks*. These are *outer activities* that you or your dreamwork partner might suggest to keep the dream energy alive. Outer Life Tasks might include taking actions that involve other people or the work you do. If your dream revealed that you had the energy to enhance your courage, you might choose to practice a simple act of assertiveness, or to stand up for yourself among your friends, or to write a letter of complaint to some company. Not only did Marie enter psychotherapy, but she also realized that without the mask she might appear angry and critical, so she chose to tolerate these unfamiliar feelings and consciously express them appropriately in public as validation that she was indeed removing her mask. Notice how each of these three kinds of dream tasks support and enrich each other.

The objective with dream tasks is to choose tasks to keep the energy alive, not to exhaust it. Therefore, you should choose tasks that you are able to accomplish in a finite amount of time and at which you are likely to succeed. Success breeds success, and a successful expression of dream energy is most likely to keep that energy alive. It is best to have a string of successes to keep you motivated and actively involved.

I believe dreamwork has made a revolutionary contribution to spirituality in recent years. Dreamwork is really a spiritual exercise that almost everyone can learn with some degree of proficiency and use effectively without having to depend upon someone else as a dream expert. Versatile and adaptable, it can be used individually, with partners, and in small dreamwork groups.

Since you dream every night, there is never a dearth of material for spiritual growth. On the other hand, there is no need to become compulsively attached to the dreamwork process. You may use it regularly without engaging in it compulsively. You don't need to do it every day. Whenever you choose to explore your dream resources, your deepest inner self will help you realize your true potential.

Deborah Jay Hillman

The Emergence of the Grassroots Dreamwork Movement

As an anthropology student in the late 1970s, I had the good fortune of meeting Montague Ullman. For several years he had been developing and teaching his small-group approach to dreams,[1] and when I heard him discuss it during a public lecture one evening, I knew that I wanted to learn more. A correspondence followed, then my first workshop in Ullman's method, and soon I was embarked on a year of participant observation in one of Ullman's weekly dream groups in New York City. It was from this vantage point that I began to see the signs of a more widespread interest in dreams in American culture. From 1979 to 1982, I explored this incipient movement, visiting groups and workshops and interviewing dreamers, primarily in and near New York City. I have since stayed close to the movement as a participant in the ordinary sense, as well as an informal observer.

Elsewhere I have written about the dreamwork movement and its relationship to the anthropological study of dreams.[2] Here I will draw on that earlier discussion to help outline a context for dream groups. It is important to note that although I focus on the dreamwork scene in America, this development extends to other Western countries as well. Moreover, in light of the cultural link between dreams and the concept of "reality,"[3] it makes sense that change is starting to take place in Western dream ideology.

For more than two decades (paralleling the upsurge of interest in dreams), a flowering of scientific research on the nature of consciousness has been occurring.[4] There is evidence that the underlying shift to a more unified view of reality, giving due weight to subjective phenomena, applies "not only to all the sciences but also to the humanities and to contemporary thought in general."[5] So as our conventional dualism, with its stress on objectivity and reason, is challenged by a more holistic model, dreams, along with other kinds of inner experience, take on new value and significance. The dreamwork movement, by encouraging public and scholarly attention to dreams, both reflects and supports the cognitive revision taking place in the culture at large.

"Dream groups are popping up like pottery classes out there," wrote one of my fieldwork correspondents, following a trip to California at the start of the 1980s. It was only a short time later, in 1982 and 1983, that the term *dreamwork movement* surfaced in popular usage. Several different paths, including that of the human potential movement, have led people to the practice of dreamwork in recent decades. One of these has been participation in a metaphysical or spiritual organization, such as the Association for Research and Enlightenment (devoted to the work of the American psychic Edgar Cayce) or the Spiritual Frontiers Fellowship. In addition, for many women, the feminist movement has been an avenue toward awareness of dreams, presenting dreamwork as a means of deepening self-discovery and strengthening their identities as women. And while therapy is not designed to encourage dream sharing outside its own narrow framework, some people trace the roots of their interest in dreams to experiences with them in that setting. Furthermore, as the dreamwork movement continues to expand, introductions to dreamwork are increasingly linked with exposure to this new social trend. This occurs through such activities as workshops, classes, lectures, and dream groups, as well as through a variety of published materials on dreams.[6]

The grassroots movement gained visibility in 1982 with the establishment of a newsletter, the *Dream Network Bulletin*. Through several editorships and incarnations, it has remained a lively forum, offering information and ideas about dreamwork, practical suggestions for starting dream groups, and a convenient means of bringing like-minded dreamworkers together.[7] When the Association for the Study of Dreams (ASD) was founded a year later to encourage professional interest in dreams, its creation caused concern among some grassroots dreamworkers that the egalitarian spirit of dreamwork might be undermined by an emphasis on professionalism.[8]

Despite an initial uneasy alliance between the two parts of the movement, a closer relationship is evolving. Professionals read and contribute to the *Dream Network Journal* and have been among its editors,[9] while the ASD welcomes dreamworkers from outside the professional realm. As the dream-work movement gains momentum, the very scope and definition of dream-related professionalism is expanding.

Within the dream field, the word *professional* is commonly used in two different ways. In one sense, it refers collectively to clinicians and dream researchers—that is, to people with varied academic backgrounds whose work relates to dreams. But it is also used to distinguish those trained to prac-tice therapy from those who lack clinical experience. This latter meaning is the one referred to by the phrase "deprofessionalizing the dream."[10]

There is some irony in the fact that as the dream becomes more "public," a new kind of dreamwork professional is appearing outside of the clinical realm. Though a "nonprofessional" in the orthodox sense, this new breed of professional earns a living through the practice of some form of nonclinical dreamwork. This might include dream-group leadership, one-to-one dream counseling, or dream education in classroom and workshop settings. Since there are currently no formal training programs in nonclinical dreamwork, the role is a self-styled one. Most—if not all—of these dreamwork practition-ers are college educated (some have graduate degrees), and virtually all are ex-perienced with dreams on a personal level.

Some dream groups are organized and led by people pursuing this kind of career, though in the area of leadership and fees they are just one permuta-tion. In addition to dream groups led by members of the new professional cat-egory, there are those whose leaders have been clinically trained. Both of these types generally involve a fee, but there are also groups run by a lay leader free of charge. Furthermore, one can find leaderless peer groups operating with-out fees, as well as groups in which the leadership role regularly rotates among the members. With all of these variations in form, the question neces-sarily arises, "What is meant by a specifically *grassroots* dream group?"

I suggest that in the context of the current dreamwork movement, we view as grassroots efforts all community-based, nonclinical dream groups or-ganized by and for lay people (in the traditional sense). These run the gamut from informal, leaderless groups that are free to groups offered by the "new" dreamwork professionals, for a fee. Excluding from the "grassroots" designa-tion groups run by clinical professionals does not deny the role some clinicans have played in furthering the grassroots cause.

Among clinical professionals encouraging and inspiring the grassroots movement, Montague Ullman, in particular, stands out. His systematic and popular approach to dreamwork is touched upon in the next section.

GRASSROOTS DREAM APPRECIATION GROUPS

There are so many variations in the structure, composition, settings, goals, and methods of dream groups that it is possible to say, "a dream group is not a dream group is not a dream group." We have noted several patterns in the sphere of leadership and fees but have yet to consider the other areas of diversity.

Composition. Dream groups vary in regard to such factors as size, age and gender make-up, and the nature of members' relationships to each other. The patterning results in varying degrees from both circumstance and design, especially since "groups can come about in a number of different ways. Natural groups can spring up among friends, members of a family, people at work, or even among strangers who find they share a common interest in dreams."[11] And while some groups arise spontaneously or are assembled through personal networks, others develop by means of organized efforts to recruit members. This is done under the auspices of community organizations like churches and schools or simply by advertising in local newsletters and meeting places. In addition, the *Dream Network Journal* lists in its classified section both regional dreamworkers' organizations and local dream groups seeking new members.

Dream groups range in size from three or four people to upward of fifteen or twenty. Sometimes they form on the basis of a particular shared core of experience, whatever similarities and differences might characterize their members in other ways. There are artists' dream groups and women's dream groups, for example, and not long ago the *Dream Network Journal* advertised a dream group for "12-Step People," meaning those involved in recovery programs modeled after Alcoholics Anonymous.

Some dream groups have a long life and fairly stable membership; others function with a high rate of turnover. Testimony to the former can be found in Jenny Dodd's warm account of the "mothers' dream group" she organized in her suburban community.[12] Originally seven women, they had grown to nine and after four years still managed to meet weekly. In contrast, I talked with a dreamworker who left a group after several sessions because, apart from a common interest in dreams, "there didn't seem to be any other thread."

Settings. Grassroots dream-appreciation groups take place in a variety of settings. Some are held in such community spaces as recreation centers, libraries, churches, and schools; others gather in the workplace. But the most common site for dream-group meetings is in participants' homes. Some groups, like

Jenny Dodd's, rotate the role of host; others meet in a single, fixed location. Occasionally groups come together in more ritualistic settings, such as a special tepee designated as a "group dreaming space." Here, members not only relate their dreams to each other, but actually *dream* them together.

Goals. Individual dream groups do not necessarily articulate their goals, apart from "working on," "talking about," "getting in touch with," or simply "sharing" dreams. But a host of reasons for engaging in dreamwork have been expressed by the dreamwork movement, and they exist as motivations within the grassroots sphere.

Broadly speaking, the goal of nonclinical dreamwork is to foster an appreciation of dreams and to make them more available as useful resources for waking life. Differences exist in the ways that sense of appreciation is engendered and in the waking domains to which the dreams are most assiduously applied. Generally, it is the psychological and spiritual dimensions of the dream that receive the greatest attention. For although dreams contain a wealth of social and cultural information, these aspects are rarely explored in dreamwork settings, at least not explicitly.[13]

Along with the more generalized dream-appreciation groups, there are those with a specific focus on a particular aspect of dreaming or way of applying dreams. Some groups, for example, concentrate on the experience of lucid dreaming (a state of consciousness in which the dreamer is aware of dreaming while it is actually occurring).[14] Others are devoted to exploring the purportedly psychic dimension of dreams, and still others to using dream images as inspiration for creative art.

Methods. Two distinct styles of group interaction are found among grassroots dream groups. These are not mutually exclusive, and most groups combine them in some way, though one or the other tends to predominate. The first style can be termed the *study-group* approach. In it, the group serves as a forum for sharing and discussing dreams in a manner that is largely unstructured and conversational. Attention may be given to skills like remembering dreams and keeping a dream journal, as well as to building a repertoire of techniques for both shared and private dreamwork. But while various hands-on methods are usually sampled in the study-group format, it lacks the consistent experiential tone of the second approach.

There, the group members act primarily as catalysts for the dreamer, using techniques to help the latter become more intimate with the shared dream. Groups that have this *experiential* style tend to be more structured, whether they stay with a single, preferred dreamwork method or opt to practice several approaches.

Ullman's *experiential dream group* process[15] epitomizes the second approach. Avoiding specific interpretive theories, it views dream images as metaphors for feelings and assists the dreamer in connecting the imagery with the life situations that gave rise to it. Ullman maintains that dream appreciation "requires work and takes energy." His group process has been carefully designed to enable the necessary work, while preserving the emotional safety of the dreamer.[16]

At the heart of this method is a projective exercise in which the dreamer listens, while the rest of the group imaginatively try to make the dream "their own." By exploring, in this way, the various feelings and metaphors suggested by the dream, they generate a pool of possible meanings to which the dreamer can inwardly respond. Afterwards, the dreamer has a chance to actively reply to the group's projections and then to engage in a kind of focusing dialogue with the group.

A principle underlying Ullman's method, and shared by most dream groups, upholds the exclusive authority of the dreamer when it comes to the meaning of a dream. Accordingly, the various methods are meant to stimulate the dreamer's inner knowledge, rather than to impose understandings from without. Since a hallmark of grassroots dreamwork as a whole is its sheer diversity of method, the full range of techniques cannot be encompassed in a chapter of this size. Unitarian-Universalist minister and dreamworker Jeremy Taylor has a delightfully inclusive attitude in the face of such abundance. He believes that "virtually all of the theories, styles of work, religious beliefs, community dream sharing practices, etc. of various cultures and periods of history have been born out of and are focused on some aspect of the multiple, whole truth about dreams."[17] In his book *Dream Work,* Taylor offers numerous practical hints for working with dreams alone and in groups, encouraging dreamers to unravel the many threads of meaning contained in the tapestry of a dream.

CULTURAL IMPLICATIONS OF DREAM GROUPS

In mainstream American culture, to the extent that it values dreams, the current perspective is a therapy-centered one. It looks to one or another technical theory of dream interpretation and calls on an expert (the therapist) to make interpretive statements about the dream. It views the dream as a form of communication productive of therapeutic insight but does not concern itself with the dream as a resource outside the consulting room. Grassroots dream-appreciation groups share the assumption that dreams have meaning, but they act on the belief that the value of dreams transcends the clinical context. They hold that dreamers themselves can appreciate the significance of their dreams without having to rely on the interpretive guidance of experts. By thus widening the social framework within which we make dreams important, dream groups play a vital role in helping to raise our cultural appraisal of the dream.

Yet the cultural function of dream groups goes beyond their promotion of the value of dreaming and to the kind of social interaction they encourage. This is suggested by the work of Alexander Randall on the effects of dream sharing on group cohesion.[18] Randall studied a group of fifteen people engaged in a month-long residential conference on themes relating to dreams, shamanism, and the work of the American psychic Edgar Cayce. Dream-sharing activities were part of the group's daily routine during the conference, and dreams were the primary focus of discussion. Randall discovered that "not only did the reflective nature of the dreams help to iron out interpersonal differences, but the very act of sharing dreams put the members on a personal level of intimacy."[19]

Dream groups can also help us in the scientific task of learning more about the phenomenology of consciousness. Regular work with dreams has a tendency to increase one's sophistication as a dreamer, bringing about a wider experience of the full range of consciousness possible during sleep. Dreaming is not a "unitary phenomenon,"[20] as conventional wisdom would have us assume, and lucid dreaming, out-of-body experiences, and other qualitatively distinct states must be included on our cognitive map. Furthermore, by learning to value our dreams, and by expanding our knowledge of dream states, we challenge the narrow cultural focus on the ordinary phenomena of waking.[21]

In addition, dream groups offer an excellent opportunity to begin exploring the social and cultural dimension of the dream itself. In one of his more recent contributions to this theme, Ullman says:

> Cultural anthropologists have long viewed dreams as useful instruments for studying the mores and value systems of exotic cultures. Logically, they should be as useful in the examination of our own society. Social in origin, our dream imagery has an intrinsic bidirectionality that points inwardly to the innermost and often hidden aspects of our personal being and outwardly to the source of their origin and to their possible connection to prevailing social realities that otherwise tend to be obscured from view.[22]

An eloquent example of how and why we should attend to this "social intelligence" of dreams is provided by political scientist John Wikse.[23] He points out that in a social environment in which dreams are customarily suppressed, we tend not to be aware of our inner knowledge of how that environment impinges on our feelings. But by sharing dreams "in a context in which it is possible to become reflective about the conditions and circumstances of social life,"[24] we gain access to that liberating intelligence.

Part of the process of tapping the social and cultural dimension of dreams is using the information to reshape the outmoded myths and images we find there. Some feminist dreamworkers, for example, in exploring their identities through dreams, have sought to transform Jungian archetypal imagery along less gender-stereotyped lines.[25] As psychologists David Feinstein and Stanley Krippner point out in their book *Personal Mythology,* "gaining a measure of autonomy from the limiting mythic images of your culture and from other early influences increases your psychological freedom and strengthens your ability to cope with a rapidly changing world."[26]

In the broadest sense, dreamwork has the capacity to help heal the collective wounds resulting from our social dividedness. Jeremy Taylor writes passionately about this transformative potential:

> As a community organizer I realized that dream work could bring people together across all the barriers of race, age, sex, class, et al. to join in the work of changing society. I came to understand that dream work has the potential to be deeply "radical," not only in the original sense of *radix,* getting to the "root" of things, but also in the political and social sense of dramatic transformation of collective fears, opinions, attitudes, and behaviors.[27]

Finally, just as the therapy process is a common dream theme for those who are engaged in it, so is the dream-group experience often depicted in the dream lives of its participants. As with other aspects of the social world, we can learn more about the role of dream groups if we begin examining our collective imagery about them. I can offer a small start by reporting one of my own dreams, which occurred when I was regularly involved in experiential dream-group work.

Our group met weekly in the living room of a Manhattan apartment, where there was a nice, but very undistinguished, carpet. Yet one night I dreamed that marking the area where we assembled was an Oriental rug of extraordinary subtlety and richness. While the transformative nature of this image speaks to my personal experience of dreamwork, it points to a larger meaning, as well. For as Taylor suggests, dream groups have a role in helping to enrich and repair the complex social fabric weaving us together.

David Feinstein

The Dream as a Window on Your Evolving Mythology

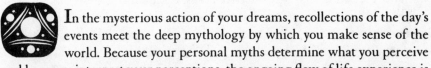 In the mysterious action of your dreams, recollections of the day's events meet the deep mythology by which you make sense of the world. Because your personal myths determine what you perceive and how you interpret your perceptions, the ongoing flow of life experience is usually sorted and stored in a manner that affirms your existing mythology.

Some experiences, however, collide with this mythology and the understanding and guidance it offers. Dreams are a primary arena for mediating such conflict. It is also in dreams that the primal and spiritual impulses of the archetypal imagination may first come to challenge the prevailing mythic structure. In the ensuing battle, the reality by which you live is further formulated and refined. By attuning your waking consciousness to your dream life, you can watch your deepest mythology evolve.[1]

PERSONAL MYTHS AND PSYCHOLOGICAL DEVELOPMENT

Your personal mythology interprets the past, defines the present, and offers guidance for the future. Myths, in the sense my colleagues and I use the term, are *not* falsehoods; they are the lens through which the human psyche perceives and organizes reality. Mythic thought, with its compelling symbolism and narrative, is the natural language of the psyche. A personal myth is a complex of images, emotions, and concepts, organized around a core theme that addresses at least one of the domains within which mythology traditionally functions.

According to Joseph Campbell, these include: (1) the urge to comprehend one's world in a meaningful way, (2) the search for a marked pathway through the succeeding epochs of human life, (3) the need to establish secure and fulfilling relationships within a community, and (4) the longing to know one's part in the vast wonder and mystery of the cosmos.[2] Personal myths explain the world, guide individual development, provide social direction, and address spiritual longings in a manner that is analogous to the way cultural myths carry out these functions for entire societies. Personal myths do for an individual what cultural myths do for a community.

Mythology, culture, and consciousness evolve in tandem. One of the most provocative facts about human evolution is that while the structure of the brain has remained essentially unchanged for at least 40,000 years,[3] consciousness has evolved dramatically. For the human species, language and myth-making replaced genetic mutation as the primary vehicles by which individual awareness and societal innovations are carried forward. Myth-making, at both the individual and the collective levels, is the fundamental though often unperceived psychological mechanism by which human beings order reality and navigate their way through life.

A dilemma of the modern era is that the ability of cultural myths to adapt to new conditions has been outstripped by the rate of social change. At the same time, human beings have achieved greater autonomy than in any previous period of history for formulating distinctively *personal* mythologies and reflecting upon those mythologies. The lack of coherence in the culture's mythology allows and, in fact, forces individuals to think and act for themselves in ways that were unimaginable in the past. Major mythic shifts—regarding issues as vital as what it means to be a male, a female, a parent, a good citizen, or a success—are being hammered out today on the anvil of people's lives. This places a tremendous burden on the individual to forge an uncharted path into the future without the benefit of the myths, rituals, and traditions that have guided previous generations.

Since the mid-1970s, Stanley Krippner and I have been developing an approach for teaching people to turn within and engage with the submerged personal mythology that is guiding their lives.[4] We believe that a well-articulated, carefully examined personal mythology is one of the most effective devices available for countering the disorienting grip of a world in mythic turmoil. By understanding the principles that govern your underlying mythology, you can learn to influence patterns in your life that once seemed predetermined and went unquestioned. You become more capable of creatively adjusting to the bewildering disarray in today's guiding myths. And you increase your capacity to stretch your mythology beyond the limitations of the culture's jumbled mythic images and beyond confining beliefs and self-images rooted in your own unique background.

DREAMS AND YOUR EVOLVING MYTHOLOGY

Personal myths are the product of four interacting sources. The most obvious are *biology* (the capacities for symbolism and narrative are rooted in the structure of the brain, information and attitudes are neurochemically coded, temperament and hormones influence belief systems), *culture* (the individual's mythology is, to an extent, the culture's mythology in microcosm), and *personal history* (every emotionally significant event leaves a mark on one's developing mythology). A fourth source is rooted in *transcendent experiences*—those episodes, insights, and visions that have a numinous quality, expand a person's perspective, and inspire more enlightened behavior.

Transcendent experiences vary in their strength and significance. Their most profound form is in the full-blown mystical or religious experience. William James reported that "mystical states of a well-pronounced and emphatic sort *are* usually authoritative over those who have them. . . . Mystical experiences are as direct perceptions of fact for those who have them as any sensations ever were for us."[5] For Philip Wheelwright, "the very essence of myth [is] that haunting awareness of transcendental forces peering through the cracks of the visible universe."[6]

Your personal mythology is continually changing as your construction of reality evolves over the course of your life. Dreams are both markers and agents in this process. Dreams synthesize, with the existing mythic structure, ongoing input from the biological, cultural, biographical, and transcendent sources of your mythology. From Freud and Jung to modern neurophysiologists, the concept of synthesis has been used to describe an essential function of dreams. Anthony Stevens has summarized neurophysiological findings that suggest that this involves a *vertical* synthesis among the brain stem, midbrain, and cerebrum, and a *horizontal* synthesis between the cerebral hemispheres.[7] In presenting their "activation-synthesis hypothesis," McCarley and Hobson note:

> Information from sensory systems, motor systems, information about the affective states of the organism are all linked together and compared with information about the organism's experiences in the past, its memories. Dreams are not a result of an attempt to disguise but are a direct expression of this synthetic effort.[8]

The essential synthetic function of dreams in relation to the dreamer's developing mythology is that *in dreams, the psyche interprets new experiences in terms of old and emerging mythic structures.* As we will see, this formulation provides you with a context for interpreting the meaning of your dreams and for better understanding your developing mythology as well.

DREAMWORK WITH A MYTHOLOGICAL PERSPECTIVE

Ernest Rossi (1977) has observed that "since ancient times, dreams have been continually rediscovered as sources of higher, intuitive or more synthetic patterns of psychological growth and understanding."[9] Recognizing that individual dreams occur within an ecology of complementary and competing personal myths yields a powerful interpretive framework. Within that framework, most established dream techniques, such as association, amplification, and identification with dream symbols, may be gainfully employed.

A principle of dream interpretation upon which most psychodynamic therapists agree is that dreams are best understood as an unfolding of the movement of the psyche and should not be distorted by highly intellectualized interpretations. My co-workers and I hold to this principle, while also wanting you to sense the relationship between the continuity of your dreams and your developing personal mythology. So in providing you with an interpretive framework, we also want to emphasize that your dream analysis not be overly intellectual or divorced from feeling.

The focal point for understanding the development of your personal mythology is the dialectic that occurs between a prevailing myth that has, in at least some respects, become dysfunctional and a counter-myth generated to compensate for the old myth's limitations.[10] "Mythical thought moves from an awareness of contradictions toward their resolution," explains Richard Cavendish, and it attempts "to mediate opposites and resolve them."[11] Thus mythical thought is dialectical in nature. The thesis is the old myth, the antithesis is the counter-myth, and the synthesis is a new mythic structure that ideally integrates the most beneficial qualities of each into a higher order. A single dream may attend to any part of the dialect—old myth, counter-myth, new synthesis—or any combination.

Initially operating outside of consciousness, counter-myths eventually crystalize into awareness and become increasingly influential. As the counter-myth develops, it poses a growing challenge to the old myth. These prevailing and emerging mythic structures engage one another, although to a great extent this dialectical drama is played out at an unconscious level. Much of our emphasis in helping people work with their mythologies involves bringing conscious attention to the underlying process. In such work, we particularly take heed of Jung's suggestion that the best way to approach the unconscious is to attain a conscious attitude that allows the unconscious to cooperate, rather than to be driven into opposition.[12] We caution against clinging to the old myth—though sacrificing its longstanding promises and familiar world-view may be painful and produce anxiety—or attempting to sever oneself from the problems the old myth creates by clutching to a counter-myth and hoping never to look back. Paradoxically, in order to grow beyond an old myth, it is often necessary to accept the role it played in your life, understand the reasons you at one time needed it, and appreciate the valid messages it still holds.

Dreams often provide the first glimpse of shifts in an individual's mythology, a process whose form we have found to be both lawful and predictable. When there is a discrepancy between your mythology and a new experience, your dream life will attempt to resolve the incongruity. Some dreams settle the difference by reinterpreting the experience so it will fit the existing mythic structure, a process analogous to Piaget's concept of assimilation.[13] Other dreams activate changes in the mythology so that it may better correspond to the new experience—similarly to Piaget's notion of accommodation. Such dreams highlight ways the mythic structure is failing you, or at least failing to adequately account for your experiences. Other dreams generate alternative mythic structures, counter-myths, to account for new experiences and an unfolding sense of possibility. Still others mediate between older mythic structures and these emerging alternatives. Dreams also may be a conduit for archetypal material and may serve as an arena for the encounter between existing mythic structures and the deeper mythic imagination.

DREAM SYMBOLS IN THE CONTEXT OF YOUR EVOLVING MYTHOLOGY

If you recognize that dreams occur within a psychological environment of evolving, often conflicting personal myths, your efforts toward self-understanding occur in a larger context. Ongoing developmental tasks are seen as part of an unfolding mythic drama. From this perspective, the symbols and events in your dreams can be interpreted according to the following framework.

A Mythic Framework for Interpreting Dream Symbols and Events

	DREAM FUNCTION		
	sustain old myth	create and strengthen counter-myth	integrate conflicting myths
reconstruct past			
process recent events			
consider possible futures			

TEMPORAL FOCUS

As the chart suggests, dream symbols and events may serve to sustain a prevailing myth, create or strengthen a counter-myth, or facilitate the resolution of a conflict between prevailing and emerging myths. We emphasize the dream's temporal focus to clarify that whether the dream is dealing primarily with an old myth or an emerging myth, or a reconciliation of the two, is independent on the dream's setting in place or time. Old-myth dreams may be set in the past, present, or future, as may counter-myth dreams and resolution dreams. A dream may, for instance, entertain future possibilities according to the assumptions of an old myth or according to a new integration of previously competing myths. Past events may be reinterpreted from the perspective of an emerging counter-myth. Or an old interpretation may be affirmed according to the prevailing myth. All nine combinations shown on the chart are possible, and many dreams include a mixture of symbols and events representing several of the categories. The value of the grid is in the perspective it offers for teasing out the meaning of a particular dream symbol or event in relationship to a changing mythic panorama.

There are strong parallels between this framework and the research findings of Rosalind Cartwright,[14] who identified a nightly pattern in which the initial dreams tend to review unresolved concerns from the day. Next are dreams that consider scenes from the past in which analogous problems have previously been confronted; then come wish-oriented dreams in which there is a sense that the conflict has been resolved. The final dreams attempt to integrate the various elements of this dream sequence into a viable resolution of the conflict.

This process is a nightly microcosm of the framework presented here for understanding how your mythology evolves over time. When conflict emerges between what you experience and the mythology you hold, your dream life will bring this unresolved conflict into focus. Dreams attempting to fit the experience into old mythic structures will follow. If these attempts fail, other dreams will reveal and develop a wish-oriented counter-myth. Eventually, these conflicting myths engage in a dialect process that functions to bring about a resolution, a higher order integration of the most viable elements of each of them. The following discussion will present in greater detail these primary mythological functions of dreams: sustaining a prevailing myth, creating or strengthening a counter-myth, and facilitating a resolution between the two.

Sustaining a Prevailing Myth

A forty-two-year-old woman who carried overbearing parental injunctions had the following dream the evening after she proudly announced to her therapist some progress in liberating herself from those injunctions. *I was walking down the street in a sort of run-down neighborhood when I noticed two men on motorcycles, both pretty stocky, pretty good size. One of them said "You're coming with us." I said, "No I'm not," but I felt absolute terror when he spoke to me.*

Like the motorcyclists in this dream, many dream symbols reveal that the old myth is still a potent force, new attitudes and beliefs notwithstanding. These dreams maintain a psychic economy by supporting prevailing myths that are being challenged by new experiences. In such dreams, we see Piaget's process of assimilation in operation. The woman's newfound experience of independence came into conflict with the domination of her internalized parents, and the dream attempted to diminish her experience of autonomy by portraying dominating figures who invoked terror in her about acting independently of their wishes. By casting doubt on her sense of independence, the dream served as a force toward discounting the progress she was feeling.

Her first response to the dream was to reframe her recent successes so they could be assimilated into her existing mythology without changing that mythology: "It makes me feel I'm not really so independent after all, and I'll bring trouble my way by acting as if I were." Her perceived behavioral changes were thus *assimilated* into her old mythology, with the overall effect that the disparity between her perceptions and her existing mythology was decreased in the direction of strengthening the mythology. We can see here the potential value of having an interpretive framework that recognizes the dream as an attempt to shore up the old myth rather than a statement from the unconscious that recent progress is illusory.

If the dream life is unable to assimilate new experiences into old mythic structures, the equilibrium of the cognitive system becomes upset. The vital function of dreams capable of assimilating difficult experiences is suggested by research evidence. One laboratory study showed that after a mildly unpleasant experience, people who dreamed about the experience (*incorporators*) woke with improved mood, frame of mind, and willingness to again approach an unpleasant problem, as contrasted with non-incorporators, who did not dream about the experience.[15] Another study, however, revealed that dreaming about a highly unpleasant experience (a gory film about accidents was shown to subjects before going to sleep and again upon awakening) may increase anxiety and interfere with future adaptations to stress.[16] In the first study, the dreamers were apparently successful in assimilating the stressful event, while in the second study they were not.

Dreams that involve a struggle to assert the validity of a prevailing myth that is being challenged by an emerging structure often feel defeating and hopeless and leave the dreamer drained of energy and vitality. Dreams that support the old myth may be set in the past, present, or future. If set in the past—such as when a childhood friend appears—old myth dreams present evidence that affirms the myth's validity, despite contradictory recent experiences. Old-myth dreams set in the future may serve to maintain the prevailing mythic structure by providing a vision of its continued domination, frequently portrayed with a sense of fatedness. Such future-oriented old-myth dreams may be as upsetting as a visit from Charles Dickens' "ghost of Christmases yet to come." Other old-myth dreams rework recent experiences. Freud observed that often, in dreams, "residues of the previous day have been left over from the activity of waking life, and it has not been possible to withdraw the whole cathexis of energy from them."[17] The most universal psychological function of dreams is, in fact, to assimilate "day residue" into existing mythic structures.

Creating or Strengthening a Counter-Myth

Prevailing myths do, through the action of dreams and other mechanisms of the unconscious, frequently distort perceptions and interpretations of experiences that are not consistent with their premises. Such systematic distortion of experience, however, paves the way for a counter-myth that will challenge the original myth, as we will examine here. Another condition that allows counter-myths to emerge has to do with the way prevailing myths are continually accommodating themselves to new experiences. Many old-myth dreams, rather than distorting experiences that do not fit the myth, adjust, refine, and update the myth itself. Sometimes, however, the old structure has been so thoroughly revised that a limit to the input it can accommodate has been reached, beyond which, according to Piaget, "the cycle forming the scheme would rupture."[18] Experiences that do not match the myth then become more likely to exceed what Piaget called the schema's *accommodation capacity,* and a *higher-order* cognitive structure becomes necessary.

Creating a counter-myth is one of the psyche's primary mechanisms for raising the existing mythology to a higher order.[19] When new experiences are not congruent with reality as constructed by the prevailing myth, when they exceed that myth's accommodation capacity, or when living according to the myth's dictates has consistently resulted in negative reinforcement, the conditions are set for the emergence of an alternative way of constructing reality. Experiences that are distorted or ignored because they clash with a prevailing myth are often unconsciously recognized and stored. Research evidence cited by Epstein demonstrates that mental content may be perceived and encoded without awareness.[20] When experiences that are inconsistent with the person's mythology are thus dissociated, they may become the core of a new mythic structure that organizes perceptions in a manner quiet contrary to the pattern of the old myth. Epstein explains that dissociated material forms its own subsystem, which is insulated from the remainder of the conceptual system.

We refer to this new subsystem as a counter-myth because it is based upon experiences that represent a counterpoint to the existing mythology. While the counter-myth may remain outside of conscious awareness for a substantial period of time, additional experiences that are discordant with the prevailing myth may increase its mass until it breaks into consciousness, often in dreams, fantasies, or changes in self-concept.

A single dream may contain symbols or portray events that serve to maintain an old myth, while other symbols or events in the same dream are fortifying the counter-myth that challenges it. In the above dream fragment, figures representing the power of the dreamer's old myth did appear and were terrifying, but she was also able to tell these figures she would not go along with their wishes. A subsequent portion of the dream gives further expression to the counter-myth that was emerging in her inner life. As the dream proceeded, there was a confrontation in which the dreamer killed the first motorcyclist, and then: *the second man started running over toward me, and I picked up the same weapon that I had used on the other man and I thrust it into his chest, and I remember feeling it sink in, it was a real strong feeling. It probably only took a split second but I remember it going into the flesh and then stopping, and it knocked him backwards and I kneeled over him. He said to me, "I don't think I'm going to die, I have too much life in me." And I said to him something like, "Oh yes you are!" At the time I said that I felt really pleased, really glad that I had killed him and that he would soon know he was going to die. So I had this victorious feeling. I was physically over him and I had slain the enemy.*

Here we see the old myth being symbolically and dramatically overcome by a counter-myth that supports a deeper voice than the parental injunctions that characterize the former. Counter-myths may be modeled largely after the myths of others who have an influence on you, may be rooted in a developmental readiness to accept more advanced myths from your culture, or may be patterned after an intuitive perception of deeper wisdom or archetypal images. Counter-myth dreams often have a wish-oriented quality. The woman wanted an end to her captivity in parental injunctions. Freud noted that sometimes "the activity of waking life during the course of the day has led to the stirring up of an unconscious wish."[21] Counter-myths, initially oriented around frustrated needs or unfulfilled desires, are often based upon the logic of wish fulfillment.

But within the counter-myth may also be found the seeds of constructive action and developmental progress, which emerge not only in reaction to thwarted wishes, but also in compensation for inadequacies of the prevailing mythic structure. In Jungian analysis, in fact, the dream is understood to be compensation "by which the unconscious expresses in symbolic form a balancing or homeostatic reaction to the one-sided position of the conscious attitude."[22]

Montague Ullman has summarized the purpose of such dreams, in which "new levels of self-revelation are struggling to gain expression in an area where outmoded techniques of self-deception are beginning to weaken and crumble."[23] Counter-myth dreams, with their strong sense of success or triumph, may, however, quickly shift to feelings of distress as the old mythic structure works to reestablish its domination. The woman who had the dream about killing the figures representing her overbearing old myth continued: "I was really feeling good [in the dream] and then all of a sudden it hit me, 'Oh my god, what have you done; you've killed two people.' And the worst part was not just that I'd killed them but that I was feeling so good about it."

Dreams in the service of the counter-myth typically feel hopeful, optimistic, even inspirational, though they are usually lacking in practical guidance. Like old-myth dreams, counter-myth dreams may invoke a sense of past, present, or future. Some rework past disappointments and defeats, reinterpreting them in a more affirming and optimistic manner. This provides an alternative to the self-limiting definitions of the old myth. Other counter-myth dreams interpret the experiences of the day as evidence of the counter-myth's promise. Counter-myth dreams also may portray future possibilities, full of hope and the promise of wishes fulfilled though lacking in the practical guidance of integration dreams.

Integrating Conflicting Mythic Structures

Once a counter-myth has become well-formulated, the psyche has the task of resolving its inevitable, often intensifying conflict with the prevailing mythic structure. This is the third function of dreams in relationship to the way personal myths develop. In the above dream segments, besides fortifying the old myth and exercising the counter-myth, the dream is also bringing the two into a direct confrontation. In a segment of the dream that occurred between the two segments described above, a dialogue took place between the figures representing the old myth and the counter-myth. The woman had gone into a sort of warehouse, and after having killed the first man, she reports: *I was really relieved and triumphant. I was sitting resting after this and I looked out the window and his friend, a sandy-haired man who looked a little younger, was climbing up a ladder to get in the back window. He said "guess who" and he laughed. I said to him "You might as well go all the way." The feeling I had at that point was not fear so much but I kind of had respect for him, that he was coming to avenge his friend's death, that he wasn't running away, and I felt we were equal, we were a match, and I was almost revved up for the competition.*

While the dream reflects only the beginning of her resolution process, you can sense how the dialectic is proceeding. In subsequent dreams, the old myth was represented in less menacing ways, and some of its strengths, such as its purpose of giving the dreamer protection, were integrated into her emerging mythology. Piaget spoke of the "reciprocal assimilations and accommodations" that occur between subsystems, eventually leading to mutual integration.[24] This is how the dialectic proceeds, and dreams often reveal the process in action.

Dreams that primarily serve an integration function tend to produce a calming, peaceful feeling, and they often provide guidance that is practical and realistic. Resolution dreams, like old-myth dreams and counter-myth dreams, may be set in the past, present, or future. When set in the past, they may reveal a new way to approach the current conflict based on the way a previous conflict was resolved. One man reported new insight regarding difficult feelings he was having about his boss after dreaming about a fifth-grade teacher he at first hated, but with whom he eventually became very intimate. Resolution dreams that focus on current difficulties sometimes provide very specific guidance about steps to take that embody the strengths of both the old myth and the counter-myth. Resolution dreams set in the future may show a circumstance in which the conflict has been resolved and provide metaphorical instruction about how to accomplish such a resolution.

SYSTEMATIC WORK WITH YOUR DREAMS AND MYTHS

There are three kinds of resolution dreams. The first focus primarily on the way the old myth and the counter-myth engage one another; the second are concerned primarily with presenting an image of a new myth, a higher-order synthesis of the most viable elements of the old myth and the counter-myth; and the third show how to bring that new synthesis into daily life. Old-myth dreams, counter-myth dreams, and the three kinds of resolution dreams each have a parallel in one of the stages of a five-stage model my co-workers and I use for helping people work with their evolving mythologies.

The first stage of our model for teaching people to work more consciously and effectively with their guiding mythology involves recognizing when a guiding myth is no longer an ally. Conflicts in the person's inner life or outer world are traced back to a prevailing myth that is out of date, is steeped in internal discord, is causing conflict with one's world, or is otherwise creating difficulties. Old-myth dreams, which often leave the dreamer drained of energy and feeling hopeless or defeated, may signal the area of the person's mythology that is requiring attention in this first stage of the process. Counter-myth dreams, and their disparity with the dreamer's waking life, may similarly point toward underlying mythic conflict.

In the second stage, the conflicting myths are brought into focus. The historical roots of the long-standing prevailing myth are identified and the circumstances leading to the emerging counter-myth are explored. Again, both old-myth and counter-myth dreams inform the process during this stage of the work. It is in the very areas in which the person's mythology is not working well, as identified in the first stage of the program, that the psyche is typically generating a counter-myth, often below the level of consciousness. We teach people how to investigate those fledgling mythic structures, examine their potential contribution, and consciously participate in promoting their wholesome development.

The third stage of the program is dedicated to promoting the natural dialectic between the prevailing myth and the counter-myth. Energy is focused on bringing resolution to their conflict. The task in this stage, once the differences between both sides have been highlighted, is to promote a process of deep reconciliation where the best of each side is integrated and elevated into a new and more effective mythic image. The counterpart to this stage of the work is seen in resolution dreams that focus primarily on the way the old myth and the counter-myth engage one another.

The fourth stage of our program has its parallel in those resolution dreams that are concerned primarily with presenting an image of a new myth. In this stage, a new mythic image that integrates the most vital elements of the prevailing and emerging myths into a higher-order synthesis is articulated, refined, and anchored into one's being. The final stage of our program has its analog in those resolution dreams that show how to bring this new synthesis into the practical world. In this stage, the task is to take concrete steps for weaving the renewed mythology into daily life.

While we have developed a program of personal rituals for assisting people through each of these five natural stages in the evolution of personal mythology, the five kinds of dreams provide an organic parallel to the model. Attending to your dreams from the perspective of your evolving mythology sheds light on both your dreams and your myths. James Hillman has suggested: "Let us reimagine psychodynamics as mythic tales rather than as physical processes; as the rise and fall of dramatic themes, as genealogies, as voyages and contests and respites, as interventions of Gods."[25] Understanding your dreams as the poetics of underlying mythic inspiration, conflict, and resolution yields a penetrating and systematic framework for perceptively encountering the mysteries of your dream life.

II

Dreams in Therapy and Healing

The only "correct" interpretation of a dream . . . is one that gives the dreamer a joyful "aha" experience of insight and moves him to change his life in some constructive fashion.
ANN FARADAY

Many well-informed and educated people continue to insist that dreams are "nonsense" and "without meaning" and that dreamwork may be dangerous to one's mental health. Philosopher Edward Erwin observes. "It might turn out that dream analysis is not only of little clinical value, but is actually harmful, although at present this is speculative."[1] Nobel laureate Francis Crick and neuroscientist Graeme Mitchison assert that "attempting to remember one's dreams should perhaps not be encouraged, because such remembering may help to retain patterns of thought which are better forgotten."[2]

As a first rejoinder, let us bury the claim that dreams are meaningless. If dream content is devoid of meaning, why have scientific studies detected differences when two or more groups have been compared? For example, Robert L. Van de Castle reported a striking relationship between the percentage of dreams containing one or more animals and the dreamers' chronological ages. Younger people, especially children, dreamed about animals more frequently than older dreamers. However, when the focus was shifted from the United States to groups of native peoples, there were cultures in which no difference was found between children and adults regarding animal content, probably because contact with animals in these societies was common among both age groups.[3] In addition, Van de Castle studied the Cuna Indians in Panama, noting that their dreams included very few acts of aggression against other people—a trait also noticeable in their daily lives.[4]

People in developing countries, living in areas with high-density populations where food is often scarce, have an unusually low frequency of food consumption in their dreams,[5] a finding that appears to refute Freud's notion of "wish fulfillment"—that we dream about those activities that we most desire. Instead, the data support Alfred Adler's proposal that there is a continuity between dream life and waking life.

Robert Levine studied three groups of male Nigerian students and found that dream content differed in relation to their tribal background. For example, the Ibo culture has a value system and social structure favoring upward mobility of its members. The Hausa culture does not support social mobility and individual achievement, while the Yoruba culture takes an intermediate position. Dream reports from Yoruba students contained more achievement themes than those of Hausa students but less than those of Ibo students, exactly what one would predict if dreamtime reflects waking life.[6]

Several studies demonstrate that people undergoing episodes of depression have more dreams set in the past than do nondepressed people. Further, depressed dreamers report more content characterized by masochism, dependency, and blandness of emotion. If the depression begins to lift, however, dream content changes; for example, more feeling and emotion begin to appear in the dreams.[7]

These studies and dozens of others indicate that dreams generally mirror waking activities and that people's dreams reflect detectable differences in age, gender, and cultural background. Those individuals who denigrate dreams insist that they "are full of sound and fury, signifying nothing." The next time you hear anyone make this claim, ask how he or she would explain the comparative data collected by Robert Van de Castle and other dreamworkers.

On the other hand, there are no conclusive studies demonstrating that psychotherapists who pay attention to dreams are more helpful to their clients than are those who ignore the language of the night. Psychotherapy is a difficult process to study, and many researchers have claimed that there is no incontrovertible evidence that it changes attitudes and behavior for the better.[8] I believe that *some* data are beginning to emerge supporting the efficacy of psychotherapy,[9] but admittedly the task is a difficult one.

In the meantime, I believe that the use of dreams in therapy and healing can serve a beneficial purpose, and this section explores the way that dreams help people deal with life issues and problems. It opens with humanistic-existentialist psychologist Alvin R. Mahrer's perceptive discussion of the use of dreams in psychotherapy and proceeds with descriptions of psychoanalytic and Jungian approaches to dreamworking by Wynn Schwartz and June Singer, both of whom are psychologists and psychoanalysts. Schwartz points out that psychoanalytic doctrines are not etched in stone, but are constantly evolving; Singer describes how Jungian dreamwork attempts to reconcile the conscious and the unconscious, the internal and the external worlds.

P. Erik Craig, a psychologist, demonstrates the trend away from Freud's emphasis on dream content as *disguise* and toward the *adaptive, problem-solving nature* of dreams originally suggested by Jung and Adler. To close this section, one of our psychology graduate students at Saybrook Institute, Adam Zwig, presents several approaches that use the dreamer's body as the point of departure in dreamworking.

Space did not permit the inclusion of some other important psycho-therapeutic approaches that emphasize the use of dreams. Especially notable is the holistic approach of Alfred Adler, who viewed dreams as purposeful and who stressed their congruent relationship to the lifestyle of the dreamer.[10] Adlerian psychotherapists do not preoccupy themselves with unconscious strivings but with the total experience of the dreamer, using the dream to detect the client's private logic, biases, and errors in thinking. For Adlerians, the dream is not significantly different from waking thoughts; like all thought, it becomes part of the process of rehearsal for future activities and achievements.[11]

Walter Bonime's work, in part, is derived from Adlerian principles. In Bonime's *culturist* (or *interpersonal*) approach to dreamworking, the dream is an unguarded expression of oneself.[12] It is not a disguise but, perhaps, an uncensored and therefore authentic self-presentation. I agree with Bonime that dreams express the individual's shifting self-images, emotions, motivations, attitudes, and actions. As a result, "Indications of what is newly materializing in the personality may be discerned in this sleeping experience."[13]

The storehouse of experiences shared by members of the same culture combine with subjective, idiosyncratic elements in creating a dream. Reciprocal effects bring the therapist and client together in the dreamwork process, enhancing the client's capacity for cooperation and honesty.[14] In addition, many therapists have found Gestalt,[15] object relations,[16] psychodrama, and various transpersonal approaches[17] of use.

In 1989, eminent dreamworker Montague Ullman articulated several premises underlying his work with dreams in therapy and healing.[18] I agree with him, and I believe that the authors of these chapters would share most or all of Ullman's premises as well.

1. Dreams are internal communications that reveal certain truths about the life of the dreamer that can be made available once the dreamer is awake.

2. If we recall a dream, we are in some sense ready to be confronted by the information in that dream.

3. If the confrontation is allowed to occur properly, the effect is one of healing, and there can be a movement toward wholeness.

4. Although the dream is a private communication, its sharing in a safe, supportive context can provide a powerful opportunity for therapy and healing.

5. Dreams can be made accessible. Anyone with sufficient motivation and interest can learn, develop, and share dreamworking skills.

In Part Three, Ullman presents his guidelines for teaching dreamwork. In the meantime, these five premises portray the battle between dreamworkers and those debunkers who brand reports from dreamtime as "meaningless" and refer to dreamwork as wasted effort.

Alvin R. Mahrer

The Role of Dreams
in Psychotherapy

 This chapter focuses on three questions: (1) What is the current status of dreams in psychotherapy? (2) What are the uses of dreams in psychotherapy? That is, what are the main objectives that therapists want to obtain from their client's dreams? (3) What are the main methods used in dreamwork? That is, what are the main ways in which therapists get whatever they find important to obtain from dreams? Overall, the purpose of this chapter is to enable the reader to appreciate the role, or perhaps roles, of dreams in several approaches of psychotherapy.

THE CURRENT STATUS OF DREAMS IN PSYCHOTHERAPY

If we look at the whole field of psychotherapy, counseling, and guidance, only a relatively small proportion of practitioners use dreams. Even including therapies in which only a portion of a few sessions deals with dreams, my impression is that dreams are used in perhaps 10 to 15 percent of psychotherapies. When we limit our field to those psychiatrists, psychologists, and social workers who agree that what is occurring is "really psychotherapy," I would estimate that dreams are used by only about 15 to 20 percent of psychotherapists, and this includes those who devote limited attention to dreams over a few sessions. Dreams are not a premium item in the field of psychotherapy.

This does not represent any reduction of popularity. It is my impression that roughly the same proportion of psychotherapists have used dreams over the past fifty years.

A Few Psychotherapies Rely Heavily on Dreams

Similarly, a few schools and approaches to psychotherapy use dreams extensively. In Jungian analysis, dreams are a featured medium of psychotherapeutic work. Dreams are also important in psychoanalysis, although some psychotherapists are concerned about a possible waning of the popularity of dreamwork.[1] Dreams are used substantially in such psychotherapies as existential therapy, Gestalt therapy, experiential therapy, and others, but it is in Jungian analysis that the use of dreams predominates. With therapists who follow dream-friendly approaches, perhaps 80 to 90 percent or more use dreams, and dreams may be used in about one-third to one-half (or more) of their sessions.

In general, these approaches hold that the very process of dreaming is therapeutic because dreaming carries out a function of regulating, balancing, integrating, healing, or adapting some aspects of the psyche. For example, Jung claimed that if waking life emphasizes the cognitive aspects of one's personality, dreaming tends to emphasize the emotional side. If waking life tends to highlight social interpersonal relationships, dreaming regulates and balances this by highlighting the personal and self-focused side of the dreamer's personality.[2] Other therapists have observed that if one has suffered a shock, trauma, or severe stress, dreaming carries out a process of healing or working through these issues.[3]

Some Therapeutic Trends Are Not Dream-Friendly

A modest proportion of therapists think of the entire human personality as containing a hidden deeper part, which lies outside of conscious awareness. This idea is represented by the classical psychoanalytic "unconscious," which plays a rather large role in determining what clients do and who they think they are. For therapists who picture personality in this way, dreams constitute what Freud called the royal road to the unconscious; therefore, they are precious.[4] Nor is this picture restricted to classical psychoanalysis. As long as the theory includes some deeper, hidden component, the dream can be valued because it is a road into this unknown aspect of the psyche.

On the other hand, many current trends are turning away from this concern with the unconscious. Instead, they emphasize the conscious thinking and behavioral aspects of personality; family, society, or culture; or neurological, physiological, or chemical factors. Perhaps a majority of contemporary therapists accept a picture of personality that has little or no place for a deeper unconscious component; therefore dreams are not seen as especially valuable. Even in contemporary psychoanalytic approaches, the emphasis on ego psychology, object relations, and self psychology has taken some of the steam out of the importance of dreams.[5] Such current trends in psychotherapy are not especially friendly to the use of dreams, and dreams are not especially valued by therapists using these approaches.

Therefore, over the past fifty to eighty years, dreams have continued to be used by a relatively stable proportion of therapists, some of whom rely heavily on dreams, with about half their sessions involving dreamwork. At the other extreme are those therapists who rarely engage in any substantial dreamwork. Overall, dreams are used predominantly in therapies that aim at deep-seated and profound personality change. It seems safe to say that those therapists who value dreams tend to use them a great deal, while those who see little value in dreams use them sparingly if at all. As a result, there is a sharp division among therapists on the issue of working with dreams.

THE USES OF DREAMS IN PSYCHOTHERAPY

What do therapists seek from working with dreams? What are dreams? What are dreams used for in psychotherapy? Dreams are used in various ways, which differ substantially from one another, and for quite different purposes.

Messages from "Alien" Sources

In many ancient cultures, dreams were thought to be messages from the gods.[6] Although this point of view is no longer generally accepted, some therapists accept dreams as being messages from various "alien" sources. In Jungian analysis, for example, some dreams are seen as revealing the dreamer's health status as well as the condition of various bodily organs.[7] Jung also acknowledged that a client may occasionally have a dream that comes from and belongs to some other person such as a spouse, parent, or sibling. In Jungian analysis, the most common alien source is contained in those dreams with collective significance that transcend the client's day-to-day life. These are known as archetypal dreams, and they contain symbolic meanings represented by a common image or activity that has a teaching function as well as a spiritual quality.

Problem Solving

Some therapists emphasize the problem-solving potential of dreams. Before falling asleep, the client formulates a meaningful question, typically about some personal problem, for example: "Should I go through with the pregnancy or have an abortion?" "Should I accept the position in the family firm or strike out on my own?" In the light of this personal question, the therapist and client study the dreams of the next few nights to see if they contain answers.[8]

Sometimes there is no explicitly formulated question when the client is ready to go to sleep. Instead, there is a more-or-less continuing question that carries over for many therapy sessions: "My marriage is getting worse and worse; should I end it and get a divorce?" "Should I stay with this boring job or should I go back to school?" If this question hovers over the therapy sessions, the dream can be examined to see if it offers answers to what the client can do or should do, or at least might seriously consider doing. The therapist uses techniques that bring these tentative answers to the dreamer's problems into waking consciousness, where they can be evaluated and, perhaps, adopted. The problem-solving function of dreams is utilized by therapists representing many dreamworking approaches.[9]

Facilitating Personality Change

Some therapists will focus on dreams in which change occurs in the dream itself, taking one of many different approaches. In one such approach, the dreamer is understood as undergoing substantive personality change in the dream itself, transforming into a new and different person.[10] The new behaviors are then worked through and reinforced in waking life.

Secondly, change occurs when the dreaming person is aware that he or she is dreaming and may even be able to direct what occurs in the dream. Having rehearsed these activities in "lucid dreams," the dreamer is often better prepared to make changes in waking life.[11]

In a third approach, dreamers interact with some other dream figure who represents them, either a figure they resemble or a figure who might symbolize them.[12] In all three approaches, the therapist can use the personality changes that occur in the dream as a model for the client to follow. For example, clients may be asked to imagine going back into the dream, observing the new behavior, and identifying ways to make that shift in waking life. Through role-playing, the client can rehearse those activities with a therapist.

Projections into the Future

In ancient times, dreams were often used to foretell the future. There are residual offshoots of this predictive function in many contemporary dream approaches. In some psychoanalytic approaches, the dream may be used as an anticipation of imminent phases of development.[13] In the Jungian approach, some dreams are seen as providing a prospective anticipation or plan of what the unconscious holds in store.

Sometimes, the therapist can use a series of dreams to monitor and predict the overall process of personality change, facilitating the next step in the client's development based on information in the dreams. For example, the therapist may monitor how a client's dreams reflect the working through of a trauma following a child's sudden death and do whatever may be helpful in complementing the healing process.

Providing Information about the Client's Personality

Most psychotherapists who use dreams attempt to obtain information from them regarding a client's personality. Not only can dreams provide material about the surface personality traits of a client, but they also can reveal a client's deeper conflicts and life issues.[14]

Sometimes dreams reveal material of which the client is largely unaware. For example, the therapist and the therapeutic process may appear directly or symbolically in the dream. Dreams can then be taken as reflecting the nature of the relationship between therapist and client.[15] Dreams that occur quite early in therapy are thereby taken as especially indicative of attitudes toward starting therapy and the feelings the client harbors toward the therapist.[16] Dreams occurring toward the end of therapy may portray the client's feelings and attitudes toward termination.

The dream often provides information about the client's unconscious conflicts, impulses, and wishes. One of the most compelling uses of dreams is to elicit information on the hidden netherworld of the psyche, the client's repressed desires and problems. Some therapeutic approaches, especially Freudian and Jungian analysis, count on dreams to illuminate the material that exists outside the dreamer's conscious awareness. Each school of dream therapy has its own version of this hidden, unconscious material and how the dream allows the therapist to obtain necessary information.

The dream also provides information about the client's inner potentials and capacities, indicating the type of individual the client can become. The therapist can use this material to identify directions and talents that are avoided or are simply latent in the client's waking life,[17] as well as emerging attitudes and goals that are worthy of replacing old ones,[18] and the qualitatively different personality the client is capable of becoming.[19] In such approaches as experiential therapy, Gestalt therapy, and existential therapy, the deeper personality is comprised of possibilities, capacities, and potentials rather than (or, at least, in addition to) negative repressed and unconscious impulses and conflicts.

How Therapists Obtain Useful Dream Material

If the therapist uses dreams as the arena in which substantive personal change occurs or to provide the functions of healing, regulating, and integrating the psyche, he or she does not need particular ways of obtaining the useful material from dreams. Sheer dreaming is enough. But this is not the most common way of employing dreams in psychotherapy. Most therapists need ways to obtain useful material from the dream.

Each of the following methods is unique. Most therapists rely on one or two of them, because they are tied to what the therapist wishes to gain.

Finding Symbolic Meanings and Reinserting Them into the Dream

According to this method, each dream is made up of elements or components that are seen as having symbolic meaning. The first step is to select those particular elements that are considered to have symbolic meaning. Since not every element (and not every dream) has such meaning, this is a matter of organizing the dream into its components and then selecting which elements are to be used to arrive at symbolic meanings.

The second step is to use a system for arriving at the meaning. Several prominent systems exist to achieve this goal, among them the Freudian, Jungian, and object relations systems. This task is complicated by the principle that many elements often have multiple symbolic meanings, even within the same overall system.[20]

The final step is to reinsert the symbolic meanings of the selected elements into the overall dream context in order to arrive at the meaning. If the therapist selects two, three, or more elements and arrives at the symbolic meaning of each, the essential overall meaning depends on the proper way of reinserting the symbolic meanings back into the overall dream content. The same symbolic meanings will yield different meanings depending upon the context.

Finding the "Essential Distinguishing Characteristics" and Reinserting Them into the Dream Context

This method is used by several dreamworkers,[21] but its leading proponent has been Medard Boss.[22] Instead of regarding elements as having symbolic meaning, this method maintains that the meaning of an element lies within the element itself. Again, the first step is selecting the key elements, then identifying the "essential distinguishing element" of each selected item. What is the essential distinguishing element of a snake, a jungle, a king, a beard, a picnic, or the color white? Almost inevitably, the answers will be different from their potential symbolic meanings. Once the therapist arrives at these characteristics of each selected element, the final step is to reinsert these meanings into the overall dream context, thereby arriving at the dream's meaning.

Discovering the Client's Ideas about Selected Parts of the Dream

The therapist, client, or both select a part of the dream or the client's associations to the dream upon awakening. The dream can be used as a whole, although there is controversy about the value of this procedure.[23]

Once the part has been selected, the client expresses his or her thoughts and ideas about it. These may relate to that portion of the dream, or they may meander to a series of related topics. Then the therapist makes some sense of this series of thoughts and ideas, as well as the entire flow of associations. The therapist may look for themes, may search out symbolic meanings, or may use other ways of making sense of the client's statements. It is the therapist's way of making sense of the client's flow of ideas that leads to an understanding of the dream.

The Client Becomes the Dream Elements

In the psychoanalytic, Jungian, Adlerian, existential, and other dream schools, there is a belief that an understanding of the dream can derive from the meaning that the dreamer has attributed to figures and objects other than the dreamer. Fritz Perls elevated this assumption into his chief method of dreamworking. He proclaimed, "All the different parts in the dream are yourself, a projection of yourself."[24]

Accordingly, this method consists of the client's "being" various elements in the dream—getting inside each element, becoming it, acting it out, and adopting its thoughts and feelings. As a result, the client supposedly begins to reown and reclaim those projected (and often rejected) portions of the personality.

The Client Enters into the Feeling in the Dream

This "experiential approach" assumes that the dream contains an underlying experience that is present and available in its moments of peak feeling.[25] Accordingly, the client reenters the dream at the moments of peak feeling, to relive it even more deeply and fully, and continue until he or she reaches a point of new inner experience. And it is this inner, deeper experience that forms the core of the kind of person the client can become.

These are some of the major methods of using dreams in psychotherapy. Each can be instrumental for particular therapists, clients, or therapy goals. The method that therapists choose depends on how they use dreams and on their notion of the nature of the dreaming process. In recent years there has been a growing interest in dreams on the part of the general public. Perhaps more clients will bring dreams to their therapists, and the use of dreams in therapy will increase.

Wynn Schwartz

A Psychoanalytic Approach to Dreamwork

Psychoanalysts have attempted to understand and interpret dreams ever since Freud first created psychoanalysis. Psychoanalysis is both a method of psychotherapy and a group of historically developing psychological theories. Along with the continuing evolution of psychoanalytic theory, there have been frequent revisions in the various ideas that analysts hold about dreams. In this chapter, I will mention some of these changing ideas about the dream, giving particular attention to the significant place the interpretation of dreams has had in psychoanalytic treatment. I will also indicate how the psychoanalytic practice of attending to *transference* and *resistance* rather than any particular theory of dreams that psychoanalysts might also hold gives the psychoanalytic interpretation of dreams its unique properties.

The validity of psychoanalytic work is not primarily dependent on any of the historically particular psychoanalytic theories but rather on the special nature of psychoanalytic clinic practice. Historically, psychoanalytic clinical practice has remained more constant than psychoanalytic theory.[1] Later in this chapter, the basic clinical concepts of transference and resistance will be clarified in a theory-free formulation.

FREUD'S THEORY OF THE REPRESSED CHILDHOOD ORIGINS OF THE DREAM

As early as the 1890s, Freud found reason to believe that adult psychopathology had its origins in childhood fantasies or traumas that had been unconsciously repressed. Freud thought that traumas stimulate unconscious forbidden wishes that are isolated and kept from resolution by the normal association to other ideas and feelings (that is abreaction and the processes of "working through"). He also believed that certain repressed fantasies are the result of forbidden wishes generated either by a traumatic encounter or by a "universal" psychological process such as the Oedipus complex. The basic pattern of the Oedipus complex is a family drama in which a child ambivalently yearns for possession of the opposite-sex parent while fearfully competing with the parent of his or her own gender.

By 1900, Freud also held that adult dreaming had as a motivation a conflict between the need to sleep and the defensively distorted and unresolved memory of some of these same childhood events. He thought that sleep was an essential restorative state and that dreams allowed safe expression of pressing unresolved memories and impulses. The dream itself is constructed as a compromise between the need for expression and the need for sleep. With this theory, dreams, as well as slips of the tongue, bungled actions, and neurotic symptoms, became Freud's primary texts in his exploration of unconscious activity. Following this belief, the dream also became a place where Freud could look for clinical evidence of the specific childhood origin of a particular patient's neurosis. His theoretical link was his idea that unconscious content was timeless—that is to say, unaltered by the passage of time and unordered by sequence.

If, as Freud assumed, dreams have their motivation from more-or-less disguised childhood wishes, his interpretation of dreams gave him an empirical or observable basis for his clinical theory of neurosis. Currently, however, there is good reason to question some of this as it bears on the reasons for dreams. Whereas Freud claimed to have discovered a childhood motivation "behind" the dream, this discovery may have been as much a consequence of his desire for an inclusive and coherent theory as of his carefully conducted clinical investigations. Freud listened to the associations given by his psychoanalytic patients and asked that they attempt utter honesty in revealing the contents of their awareness during the psychotherapeutic session. The attempt to reveal "free association" is the fundamental activity that the patient will try to accept, evade, and so on. Freud believed that this activity, which includes the revealing of dreams, would allow for a construction of origins.

Freud listened to the dreams and associations of his patients and interpreted them by listening to their rhythm and pattern, their similarity to other thoughts and feelings, and his own associations to them, and, increasingly as his work advanced, by their transference and resistance implications. All of this therapeutic activity has a potential validity separate from the various theories used in understanding and explaining the practices.

I do not make the claim that analysts do not learn about their patients' unconscious activities from their dreams, but rather that it is not necessary to assume that the dream originates in a childhood wish in order to understand it psychoanalytically. I am also not saying that dreams do not reveal material that is helpful if the analyst intends to construct a biography of the patient's childhood. Distorted or clear childhood wishes might be recognized or constructed from a patient's dreams, but this is a matter of empirical possibility and not a formal necessity. Childhood events and concerns *might* be involved in a specific dream. The analyst is free to make interpretations and constructions about the patient's childhood if there is evidence that is personally meaningful to the patient. However, analysts use what they hear in dreams to make other sorts of interpretations as well.

FREUD'S DRIVE THEORY OF THE DREAM

Freud's conception of the unconscious was that it exists as a group of memories and instinctual drives organized by what he called the *primary process.*[2] The instinctual drives organize these memories into wishes that are repressed or made unconscious because they are in some fashion forbidden or overly traumatic. The *wish* was Freud's psychological equivalent to the biological drive. The contents of these wishes are memory traces—structures that in their most complete form are an association of words, images, and affects of pain or pleasure. This psychological content remains in a permanent unconscious storage but, under the sway of the primary processes, is able to undergo transformation and presses for immediate expression in action or thought. An individual defends against this instinctual satisfaction, as it appears in the form of a discharge of image and feeling. There is conflict built into the system.

Unconscious content may become connected to elements of current memory, or day residue. This connection can be based on almost any principle of similarity. The connection does not have to be intrinsically significant, and apparently trivial waking experiences and thoughts can serve as an escape valve for the unconscious content. This content, repressed because it was traumatic and beyond the developing child's ability to master, is then discharged in the disguised form of dreams, slips of the tongue, bungled actions, and neurotic symptoms. The disguise is a consequence of the person's continuing need to avoid recognizing the memory as a memory of an actual childhood trauma or fantasy because this would disturb sleep.

The memory unit itself is capable of transformation through *displacement, condensation,* and *symbolization.* Primary process allows for the memory unit of image, word, and affect to separate into subunits and recombine through displacement and condensation into a form different from that of the original memory. Freud's concept of displacement was that an affect or emotion originating with a particular memory could recombine with the image or sounds of a different memory. Condensation worked on the model of the Galton photograph, in which similar negatives are stacked one on top of the other before a print is made. The resulting image combines elements of both negatives with their common features amplified.

Freud organized this theory along an energic parameter in which certain thresholds of "energy" must be exceeded in order for an element to reach consciousness. Condensation and displacement also had to create energy levels in combination with the "energies" still existing in the day residue to allow for conscious attention and discharge. This "metapsychology" of energy has been rejected by many psychoanalysts on both philosophical and physiological grounds.

A central claim of drive theory is that a traumatic or forbidden memory can be discharged safely when it is censored and disguised. The censorship in dreams is a result of a vigilant set of preemptive moral concerns known as the superego, which remains somewhat active even during sleep. Freud first developed this model of unconscious transformation in his concept of the "dream work," which provided him with a model that he then applied to both the exploration of dreams and his analysis of neurotic symptoms. In effect, by using this model of the dream as containing a distorted childhood representation that had been stored in a timeless unconscious, he was able to argue that the dream could supply evidence of the childhood events that created the neurosis. Of course, this requires interpretation of the dream's apparent or *manifest* content into its disguised or *latent* content, but Freud and other psychoanalysts have always had other ways of hearing dreams as well.

For Freud, the repeating nightmare as a symptom of a traumatic disturbance was the only dream that had some of its central motivations in events beyond childhood.[3] The war neurosis and the traumatic neurosis was always recognized as exceptions to the doctrine of the childhood origin of neurosis in that these conditions are precipitated by traumatic experiences beyond the adult's ability to psychologically cope. In response to overwhelming trauma, nightmares occur that disrupt sleep's restorative function. When these dreams offer uncensored and overwhelming versions of the actual trauma, they literally wake a person up. Freud held that the nightmare is repeated over and over as the ego tries to actively master a passively experienced trauma that cannot simply be repressed. For Freud and the psychoanalytic community that followed him, dreams have always been seen as involved in some sort of function significant to adaptation, resolution, psychological synthesis, and so on. Freud viewed the nightmare as a psychological action that attempted to restore adaptive function. Its repetition is an inherent part of the ego's adaptive function of attempting to turn passivity into mastery through self-generated activity.

Two Meanings of Dreams

Dreams are remembered before or during the time they are related to the analyst. This highlights the fact that analysts do not work with dreams directly, but rather with the memory of the dream as it is told by the patient. Freud recognized this in his concept of the dream narrative as a *secondary revision,* which carries the dream content another step from its supposed latent content. The classical Freudian view is that the dream has a manifest content created by the transformation of an underlying unconscious latent content and that this manifest content is further subjected to a secondary revision when the dream is told.

Stein has pointed out that this revision allows the patient to make use of the roles of critic, editor, and plagiarist in the presentation of what was dreamt.[4] Clearly, this telling is shaped by the patient's varying needs for coherence, attention, deception, and other factors influenced by the transference and resistance. What is told to the analyst is shaped not only by the dream's original content but also by the dreamer's feelings about the dream and in the context of the complexities of the relationship to the analyst. Transference and resistance can always be an aspect of the dream told to the analyst.

The psychoanalytic view of dreaming has been attacked by some professionals as an orientation that requires the dream to be generated by and translatable back into latent and hidden childhood wishes. Although some analysts hold this position and find it clinically useful, it is possible to do psychoanalytic work without being bound by a search for "latent" childhood content as the dream's motivation. Generally, however, psychoanalysts do ally themselves with two positions, the first of which is that dreams are meaningful. This position has been supported by considerable clinical practice. The second position, less well established, is that dreams have an adaptive function beyond merely providing interpretable content.

If dream interpretation is not by any formal or theoretical necessity a search for some childhood event that has undergone distortive transformation, the interpretation of the dream can remain with the manifest dream, its associations, elaborations, and analytic context. Clinical and laboratory research indicates that the manifest dream content consists of psychodynamically meaningful content. Practically speaking, analysts always have paid attention to manifest content, although they may sometimes feel that this content stands for something else that is "deeper." Freud held that dreams are tied to Oedipal or pre-Oedipal experiences or unresolved later trauma, and indeed they might sometimes be. This is a question that is open for research. However, in research done over the last decade at the Boston Psychoanalytic Society and Institute, it has been established that manifest dream content involves the direct, metaphorical, or symbolic representation of ongoing problems or dilemmas in the dreamer's life.[5] These problems might follow from the dreamer's childhood, but they are directly understandable given the dreamer's self-experienced current dilemmas, which in the case of a person in psychoanalysis naturally involves the dilemma of analysis itself.

The Boston group also found that sometimes there is a more-or-less successful resolution of the dilemmas represented in the dreams. There was also some evidence that the presence or absence of a problem's resolution affects the dreamer's later waking life. Essentially, the Boston group's point of view is that what is dreamt about is what is found by the dreamer to be problematic or in need of resolution. In listening to dream content with an empathic ear tuned to the patient's dilemmas and styles of attempted resolution, the analyst is in a position to help understand how people are finding and creating their worlds of personal concern.

THE PSYCHOLOGIES OF DRIVE, EGO, OBJECT, AND SELF

Freud's narrative of his psychoanalytic dream studies was like that of an explorer using the dream as a vehicle in which the listening therapist and the patient could travel to the latter unconscious and childhood past, where the assumed origins of neurosis remained. Through empathic and nonjudgmental interpretation, the analyst could attempt to make these unconscious memories and wishes conscious. The adult patient, no longer as vulnerable as a child, would have a chance to come to terms with these matters from a more secure position. Further, the analyst's empathic stance would provide an opportunity to think and feel things through with less fear, shame, and guilt than if the patient assumed there was something forbidden or evil about these thoughts.

Freud's clinical theory assumed that certain instinctual drives associated with zones of the developing body and in the form of sexual or aggressive wishes are forbidden direct expression in childhood. These drives can be stimulated by natural developmental processes, such as the Oedipus complex, or by "toxic" environmental occurrences, such as seduction or abandonment. What makes them significant for dream formation is that they involve experience that, if it became conscious, would be more than a child could handle. An overwhelming adult trauma is analogous. Freud's clinical theory also allowed for the transference of these same drive-generated yearnings onto the analyst, who is then represented accordingly in the patient's dreams.

Historically, as psychoanalysis developed, interest began to shift from drives or forbidden wishes toward the relationship between wishes, defenses, and adaptation. With these concerns the analyst turned to the patient's *ego*. This term is the concept for a collection for activities and attributes that consciously, preconsciously, or unconsciously regulate the major psychological functions. Self-control, adaptation, planning, and affect regulation are among its central activities. But most essentially the ego is the site of the attempted resolutions of the dilemmas of the intrapsychic and the interpersonal worlds, grappling with the contradictory demands of the *superego* and *id*. Freud's ego psychology involves an id with its instinctual sexual and aggressive urges, desires, and wishes in conflict with the superego's unconsciously enacted representations of parental and cultural prohibition and constraint.

Psychoanalysts listening to dreams and their associations from the perspective of ego psychology observe how conflict is characteristically represented. They wonder whether and how it is resolved. They also speculate on what the dream representations suggest about other situations in the patient's life, including childhood, and almost always wonder how the analyst and the psychoanalytic encounter might be represented, during which they attended to the the issue of *transference*. When they hear themes that can be interpreted in terms of the patient's restricted freedom of thought and feeling, they attend to *resistance*.

Psychoanalytic practice consists of one person, the analyst, facilitating another person's attempts at verbal free association, especially by interpretation of transference and resistance. The analysis of the resistance is the interpretive act of understanding, pointing out, clarifying, and sometimes confronting and explaining why there are restrictions in the patient's "freedom of association." Restrictions in freedom can occur consciously or unconsciously, although psychoanalysts have traditionally been most interested in unconsciously motivated limitations and inhibitions.

The analysis of the transference is the interpretation of the relationship between analyst and patient, with specific reference to why the patient has particular associations, feelings, and resistances within the context of an idiosyncratic or personal vision of the analyst. Naturally, the patient's important past relationships will figure into this. Thus the analysis of the resistance involves understanding why there are restrictions in association of thought and feeling, and the analysis of the transference involves understanding why the quality of the present analytic relationship facilitates the specific associations and resistances that occur.[6]

The dream representations are psychological objects, as is the psychological field of the dream itself. The dream content involves particular objects, processes, events, concepts, affects, and relationships. This entire state of affairs of "actors" and "stage" is subject to critical inquiry. When the analytic focus is on the themes of intimacy, merger, closeness, individuation-separation, dependency, dyads versus triads, and so on, the relevant psychoanalytic theories are concerned with *object relations.* Is there a figure represented in the dream? Is the figure lonely, alone, happy, terrified, desperate, erotic, secure, engulfed, strong, enraged, or autonomous? Does he or she resemble mother, father, sister, or brother?

If the field of the dream is cohesive, fragmented, or narcissistically relevant in terms of self-esteem, idealization, ambition, admiration, and so on, the analyst may be attending to the concepts found in psychoanalytic *self-psychology.* And as psychoanalysis continues to evolve, there will be more perspectives through which the dream may be viewed.

Analysts listen to the dreams and associations told to them and wonder what purpose the telling serves. They try to determine why a dream is related at a particular time, what else is happening in the patient's life that makes the dream understandable, and most importantly, what it says about the ongoing psychoanalysis. The analysis may be five-day-a-week, fifty-minute meetings of intense personal investment. Therefore, expecting to be an object of the patient's dreaming does not signal an analyst's vanity.

INTERPRETATION, DREAMS, AND THE UNCONSCIOUS

The psychoanalytic concept of the unconscious and the clinical act of interpreting resistance and transference are interdependent. In interpreting something psychoanalytically, the analyst recognizes in the patient's associations something that the patient does not consciously recognize and then renders that recognition less problematic. Traditionally this has been stated as a transformation of the *unconscious* into the *conscious,* when the focus has been on the availability of self-knowledge, and the transformation of *id* into *ego,* when the focus has been on competence, including the competence to tolerate one's own cognitive and feeling states. From this perspective, resistance invoves the unconscious barriers to self-knowledge and competence.

Freud's advice is still heeded.[7] Patients are asked to associate to the feelings or images present in the dream—to the whole or to some part of the dream that may bear on issues of current emotional significance. Usually, however, analysts let patients do as they wish, and they may wonder whether the telling of the dream itself is an act of resistance or avoidance in contrast to a desire to understand more. Generally the patient already knows the dream that is to be told to the analyst, so the dream-telling could be used to avoid anything new and unexpected from happening during the therapeutic hour. As Roy Schafer has reminded analysts, ". . . true dream analysis must be open to the unexpected; otherwise there is no point in doing it."[8]

Feelings of pain and pleasure have had an especially central role in traditional psychoanalytic dream interpretation. Although Freud felt that the dream narrative reflected the experience of distorting transformation, he also held that affects are not transformable except when displaced onto new objects.[9] This observation grounded in early theory has kept analysts especially attuned to what patients say about what they feel in the dream even if it somehow seems out of place given the other content.[10] Often patients will appear to feel or to remember a feeling that is inconsistent with their verbal reports, and analysts speculate about this too.

The interpretation of symbols is an especially thorny piece of psychoanalytic clinical theory. Freud was clearly a Lamarckian believer in the inheritance of acquired characteristics. He felt that symbols were part of a deeply repressed ancestral heritage common to humans. This position rarely has been accepted by other analysts. Generally, analysts seem to view symbols as an aspect of the general cognitive ability to create likeness and metaphor, and with this belief no one-to-one correspondence between symbol and object is required. Psychoanalysts are not fond of "dream dictionaries," except perhaps as providers of hints to culturally common usage.

Psychoanalytic interpretation is an action that centers on the unconscious acts of the patients as they appear during analysis. Seen this way, the unconscious is a state of affairs constructed by the analyst and patient and used during the study of the patient's transference, resistance, and other disclaimed or unknown actions. A major implication of this viewpoint is that the concept of the unconscious is a domain of possible fact that in order to become conscious must first be constructed. The interpretation of the unconscious is a social activity in which one person thinks that he or she sees what the other doesn't. But for therapeutic interpretation to be effective, both parties must be ready to share.

Another implication of this view of a mutually constructed unconscious is that the unconscious is not an object or domain filled with a specific content for which there is only one correct understanding. The same necessarily holds for dreams. Just as there are various versions of psychoanalytic theory, there are various correct interpretations of dreams possible at any given moment. Descriptions, constructions, and interpretations are always and only versions of the possible. They are of value to the extent that they are useful and help the analysis to progress.

The psychoanalyst listening to a patient's dreams may find that the words and images are understandable given the patient's current dilemmas. Conversely, a patient's current problems may be made more understandable given what is heard in his or her dreams. I have suggested in this chapter that dreams involve a representation of the problems and issues that confront us whether or not they are primarily motivated by a childhood memory or wish. Nonetheless, a person's manner of framing the world has a history and development leading back to childhood. Dream content may be motivated by current concerns, but it is good to remember that concerns are characterized by the personality of the dreamer. Character and personality may develop throughout a person's life, but the psychoanalyst generally believes that the dilemmas of childhood are crucial in setting the course.

Freud's position has kept the analyst interested in the dream's place in the dreamer's developmental history and as a representation of the dreamer's resolution of the conflicts between the real world and personal life, which naturally includes the problems that come with biology and sexuality. These, of course, are among the most significant matters that confront the psychoanalytic therapist and the issues that inhibit, distort, and motivate the patient's quest for greater freedom. Freud still provides us with excellent reminders in our efforts to understand the dream's place in our lives.

June Singer

A Jungian Approach
to Dreamwork

Dreamwork is and always has been an important part of Jungian analysis. Dreams are seen as compensatory to our conscious attitudes, for they occur at times when the defenses we employ to cope with a problematic world are put away, and sleep opens the door to that other world where all that consciousness cannot accept awaits an opportunity to express itself. Yet a trace of consciousness remains, even in sleep, as a guardian of the gate to devilishly transform the messages from the dream side into codes that have to be deciphered to elicit their meaning. When we waken, we have a choice: let sleeping lions be, or take the risk to discover the energy and power of the dream.

The analytic process is based to a large extent on breaking down into its polar opposites something that is essentially whole. For example, we divide the psyche into "consciousness" and "the unconscious." We talk about relations between the ego and the unconscious, subject and object, individual self and world self, within and without, and so on—always as though the opposites were two different and basically irreconcilable things. Nevertheless, the task in analysis is supposed to be to reconcile them. We are told that in analytic work we are to attempt to make unconscious material conscious; but we are also told that the unconscious is so vast, and most of it so unknowable, that we can never make it *fully* conscious. We must strive to establish relations between the ego and the unconscious, yet the ego is so small and the unconscious so vast that we cannot expect to understand unconscious material completely. Analysis requires polarization or dualism—always the protagonist and the adversary; always the struggle, the hero's quest against the dark forces that would undermine him, the heroine's effort to activate her special powers.

Surely there is some virtue in taking the psyche apart (metaphorically) and identifying the various pieces in their relationship to one another—especially in cases involving psychopathology. Even an automobile has to be taken apart sometimes when it will not operate properly. However, the automobile will not function except when it is working as a whole; the value of its parts lies in their being in a correct functional relationship to one another. And so with the human organism.

For certain purposes it is useful to identify the "parts." If one wants to correct the human organism when it is malfunctioning, it is important to know what its components are, how they are organized, and how they function. This pertains not only to the body but also to the structural maps of the psyche and to enough different views of psyche and body to avoid the predicament of the blind men, each of whom insists on his individual perceptions of the nature of the elephant. So there is value, when training therapists, to teach about psychic process by identifying the "parts of the psyche." However, if we stop there, we stop with the five-finger exercises and will never play the concerto.

When I was invited to contribute to this volume, I decided to sleep on the offer before responding. This is the dream I had that night.

I have a small child, a newborn baby, and my husband and I are utterly delighted. We are busily rearranging our house to accommodate the child. My husband is doing most of the caretaking; he's very busy cleaning up the house, washing the windows, and preparing a place for the child. I'm very excited and feeling very spiritual, also extremely tired from just having given birth to the child.

The next morning it occurs to me that I haven't fed this child, I haven't diapered it, I haven't done anything for it. I've just been rejoicing about the child. I go into the child's room and the child is in its little crib, but it has grown tremendously. It is now the size of a one- or two-year-old. I decide I'd better change the child's diaper. I go to get a damp cloth to wash the child, and when I come back the child is moving about and then gets up and walks. I think to myself, "This child is one day old and it's already walking." By now it's talking, too, in a fairly coherent adult way! I'm a little surprised, but I think that with two such intelligent parents, it's really not that surprising.

I'm thinking about that when all of a sudden I'm jerked into being awake. It's early in the morning and my first analysand is ringing the doorbell. I let the person in, but I'm somewhat disoriented because of having been awakened so suddenly. We go into the room where I ordinarily see my clients and I find twin beds made up there. I'm embarrassed, because ordinarily there are no beds, but a couch and a chair in that room. It dawns on me that the dream I had was so realistic that all during the night I must have been moving furniture to make room for the child. The only thing I can do—and it seems so ridiculous—is to say honestly to my analysand, "Look, I had a dream last night that I had a baby, and it was so realistic that I must have gotten up in my sleep and moved the furniture around, so we'll have to go into my study and I'll see you there instead of here." In my study the furniture has been moved around and there is extra furniture there. It's totally chaotic. But we manage to find places to sit. I think to myself how realistic dreams can be, and how awful it was that I got carried away with this dream and let it become so real that it intruded into my life and interfered with my carrying on my analytic work. I can hardly get through the analytic hour, so filled am I with emotion.

Suddenly the alarm goes off. I am back in my usual bed, *really* awake. I realize that the whole episode with the baby was a dream, as was the whole episode with the analysand and the furniture moved around, and in reality everything is as it was. The dream was a dream, and the dream within it was a dream. Then I say to myself, "So this is reality!" And then I think about the Hindu god Vishnu, reclining in the interval between several creations, having withdrawn the universe into himself. In my mind's eye I see him within the golden egg in his threefold aspect: as himself, as the serpent Ananta Sesha who forms his bed, and as the cosmic ocean upon which he and the serpent float. All creation is like a dream within him, ready to manifest from the potentiality of the primordial waters, as he exhales. I think, Vishnu dreamed the whole world, and maybe all that *we* do is a dream. Perhaps true reality is an entirely different kind of consciousness from the world of insubstantiality that the Hindus call *maya,* and that we take for substance.

REFLECTIONS ON THE DREAM

My first impulse was not to try to interpret the dream in any methodical way, although I am sure that the dream would lend itself to the classical Jungian method. I have used these methods over the years and found that they sharpened my perceptions and gave me a structure within which to work. But more recently I have learned that if I do not begin grinding away at the interpretation of a dream according to the rules I have been taught, but allow the dream to have its own way with me (or with my analysands, if it is their dream), then I begin to enter another state of awareness, in which the dream delivers its own message.

With the dream I have just related, I allowed myself to be open to the question of what its overwhelming sense is. The first part, *the joy of having the child,* evoked the strongest feeling. Then there was the surprise that although I did not really take care of the child; it grew by itself in a fantastic way. There was some support from my husband, yet I did not have the feeling that he actually took care of it. I felt I made space for the child but that it grew independently of my efforts and took care of itself.

The next strong feeling was *the confusion*. I had moved all the furniture without having been aware of it. There was this whole autonomous side of me of which I had no consciousness whatever.

Lastly, I recalled that I had not committed myself to writing a chapter on dreams but had decided to sleep on it, waiting for some sign from the unconscious.

I had a couple of associations to the dream. The first was that I had planned to see my first analysand that morning in my study, since I had some company over the weekend that had necessitated rearranging some furniture in my consulting room. As far as having a baby, I associated to that a new project that I had begun to work on, which was growing and developing very quietly, and I had felt pregnant with it.

I realized that I could not seek an interpretation of the dream on an objective level, that is, by taking the objects in the dream as literally representing themselves. It simply would not fit the facts of my life: I was unmarried at the time and past the age of childbearing. It would be necessary to look at the dream from the subjective level, in the sense that Jung used this term:

> The whole dream work is essentially subjective, and a dream is a theatre in which the dreamer is himself the scene, the player, the prompter, the author, the public, and the critic. This simple truth forms the basis for a conception of the dream's meaning which I have called *interpretation on the subjective level.* Such an interpretation, as the term implies, conceives all the figures in the dream as personified features of the dreamer's own personality.[1]

So the elements of the dream are symbolic representations of the dreamer. I am in a creative process, and there is a "brainchild," or a child of the spirit, growing inside me. Just as Buckminster Fuller once pointed out, after conception an embryo does not have to be told how to develop into a baby, how many hands and how many feet to grow; so the child of one's own creativity does not have to be forced or prodded or fitted into a pattern of what some "public" is supposed to be buying this year. The creative process is a function that involves making space for what is growing within, living in a way that provides stimulus and nourishment, and then letting the "child" speak for itself.

OUR HOLISTIC HUMANNESS

The nature of our humanness is holistic. No matter how fragmented we may feel at times, the psyche inevitably seeks wholeness. I have long been troubled by the disjunction between consciousness and the unconscious in the analytic tradition. The dream of the child provides an example of this disjunction. We have been told that dreams are "unconscious material"; yet if I have a dream, can remember it and repeat it, is it unconscious material? The dream that I presented was fully conscious to me, yet it occurred while I was asleep, surely not the state of ordinary consciousness. But I cannot say that even then it was fully unconscious because, as my associations showed, there were elements in the dream that were clearly related to my conscious processes during the day. It appears that one is neither altogether correct in saying that the dream is unconscious material nor in saying that it is conscious material. The dream is not something that can be located in one or the other area, conscious or unconscious. Rather, it makes more sense to speak of a *dreaming process* that transcends the apparent dichotomy of consciousness and the unconscious.

Whenever we break down things, concepts, or dreams analytically, we divide unitary realities into parts and pieces. If we concentrate our efforts on taking the dream apart into its components, we may very well lose its impact. I recalled the delight in my voice at having given birth to the child. The energy vibrating in me overcame the fatigue I felt after the actual labor. This was a feeling I could recognize. I did not need to dissect the dream to know that the project I was engaged with was going to demand a great effort from me, but that it would be a labor of love. I could also see that I needed to make space for the work, and that the "child" would grow of itself. I could follow the energy in the dream and so experience the absurd self-confidence that is required of anyone who embarks upon a creative task that is unconventional by its very nature and has little if any external support. This is how I could say, half-seriously, "Why shouldn't this child be able to speak, with two such intelligent parents!"

LEVELS OF CONSCIOUSNESS

But then I found myself in another level of the dream. Within the dream I believed that I had awakened, and that I was paying with my confusion for the delight I had experienced in my absorption with my child—I was now distracted from my other task, that of meeting with my analysand. Consciousness must function on many levels and in many ways within a short span of time. One has to cultivate as much awareness as possible in order to be able to shift from one level to another, so that what is at one moment foreground can become background in the next. If we cannot do this, we are in danger of becoming one-sided, one-dimensional beings, unable to utilize fully the potentialities with which we have been endowed by the nature of our humanness.

Just as the line between what we can remember of a dream and what we cannot call back into awareness is often very fuzzy, so also is the line between the dream itself and the moment upon awakening when we first become aware of it. It was in that hypnopompic state when I was neither fully awake nor fully in the dream; that I had the insight that perhaps the state we think of as "ordinary awareness" is not necessarily a "higher" state of consciousness; that in another, broader context, what we call "ordinary awareness" is a state of "being asleep" when we compare it, for example, with what the Buddhist calls "enlightenment."

I am indebted to John Welwood[2] for calling attention to statements like the following made by Jung, which ascribe an autonomous agency to the unconscous: "The unconscious perceives, has purposes and intuitions, feels and thinks as does the conscious mind."[3] Welwood proposes a redefinition of the unconscious as an *unconscious process,* "a holistic mode of organizing experience, a mode of relationship which transcends the normal working of focal attention by grasping multiple connections as a whole, without serial differentiations."[4]

This definition fits the dreaming process quite well. Instead of looking at dreams as things—as dramas, with their settings, plots, casts of characters, and symbolic meanings—we can view them as evidence of the *dreaming process.* This process warrants our concern, for it transcends the dichotomy of what we have formerly thought of as consciousness and the unconscious. The dream gives us imagery in action. We do not dream piecemeal; we receive the dream as a whole, with an emotional impact, an energy, an impression, a feeling, and an impetus to thought or action. In the dreaming process we are no longer confronted with a totally dark and unknowable area of the unconscious, but are aware of the process by which the unconscious filters into consciousness. We see it, feel it, hear it, taste it, and smell it, but not serially—rather all at once, as a whole.

FOCUSED AND DIFFUSE ATTENTION

Interpretation works through a process of directing focused attention to details. Through dream interpretation we may grasp intellectually certain implications of the dream, a limited sense of meaning. But as Welwood points out in writing about the unconscious, "It is unknowable through focal attention which would necessarily distort its nature by breaking it into serial discrete elements."[5] However, we can approach the unconscious through another type of attention, diffuse attention. This allows the whole field to be experienced all at once in its wholeness.

Welwood suggests a more dynamic concept of the relationship between what we are used to calling "consciousness" and what we are used to calling "the unconscious." Instead of looking at them as polar opposites, it is proposed that we understand the relationship between conscious and unconscious as a continual shifting between figure and ground. The ground of our being, the ground of our awareness, is the rich background of feelings, observations, sensations, intuitions, things we have learned and forgotten, our bodies and their conditions, our levels of energy and our genetic inheritance. All this is not simply an amalgamation of psychic substance lodged in some area called "the unconscious," but rather the fusion of everything that has happened in our personal and collective past to contribute to this moment. This is the ground of consciousness. It is perceived directly, in the form of the overwhelming feelings we know and which, to a great extent, guide our feelings and behavior. Eugene Gendlin says, "The feel of doing *anything* involves our sense of the *whole* situation at the moment, despite our not focally reflecting on it as such. This is the myriad multiplicity. . . ."[6]

As the "ground" is implicit in the figure, so the "unconscious" is implicit in consciousness. The ground is perceived holistically, not through the effort of the intellect alone. Interpretation is a function primarily of the intellect; which is why the dreaming process cannot be grasped through interpretation alone. The intellect works through a conceptual separation of the organic whole into its parts; but the whole is greater than the sum of its parts. Accordingly, the dream is greater than the effort of interpretation allows us to perceive.

Consciousness, then, is the foreground—what emerges into focused awareness from the unconscious background, the "ground of consciousness." Consciousness emerges discretely from this ground at a particular moment and stands against it, commanding our attention as a specific event or as a specific and defined process. Consciousness and its contents or processes will naturally vary from moment to moment as certain movements occupy the center of our attention while others are relegated to the periphery. If we allow our attention to flow freely between foreground and background, realizing that what we are aware of at a given moment is only the foreground at *this* moment, we become actively and dynamically involved in the interpenetration between what we have been used to calling "consciousness" and "the unconscious." In this sense, the unconscious does not have "a mind of its own" (as Jung asserted), nor does it have an existence separate from consciousness, but the unconscious is *actually present* implicitly in whatever is going on at the moment.

FOUR LEVELS OF THE DREAMWORK PROCESS

With this in mind, I propose a restructuring of the dreamwork process on the basis of four approaches to the dream, which correspond to four levels of the psyche. These are inspired by Welwood's "four levels of conscious experience," but I have altered them to apply to dreamwork.[7] The levels which are not hierarchical in nature but, as I indicated earlier, interpenetrating are the contextual level, the personal level, the transpersonal level, and the holistic level.

The *contextual level* is the background of the dream, the field upon which the action is played, the life experience of the dreamer up to the moment of the dream's appearance, mostly forgotten and certainly not in the focus of the dreamer's awareness during sleep. The context supports the action of the dream and provides the reservoir out of which the motifs and actions of the dream may emerge.

The *personal level* deals with personal associations to the dream process or the dream story—what those images evoke in us. Here the dichotomy between the dream as objective and the dream as subjective breaks down: we experience what the dream process brings up in us; we look at the data presented in the dream and react to them out of the flow of energy that surges up from the background as we let the dream have its effect upon us. (I did not need to ask myself whether it was a real baby in my own dream or whether the growing, developing new thing coming out of me was being symbolically represented as a baby. I simply knew that this autonomous being was being born through me, but that it had its own life.)

The *transpersonal level* reflects the way in which the whole organism of the dreamer is "attuned to the patterns and currents of the universe and the life process itself."[8] This includes the archetypal dimension of experience, but is not limited to it. Also included is what Jung called "the objective psyche," the consciousness present in all life processes, of which you and I are mere minuscule participants.

The *holistic level* encompasses the other three. I believe that Jung stood on the threshold of holistic awareness. He attempted to cross that threshold using the tools of intellect and reason, but these tools proved insufficient. Close to the end of Jung's last great work, *Mysterium Coniunctionis,* the frustration he felt when he had reached the high point of his insight seems evident. He discusses the production of the lapis in alchemy as the achievement of the Unus Mundus, the unitive or holistic consciousness:

> The production of the lapis was the goal of alchemy in general. . . . For us the representation of the idea of the self in actual and visible form is a mere rite d'entrée, as it were, a mere propaedeutic action and a mere anticipation of its realization. The existence of a sense of inner security by no means proves that the product will be stable enough to withstand the disturbing or hostile influences of the environment. The adept had to experience again and again how unfavorable circumstances or a technical blunder . . . hindered the completion of his work, so that he was forced to start all over again from the beginning. Anyone who submits his sense of inner security to analogous psychic tests will have similar experiences. More than once everything that has been built will fall to pieces under the impact of reality, and he must not let this discourage him from examining again and again, where it is that his attitude is still defective, and what are the blind spots in his psychic field of vision. Just as a lapis philosophorum [the philosopher's stone, which is a metaphor for the goal of the alchemical work], with its miraculous powers, was never produced, so psychic wholeness will never be attained empirically, as consciousness is too narrow and one-sided to comprehend the full inventory of the psyche. Always we shall have to begin over and over again from the beginning.[9]

This is a distressing prospect. Examination and reexamination of one's attitudes to discover the blind spots does not necessarily lead to psychic wholeness. One can, and often does, avoid the same blind spots over and over. So the intellectual, or interpretative, approach to the dream is insufficient in and of itself.

Beyond Interpretation

It appears that Jung penetrated the realm of human experience as far as he could with the instrument of the intellect. He found, at the end, a barrier, "the still unknown or unconscious facts" that would not yield to symbolic interpretation. The alchemists, on the other hand, broke through the paradox of reason and saw that the dichotomy between consciousness and the unconscious was a false duality. They did not work solely with the *idea*; they worked with the *stuff* as well, the *prima materia*. They maintained an immediate, tactile involvement with the concrete realities. That is why they would talk of the *Unus Mundus,* the unity in which "one is the stone, one the medicine, one the vessel, one the procedure, and one the disposition" without feeling any dissociation. In the alchemical work, the adept, the process, and the outcome were one. The experience was successful to the degree that it arose from bodily participation in the work.

When we read Jung, alchemy, or any other system, we need to remember that behind the words lies the living experience and that the experimenter is united with the process. But when we step back to formulate it, we get a secondary product, an abstraction of the work. Instead of the experience, we get a structure built up from the bricks of many experiences that have been generalized.

This applies to dreams as to any other experience. In the dreamwork itself, we do better to deal directly with the totality of each dream, unique unto itself and specific to the individual dreamer, which represents the culmination of the dreamer's life until the moment of the dream. This makes it possible to see the dream as a whole and complete product of a whole and complete organism.

P. Erik Craig

An Existential
Approach to
Dreamwork

The orientation for understanding dreams used here is European in origin and grows out of an approach to philosophy and science that began with the twentieth-century philosopher Edmund Husserl and especially with his simple, straightforward appeal "to return to the things themselves." This approach, called phenomenology, strives to avoid the use of unexamined assumptions and presuppositions in order to study phenomena as they present themselves directly in our conscious experience. Such philosophically informed phenomenology is not merely concerned with describing surface appearances, but extends beyond this to investigate underlying or "essential" structures and meanings. Phenomenology is, therefore, particularly well-suited for the study of the meaning of dreams.

The term *phenomenology* is perhaps best understood by tracing it back to its ancient origins. The word *phenomenon* comes from the Greek work *phainesthai,* which means "to shine forth," "to appear," or "to show itself." The Greek *logos,* on the other hand, means "discourse," that is, the act of revealing something or making something manifest. Phenomenology, then, is simply the revealing of that which shows itself from itself.[1]

What this suggests is that when we approach things phenomenologically, we want them to reveal themselves as the very things they are. If, being phenomenological, we were to meet someone on the street, we would want that person to appear as the unique and particular person he or she is. Conversely, we would *not* want our prejudices or assumptions about that person to be what is revealed. Likewise, with dreams, we want every dream we remember or hear to reveal itself *from itself* and not from our ideas or assumptions about it. Having a phenomenological attitude is the most loving way we can approach the world, because, with this attitude, we want whatever *is* to be just what it is and what it is becoming.

Because of its careful, unbiased approach to understanding phenomena in an objective, open-minded manner, the phenomenological manner of inquiry was adopted by various European philosophers and psychiatrists, known as existentialists, who were especially concerned with understanding the depth and meaningfulness of human existence. In its broadest sense, existentialism was simply the application of phenomenological methods to the study of human existence as it manifests itself directly and concretely in our own experience. Consequently, the existential approach to dreams emphasizes the manifest meaningfulness of dreaming not only as it is significant in and for itself but also as it relates to our lives while fully awake.[2]

THE SIGNIFICANCE OF DREAMS

In this chapter I shall show how the existential-phenomenological use of dreams in psychotherapy may reveal and facilitate an individual's capacity for a fuller, freer, more authentic existence. But first we must raise a critical question: "Of what does the meaningful content of a dream consist?" While this question has been asked many times throughout the history of oneirology, almost without exception the answers have relied upon theoretical formulations that are not apparent in dreams themselves and that must either be assumed or persuasively demonstrated with each new dream. But, proceeding phenomenologically, we are uniquely concerned with what dreams themselves show us, from themselves, about their meaningful content. Let us try an experiment.

Imagine yourself slipping off to sleep. As your world becomes increasingly dark, vague, and sluggish, you surrender to a profound condition of relaxation and stillness, a quiet and memoryless sleep. Soon you are enveloped by the black, black night. Space disappears, and you let time pass by without you. A while later you begin to notice a soft light spreading silently through your existence. This is not the light of the sun, not a physical light, but rather the light of being, of things coming into being in your very presence. Sound and smell may also appear, as well as moods. Gradually you find yourself opening to a whole world in progress. You may encounter family members, friends, lovers, enemies, colleagues, or strangers. You may be active or passive, cheerful, angry, frightened, sexy, loving, or inspired. You may find yourself involved in a number of activities within any number of settings and situations, from the extravagant to the mundane. The possibilities are vast and they are simply that—possibilities; they are the particular possibilities for being-in-the-world to which you are open while dreaming—nothing more, nothing less.

So in answer to the question, "Of what does the meaningful content of a dream consist?" we can simply say, "Of our relationship to a specific constellation of existential possibilities." We can even say that there are three general kinds of existential possibilities to which we are open while dreaming. First, we are open to possibilities of our existence that we observe and readily acknowledge while fully awake. Second, we find ourselves relating to existential possibilities that we acknowledge in our waking life but often choose to ignore. And finally, we are concerned with possibilities that, because of our own blurred and constricted vision in waking, we fail to see at all. Drawing from dreams of individuals in therapy, I would like to show how each category of dream possibility may be used in psychotherapy.

DREAMING OF RECOGNIZED POSSIBILITIES

We might be tempted to avoid considering dreams of already recognized existential possibilities, because they supposedly reveal only what we already know. However, a concern for what we believe is "merely" obvious often turns out to be surprisingly rewarding.

Ted, a social-work student in his mid-twenties who was having difficulty separating from a former lover, dreamed that he was waving good-bye to her while he was sitting backwards on a motorcycle, trying to get it started so he could go to a new job in the city. When he woke up, Ted immediately recognized the similarity between his dreamed and waking predicaments: he couldn't pull away from this relationship and get on with his life. Reflecting further on his dream, Ted realized that if he had sat down facing forward on the bike he could have easily started it. Nudged on by his dream experience, in waking life Ted decided to stop thinking so much about the past and about "saying good-bye."

A few weeks later, however, Ted had another dream in which he got a ticket for driving the wrong way down a one-way street. This time he was facing forward in the driver's seat, but unfortunately, he was driving backwards and at fifty miles an hour! The policeman was so annoyed that he wrote Ted a ticket for going the wrong way at *seventy* miles an hour! At this point Ted woke up, recalled the dream, and burst into laughter, recognizing at once that over the previous days he had once again been dwelling on the past instead of looking ahead to the future. Heeding the dreamed admonition, Ted quickly put his waking life back in "forward gear."

Ted's dreams show how thinking about our dreams may help us consider new possibilities for dealing with ongoing enigmas in our lives. While dreaming, Ted lived out his familiar conundrum in such farcical extremes that the mere humor evoked constructive change. Likewise, reflecting on dreams may underscore our awareness of our own immediate existential posture, enhance our self-acceptance, and open the way to personal growth.

DREAMING OF RECOGNIZED BUT IGNORED POSSIBILITIES

Stephanie, a vivacious woman in her early twenties who was a member of a psychotherapy group, described a recurrent dream of horrifying encounters with small, hairy creatures who woke her up as soon as she fell asleep, grabbed her by the feet and tried to pull her out of bed. Stephanie was always paralyzed by the mere sight of these ugly little beasts.

These encounters seemed so real to Stephanie that she wasn't sure that they hadn't actually happened. Consequently, she no longer dared fall asleep and her sleeplessness soon led her to join the therapy group.

On several occasions during the first few weeks of her group Stephanie talked about her nightmares but, each time, she remained perplexed about the significance of these shaggy dwarfs in her life. One day the therapist suggested that she forget about her dreams for awhile and simply talk about her waking life. Stephanie described many very positive experiences. An exchange then ensued roughly as follows.

THERAPIST: So your life seems to be going quite well lately.

STEPHANIE: Yes. Things are just great and I feel so lucky with the exception of these dreams—or whatever they are—and the fact that I can't get to sleep anymore. I don't understand it.

THERAPIST: You certainly *do* seem fortunate, though, of course, no one's life is perfect. You mean to tell me that there aren't even a *few* things, as there naturally are for *all* of us, about which you feel at least a little bit disappointed?

STEPHANIE: No, not really. Really nothing at all! Well, I do miss playing my guitar but that's no big deal. I used to play guitar and sing for a folk group. I miss that a lot. We had a wonderful time playing at clubs and schools. We called ourselves "The Gremlins" and we really . . ."

Within moments, other members of the group had interrupted Stephanie to ask if she saw any connection between these gremlins and the little monsters in her nightmares. Stephanie responded that it had occurred to her as soon as she mentioned the word but that she couldn't believe it would be so obvious. Nevertheless, with the support group's encouragement, she began to explore that period in her life during which she had felt a deeply satisfying sense of purpose, self-esteem, and personal and group identity that she had never known before or since. Her experience with The Gremlins had clearly met important developmental needs, and when the folk group collapsed, so had the opportunity to address these needs. While dreaming, Stephanie was confronted by the emissaries of her own ignored possibilities for self-development and, upon recognizing the significance of their appeal, she was able to consider new ways to fulfill these needs.

Stephanie's experience shows that if we simply attend to that which stands before our eyes while dreaming *and* are able to grasp the relevant contexts to which it alludes in our waking hours, we may then shine these two lights of dreaming and waking on our single human existence. It is this *combined luminosity* of dreaming and waking that is so effective in penetrating darkened areas of our lives, wherein lies a wealth of possibility for enhancing our development as persons.

DREAMING UNRECOGNIZED POSSIBILITIES

This brings us to ways in which we are concerned, while dreaming, with existential possibilities to which we are not at all open while awake. For example, Nancy, a twenty-three-year-old secretary, dreamed that her father had died in an automobile accident. Although upon waking she was initially alarmed, she soon composed herself. Later that day she told her short-term psychotherapy group that she thought her dream was silly, since her father was in perfect health and was an extremely careful driver. When other members questioned her about her father's health, she laughed and said there was nothing to worry about. She had even called him, she added, "just to make sure!" When several individuals confronted her with her feelings about her father's mortality in general, Nancy asserted that she had never thought about his death and saw no reason for doing so now.

When one of the group members asked me if this was an example of resistance, I simply responded, "Well, we can only say that, while dreaming, Nancy was open to considering the possibility of her father's death and, now that she is awake, she is no longer open to considering this possibility." I then turned to Nancy and said that even though her dream deserved careful thought, I was impressed by her ability to maintain her own point of view in the face of social pressure. Two weeks then passed before Nancy surprisingly confessed that, as a result of her dream, she had begun to think about the implications of her father's mortality and, especially, about the importance of spending "quality time" with him while he was still alive.

Although Nancy was eventually able to use her dream to consider waking possibilities that she had previously denied, we are not always so fortunate. Sometimes we are so radically closed to certain existential possibilities that we remain so, regardless of how striking our dreamed experiences may be.

John, a businessman in his early forties, learned one fall that his best friend, Kenton, had cancer of the lung. In spite of the seriousness of the diagnosis, John firmly believed that the cancer was treatable and that, even if it did get worse, he would stand by Kenton in every way possible. One day he happened to mention in therapy that he had just visited Kenton and was surprised to find him so weak that he was unable to sit up for ten minutes at a time. Then, after discussing several other matters, John happened to mention a dream of the previous night. In the dream, he was standing in a morgue at the foot of a vault, in which lay the corpse of an old high-school buddy. The corpse suddenly sat up and tried to pull John into the vault with him. Stricken with horror, John grabbed a stick and jammed it into the friend's face while crying out for help.

Incredible though it may seem, John failed to see any connection between this dream and his relationship with Kenton. Rather, he thought it related to a colleague who was being fired and was asking for John's support. John's trenchant denial of the possibility for anxiety in relation to Kenton's situation led him to dismiss his dream with an astonishingly shallow explanation of it.

Kenton died a month later, and only then did John realize the extent of his denial. In the midst of his grief, he suddenly recalled his dream, which he had completely forgotten. He was shocked by his blindness, not only to the possibility of Kenton's death, but also to that of his own anxiety and violence in response to a friend's urgent plea for closeness. John then saw that if he had been open to considering these possibilities earlier, he might have found the courage to be more authentic with Kenton in the final weeks of his life.

John's experience demonstrates how dreaming is not enough to enable us to recognize possibilities to which we are obstinately blind while awake. Ultimately, we, as the awakened dreamers, are the ones who must be ready to acknowledge the possibilities embodied in our dreaming. It is only this open *wakeful* recognition that enables us to choose to carry out a fuller range of our own possibilities in waking life. While dreaming may help us become aware of our existence, historically determinative choice and action are the prerogatives of our wakefulness.

DREAMING OVER TIME:
A DREAM'S-EYE VIEW OF CHANGE IN PSYCHOTHERAPY

Thus far we have been concerned for the most part with single dreams and their relation to psychotherapeutic change. However, as Paul Stern, an existential psychologist, noted, "Dreams read . . . along phenomenological lines [not only] present poetically condensed images of a person's life situation at a given moment [but] . . . also accurately reflect changes in their situation over time."[3] Medard Boss, an existential analyst from Switzerland, illustrates this aspect of the clinical use of dreams in a report on a series of 823 dreams dreamt over a three-year period by a forty-year-old engineer who entered psychotherapy for depression and impotence."[4]

In the first dream the engineer had ever recalled, occurring two days prior to his first therapeutic consultation, he dreamed himself imprisoned in a dungeon with only a small window barred with wrought-iron work in the shape of mathematical signs and numbers. He then proceeded, over the next six-and-a-half months, to dream incessantly of turbines, cyclotrons, automobiles, airplanes, and other technical machines and devices. There were no human beings, indeed, no living things at all in these early dreams and, during this period, the patient became acutely aware of how imprisoned he was, in waking life, by the domination of his own "gray" mechanical intellect, seeing himself as "essentially no more than a useful cog in an industrial machine."

In the seventh month of therapy, the engineer finally dreamed of the presence of a living thing. At first there was a single potted plant; then, a green pine tree and red roses, though "the roots of roses appeared worm-infested, their buds sickly and leaves withered." After a four-month hiatus, during which he remembered no dreams, the man began to report dreams of insects. Over the next year, 105 insect dreams mingled with continued dreams of plants and machines. Six months followed of grey toads, frogs, and snakes, when finally, one night, "a bright red snake of tremendous thickness and length" startled him. At last, the first mammal appeared; it was a mouse darting into its hole. It is noteworthy that the mouse was tempting no cat, romping in no field, basking in no sunlight, and gloating over no cheese. The man's existence was still so constricted that he could be open to warm-blooded existence only in the form of mousy retreat, of dashing for cover.

Despite the apparent impoverishment of these dreams, it was during this period of plant and, especially, animal-life dreams that the man began, in waking, to regain what many existentialists would consider his full human potentiality and to experience his own possibilities for living corresponding to the nature of these creatures. For example, when the mouse dream was followed by a long series of pig dreams, and when these gave way to dreams about lions and horses, the man at last began to experience his sexual potency in waking life.

The patient's first dream of a human being, after two years of therapy, was of a larger-than-life unconscious woman "in a long blood-red dress, swimming in a large pond far below a vitreous cover of ice." Many maternal figures followed, including a gigantic good fairy with long blond hair and "mighty breasts from which there sprang waterfalls of milk." During this time, the patient became greedy for solicitude and his therapist "looked much more feminine than before." In other words, the man's entire existence, both sleeping and waking, was characterized by childlike concern with maternal care. One night, after two-and-a-half years of therapy, he dreamed of another woman dressed in blood-red, with whom he was dancing at a country festival. This new dream woman was "fully awake and passionate" and the man "fell deeply in love with her."

As you may have guessed, the dreamer in waking life was finally beginning to open himself to living a more fully autonomous and adult relationship to persons and things, to carrying out an existence that recognized and incorporated a more complete range of human possibilities.

A direct, phenomenological reading of dreams can be a powerful vehicle for change in psychotherapy. Dreams offer limpid portraits of our own existential standing, revealing not only those existential possibilities that we acknowledge while awake but also those we ignore or deny entirely. Seen over time, dreams also disclose shifts in the overall openness and quality of our lives as surely as blood pressure and pulse indicate changes in the more quantifiable aspects of our being.

Existential psychotherapists attempt to follow the significance, direction, and pace of the individual's development as they are revealed directly in dreams. Such therapists try never to tire of nudging gently at those as-yet unrecognized, feared, ignored, or denied possibilities of human existence that appear so shamelessly in dreaming. While an individual may not yet be open to seeing, while fully awake, what he or she was quite capable of seeing while sound asleep and dreaming, the therapist never loses faith in the manifest meaningfulness of the dreaming mode of existence.

Indeed, it is while dreaming that an individual may first dare, albeit timidly, to actualize some of his or her own authentic possibilities for being human. Like waking, dreaming is an opportunity for realizing a richer, more complete human existence, bringing flesh and blood to the bones of possibility. Individuals who see their own existential possibilities so concretely embodied in dreaming may be emboldened to carry them out of dreaming into a fuller, freer waking life.

W. H. Auden's poetic tribute to Sigmund Freud voices this potential of human dreaming as follows:

> But he would have us remember most of all
> To be enthusiastic over the night
>   Not only for the sense of wonder
>   It alone has to offer, but also
>
> Because it needs our love: for with sad eyes
> Its delectable creatures look up and beg
>   Us dumbly to ask them to follow;
>   They are exiles who long for the future
>
> That lies in our power. They too would rejoice
>   If allowed to serve enlightenment like him. . . .[5]

Adam Zwig

A Body-Oriented
Approach to
Dreamwork

Using body-based methods for working with dreams can be a powerful and transformative experience. Dreams are not only stories that occur during sleep; they are also mythical patterns encoded in our waking body experiences, which encompass everything from general feelings of nervousness, excitement, and sexual arousal, to minor symptoms such as headaches and stomachaches, to major life-threatening diseases such as cancer, heart disease, and AIDS. Working with dreams using body-based methods enables us to integrate our dreams and body experiences into a coherent and meaningful whole and to understand the meaning behind our physical symptoms.

The idea that dreams and body processes are interrelated is widespread and dates back thousands of years. Aristotle said that dreams were caused by the "heart," which he thought was the center of feeling, and that the skilled dream interpreter could predict illness and discover cures from dreams.[1] However, not all dreamworking systems have conceived of the same type of interrelation between dreams and the body, and there have been and remain relatively few systems that approach dreamwork by working directly with the body.

In order to give the reader an overview of body-based dreamworking methods, I have classified a variety of dreamworking systems into four categories, each of which understands the dream through a different set of ground rules or beliefs. *Philosophically based* systems do not apply dreamworking methods to the dreamer; instead, they create dream interpretations directly from specific philosophical, religious, or cosmological beliefs. *Analytical* systems use the method of mentally dividing the dream into parts and creating an interpretation based on the apparent interrelation between them. *Empirical* systems find the meaning of the dream in the dreamer's own experience of it. The *process-oriented* system uses the individual's psychological and physical experiences to discover how nighttime dreams live and express themselves in the dreamer's life during the day.

PHILOSOPHICALLY BASED AND ANALYTICAL SYSTEMS

These two categories include a variety of dreamworking systems that may interpret dreams as commentaries on the physical and existential conditions of the dreamer. Typical of these systems is the fact that they do not derive their interpretations from the dreamer's own physical experience; instead, they invoke philosophical "truths" or psychological analyses to apply a specific interpretation to the dream. In this sense, the systems in these two categories are not truly body-based; however, it is important to take a brief look at them and to differentiate them from dreamworking systems that work directly with the body.

The philosophically based category includes a number of ancient dreamworking systems. Babylonian, Assyrian, and Egyptian dream interpreters, as well as ancient Chinese and Indian physicians, created dream interpretations directly out of their religious, philosophical, and cosmological beliefs.[2] For example, Babylonian priests automatically interpreted dreams in which dead people were present to mean impending illness or death for the dreamer.[3] In classical Chinese medicine, which is based on the Chinese cosmological system and which uses dream interpretation as one of many diagnostic methods, dreams of weeping and sorrow are thought to indicate automatically a lung condition.[4] In both of these examples, interpretations about the body are based directly on philosophical systems, not on the actual physical experience of the dreamer.

Analytical body-oriented systems include modern psychological dream theories that postulate theoretical links between the meanings of various dream contents and specific physical processes; however, like the philosophically based systems, they do not work directly with the dreamer's body. Whereas a philosophically based system would automatically decide that a certain type of dream indicates a specific physical condition, an analytical system would mentally break the dream into parts and interpret each part as symbolizing a condition or process in the dreamer's body.

For example, in 1933 C. G. Jung correctly interpreted a patient's dream as an indication of a blockage of cerebrospinal fluid (probably due to a tumor). In the dream, the dreamer was asked about oiling something and milk was suggested as the lubricant; however, the dreamer preferred "oozy slime." In addition, there was a drained pond and in its slime were two extinct animals, a small mastadon and a second animal that escaped the dreamer's memory. Jung based his interpretation on two facts: one, that the Latin word for phlegm, which is one type of bodily "slime," is *pituita*—a part of the brain; the other, that *mastadon* is derived from the Greek words for "breast" and "teeth," referring to the mammillary bodies—breast-shaped structures in the brain that form a sort of pond of cerebrospinal fluid.[5]

Freud and Adler also sometimes applied dream analysis to their patients' physical conditions. However, like Jung, they did not work directly with their patients' ongoing physical experiences as a dreamworking method.[6] Reich and Lowen worked directly with their patients' body experiences, but they did not use their bodywork methods as a way of working with dreams.[7]

EMPIRICAL AND PROCESS-ORIENTED SYSTEMS

These two categories include dreamworking systems that approach dreams by working directly with the dreamer's body experiences. Interpretation in the sense used in the first two categories is replaced by *experiential understanding*; body experiences can help one interpret the dream, and the dream can aid one in understanding the meaning behind physical states. Further, while the empirical systems work directly with the interrelation between dreams and the body, the process-oriented system postulates a unified concept called the "dreambody."[8]

Specifically, the empirical body-based systems include those theories and methods of dreamworking that derive an understanding of the dream through the dreamer's physical experience and expression of the dream content. This approach is in radical contrast with the idea of purely cognitive dream interpretation; the dreamer consciously relives the dream in present experience and behavior. The major systems comprising this group are Gestalt therapy, Focusing, and Jungian Dance-Movement therapy.

Gestalt therapy, developed by Frederick Perls, aims at helping the individual reclaim buried and dissociated parts of the personality by working with behavior patterns, body symptoms, and dreams. The dream in Gestalt therapy is seen as an existential message from the unconscious that informs dreamers of their current relationship with self and with the outer world.

Gestalt dreamworking deals directly with the dreamer's physical experiences in the following manner. Every image in the dream is considered to be an alienated part of the self that the dreamer projects onto that image. The dream is worked with in the present tense, and the dreamer acts the part of each of these images. In doing so, the dreamer embodies each image and experiences its unique psychophysical reality. The dreamer then allows the various dream images or characters to encounter one another, and each one is encouraged to say and do what it wants. The ensuing interactions bring the dreamwork to a culmination and help the dreamer understand and utilize the dream's meaning. Thus, the dreamer does not make or receive a cognitive/verbal "interpretation"; he or she instead embodies the dream's contents and thereby allows the dream to reveal its message through direct experience.[9]

For example, Nancy was trying to make the difficult decision of whether or not to leave her husband of ten years. During this time, she dreamed that she was planting new plants around the border of her garden and was being helped by her husband and her father. Nancy used the Gestalt method to work with her dream.

First, she acted the part of the garden. The garden said, "I am the fruits of your labor in life. I contain your love of life and of your relationships with people." Second, she acted the part of the border area of the garden. It said, "I am made of rich earth. I am changeable. I am hopeful because I can evolve and grow whenever I need to." Third, she acted the part of her father and said, "Planting is the essence of life. I want to help you to enlarge your garden, to change its boundaries and its old patterns." And finally, she acted the part of her husband, saying, "I love this garden and I will stay and help you remodel it." Nancy felt the dream was telling her not to leave her husband but to change their current relationship by making new boundaries and allowing it to grow in new directions.[10]

Focusing, developed by Eugene Gendlin at the University of Chicago, is a body-based system used for psychotherapy, meditation, and dreamworking.[11] Focusing helps the dreamer to discover what the dream is about and to understand the growth direction that it suggests. This dreamworking method borrows techniques from several other fields; it employs the Gestalt method of acting out the part of dream figures and the Jungian method of making personal or collective associations to dream contents. In addition, focusing emphasizes a deep somatic appreciation of the dream.

A somatic understanding of the dream is achieved through the dreamer's focusing on a *felt sense* of various dream contents. A felt sense is a physically based intuition similar to the experience of "having a hunch" but is explicitly somatic in nature. Gendlin differentiates this concept from "gut feelings," emotions, and purely physical sensations. For example, if you think about someone you know and focus on your own physical sense of that person, it will be a diffuse and indescribable sense that is unique to your experience of that person. If you try this again thinking of another person and get a felt sense of these two people, you will notice an undefinable but different quality between your two experiences.

In Focusing, the dreamer poses questions to himself about the dream and allows the felt sense to provide the answers, then gets to know these felt senses by following their somatic evolution. Sometimes this may involve making movements that express the felt sense or creating mental images that illustrate it. True insights and understanding of the dream result in a physical release called a *felt shift*.[12]

Jim is a successful commercial artist who became depressed when he realized that because he was spending all his time at work, he was losing his friends one by one. During this time, he dreamed that a mermaid went to work with him and disturbed his concentration. He used the Focusing method to work with this dream.

Jim asked himself, "What part of myself or of my life is this mermaid?" He then focused on his felt sense of the mermaid. At first, he found it difficult to attain a felt sense, because he disliked the mermaid figure so much. However, he persevered and attempted to let his experience evolve. He discovered to his surprise that his felt sense of the mermaid made him feel very relaxed and comfortable. In this state, he noticed that his usual attitude toward his career—one resembling a typical achievement-oriented personality—did not go along with his felt sense of the mermaid, which made him feel relaxed, soft, and desiring friendships. Then he had a sudden insight: the mermaid represented his "feeling" or "feminine" side disturbing him in order to get his attention. The week after working on this dream, Jim decided to cut back on his work hours and put more energy into developing his personal relationships.[13]

Jungian Dance-Movement therapy, developed by Mary Whitehouse, utilizes Jung's concepts of the unconscious/conscious polarity and individuation and his method of *active imagination*.[14] This approach to dreamworking involves using dream images and experiences as the catalysts for spontaneous movement processes. Dream contents are visualized, "felt," and are then expressed in movement. The interactions and events contained in the dream are thus embodied in the dreamer's physical expressions.

Movement patterns are observed by the practitioner and dreamer in terms of polarities such as voluntary and involuntary, curved and straight, closed and open, narrow and wide, and heavy and light. In addition, White-house differentiates between *authentic* and *invisible* movement. The former is natural, congruent, simple movement coming from the self and executed with full awareness; the latter is mostly ego-directed, is done with less awareness, and appears awkward or incongruent. Whitehouse's approach helps clients to explore their invisible movements and develop them into authentic expressions of the self.[15]

Kay is a thirty-year-old woman who had been in therapy for two years. Her individuation process centered around the problem of needing to separate psychologically from her parents, whom she feels never provided her with adequate emotional support. She dreamed that she kept falling onto her back on her parents' front lawn. A friend, Susan, was trying to teach her to fall with a curved back instead of a flat one, in order to prevent pain. Kay used Jungian Dance-Movement therapy to work with her dream.

Kay recalled the dream and visualized herself falling onto her back. She let this image create a body feeling and then stood up and began making short, jerky motions with her arms to express this feeling. She said she felt as if she were punching something hard. The therapist encouraged her to continue; however, shortly thereafter, Kay became exhausted and said she couldn't go on. At that point, she stated that the exhaustion she was experiencing felt identical to how she often felt in waking life.

The therapist noted her statement and suggested Kay feel and express Susan's idea from the dream—falling with a curved back. Kay lay down on the floor and curled up. She rocked from side to side and said she felt much better. "It's just doing what you feel—not trying to change anything. When you feel like studying, you study. When you feel like sleeping, you sleep," she said. At this point, Kay felt she understood the message in her dream: her parents had never encouraged her to pay attention to her own feelings but instead had actually taught her to ignore them, which was an exhausting and un-fulfilling way for her to live. She began developing her ability to pay attention to her feelings, finding that this shift in orientation enhanced her vitality and her energy level.[16]

The process-oriented approach aims at unifying the various schools of psychotherapy and dreamworking. Developed by Arnold Mindell in Switzer-land, this system is known as Process-Oriented Psychology.[17] The term *process* refers to the way in which the dreamer's waking experience naturally evolves through a series of meaningful perceptual changes, which form the patterns expressed in dreams. Further, it refers to the way in which various psycho-therapeutic and dreamworking systems arise and change spontaneously as part of the individual's own natural psychotherapeutic or dreamworking methodology. Thus, methods such as Gestalt, Focusing, and Jungian Dance-Movement therapy do not have to be *applied* to the dreamer or dream. They instead may be *derived* from the dreamer's own process; the methods exist within the dreamer, and they manifest and change spontaneously.[18] This concept of process is also applied to therapeutic work with couples, families, and groups.[19]

Let us look at an example of this type of dreamworking and then identify the basic principles and methods involved. Esther, a client of Mindell's, was a well-behaved, well-adapted, accommodating woman. She had considerable difficulty being direct and honest with people, especially if it involved expressing negative feelings. In one session, Esther complained to Mindell of "pressing pains" extending from her neck down to her lower back which had been preventing her from sleeping. As she said this, she placed her hand on the back of her neck. Mindell noticed this and suggested that he place his hand on her neck and that she direct his hand.

Esther agreed to the idea and asked Mindell to apply pressure to her neck. He did so; however, it was not intense enough for Esther. She kept asking for more and more pressure until eventually, Mindell was pressing her neck right to the floor. At that point, Esther spontaneously recalled a recent dream in which a devil had thrown her into a hole. She said that Mindell's actions reminded her of the devil figure in the dream—in other words, that he was playing the part of the devil and she was being put into a hole!

Mindell then suggested that Esther play the part of the devil. She stood up and while pressing his neck to the floor, said, "Either you take me with you when you go out or you will have to remain in a hole." With this statement, Esther had an insight into her process. The devil in the dream was her own capacity to be direct, honest, and even negative with people. In contrast with her usual adapted and accommodating behavior, she considered this "devilish." The "devil" part of her was demanding to be noticed and utilized.[20]

Esther's "devilish" nature did not only express itself in her dream—the "devil" was also pressing on her neck and back. The dream of the devil actually arose from work with the body symptom. In this sense, process-oriented psychology works with the dreaming process rather than with the dream itself. The dream is seen as a picture or map of the process that may unfold in any number of ways.[21]

This brings us to one of the basic concepts in process-oriented psychology. The patterns contained in dreams and in body symptoms inevitably mirror each other, as they did with Esther. This discovery has led Mindell to the idea of the dreambody—an experiential body consisting of physical sensations with associated dreams and fantasies.[22] In addition, the dreambody may include the dreamer's surroundings, other people, and the inorganic world.[23]

In terms of the individual's experience, the dreambody concept replaces the idea that the individual consists of mind and body and introduces a paradigm that looks at experience in terms of information. Instead of purposely dividing the human being into compartments called "mind" and "body," human experience can be approached neutrally, calling it "information." The mode or channel through which the person is perceiving that information then can be determined.

Esther's process began in the auditory/verbal channel as she spoke about her problems. Her process then switched into the proprioceptive (body feeling) channel as she focused on her neck and back pains. Shortly thereafter, it changed into the visual channel as she spontaneously recalled her dream. As she acted the part of the devil pressing on Mindell's neck, she was operating in the kinesthetic (movement) channel. Finally, her process reverted to the auditory/verbal channel as she discussed her process with him. This evolution of experiences in different channels constitutes "process." Other channels used in this approach are the relationship channel, the world channel (one's experience in relation to the world at large), and, less commonly, the channels of smell, taste, the parapsychological, and the spiritual.[24]

The central intervention used in process work is called amplification. Instead of trying to relax Esther's neck and back muscles, Mindell amplified her pain. The purpose of this method is to help the information and pattern encoded in the symptom to unfold and reveal itself, as it did with Esther.[25]

Using the process-oriented approach with dreams and body symptoms involves noticing the sensory channel in which the client is perceiving the symptom, amplifying the experience in that channel, processing that experience to completion, and using the dream as a visual map or guide in the work. Dreams may arise spontaneously, as occurred with Esther, or they may be intentionally used for visualizing the process that is unfolding.

Esther's own personal dreamworking methodology consisted of a variety of approaches. First, the method of talk-therapy was used as she discussed her initial problems; second, as Mindell pressed on her neck to amplify her pain, a form of bodywork resembling massage or acupressure was employed; third, gestaltlike work with dream figures was done as they switched roles; and fourth, analytical work on integrating the "shadow" (Esther's "devilish" nature) was employed, a concept central to Jungian therapy. Most likely, Esther's next step would occur in the relationship therapy mode when she attempted to try out what she had learned.

Body-based methods for dreamworking offer us many possibilities for bringing dreams out of the realm of the distant and the ethereal and into our everyday physical experiences. You can dialogue with dream figures, use your felt senses to experience them, express them in movement, or amplify your body symptom and discover your dream. In all of these cases, you are discovering the living reality of dreams in your body.

III

Dreams in Creativity and Education

What the psychoanalysts stress, the relation between dreams and our conscious acts, is what poets already know. The poets walk this bridge with ease, from conscious to unconscious, physical reality to psychological reality.
ANAIS NIN

There is no agreement on the functions that dreams serve the dreamer. Are they sleep-preserving disguises for forbidden wishes and impulses? Are they waste products that are "excreted" to streamline memory storage? Are they chaotic byproducts of the brain's periodic attempt during sleep to attain neurochemical equilibrium? Or do they serve, to some extent at least, a problem solving function?

The authors in this section would argue for the latter option, a thesis originally articulated by Alfred Adler.[1] Unlike Freud, who saw the dream as the "royal road to the unconscious," it might be said that Adler saw the dream as the royal road to consciousness.[2] Adler's approach to dreams was flexible and not bound by strict rules, but he held that the dream's purpose was to reinforce dreamers' emotional power, motivating them to use that power in attaining their goals.

At the present time, there is little experimental evidence that waking creativity is directly connected to the thought processes underlying dream production. However, psychologists James M. Wood, David Sebba, and George Domino have suggested that future research may attempt to establish whether individuals who are more creative while awake are also more creative in their dreams. Past research findings have supported this possibility but have not adequately controlled for the length of dreams; creative people usually provide longer dream reports, which in turn tend to contain more creative, bizarre, colorful elements.[3] It also may be that most individuals' thought processes become more innovative while dreaming. The eminent neuroscientist

J. Allan Hobson, a contributor to this anthology, notes: "Each of us is a surrealist at night during his or her dreams: each is a Picasso, a Dali, a Fellini—the delightful and the macabre mixed in full measure."[4]

Dreams have been found to facilitate creative problem solving in a few experiments, such as the one reported by psychologist Robert Davé, who worked with twenty-four people who had reached an impasse in attempting to solve a creative task. In one of Davé's groups, six of eight subjects who were hypnotized reported nighttime dreams that provided a solution to their problems. However, only one member of a group of eight who were given rational thought exercises, and no member of the group of eight who were merely interviewed about their problem, obtained insights.[5] M.V. Barrios and J. L. Singer queried forty-eight subjects about their creative impasses, then divided them into three groups. Those who were led through either waking fantasies or "hypnotic dreams" attained greater success in breaking their creative blocks than those who were taught how to logically examine their creative projects.[6] In both studies, the exercises involving dreams or imagery were associated with creative breakthroughs.

Imagery, whether in nighttime dreams or in waking fantasy, is a neglected resource in creativity and education. Imagery can take the form of symbols and metaphors, both of which can foster practical solutions to perplexing crises in health, professional projects, or personal problems. A symbol is an image that stands for an idea, quality, experience, life issue, or process. In a dream, the image of a sun can stand for the "clear light" of a spiritual discipline, a person or project bringing warmth and nurturance to the dreamer, a literal or figurative "son" of the dreamer, good news that "shines like the sun" at the end of an ordeal, or a combination of two or more referents. On the other hand, to dream about the sun may not be symbolic at all, but the consequence of a heat wave, a newspaper story about a solar eclipse, or a recently seen film (*Duel in the Sun, Sun Valley Serenade,* or *The Sunshine Boys*).

A metaphor is a word or phrase (or a series of images) that stands for an actual life problem, event, or process. Everyday speech uses metaphors constantly: "the ship *plows* the sea"; "he uttered a *volley* of oaths." While asleep, a dreamer may jump off the ground and begin to fly. This activity may be a metaphor for "rising above" one's problems, trying to escape responsibility, advancing oneself spiritually through meditation or prayer, or engaging in more playful activities, thus balancing one's serious side. Again, a dream metaphor's meaning may be a combination of two or more referents, or it may simply mean that the dreamer has turned around in bed, stimulating bodily reactions and sensations that are incorporated into the dream as flight.

During the siege of Tyre in 332 A.D., Alexander the Great dreamed of a satyr, a demigod who supposedly lived in wooded areas. Aristander of Telmessos, a seer who accompanied him, was called in and observed that the Greek word *satyros* could be divided into *sa* and *Tyros,* which translates as "Tyre is yours." The dream symbol encouraged Alexander to wage the war vigorously and win the city.[7]

In 1844, the inventor Elias Howe dreamed that a savage king ordered his execution because he had not been able to perfect a lockstitch sewing machine. As the warriors' spears approached his body, Howe observed that they had eye-shaped holds near their heads. Awakening, Howe went to his laboratory and whittled a model of the needle, placing the hole near the tip, thus bringing his efforts of several years to a successful conclusion.[8] Here the spears symbolized the needle that Howe needed to invent, while his capture by savages probably was a metaphor for the stress brought about by his unsuccessful efforts up to that time.

Francis of Assisi, the thirteenth-century monk who founded the Franciscan order, supposedly dreamed that he had grown exceptionally tall in order to restore the balance of a Vatican basilica, which was on the verge of collapse. This metaphor gave St. Francis the courage he sought to tell the pope that his new religious order was badly needed to restore vigor to the Roman Catholic church.[9]

However, a dream need not contain symbols or metaphors to solve a problem. The naturalist Louis Agassiz dreamed about how he should break open a certain stone to obtain a fossil. Upon awakening, Agassiz located a chisel, followed the directions, and discovered a perfect specimen. Sir Frederick Grant Banting discovered a procedure for the mass production of insulin in a dream; again, the images were realistic, not symbolic.[10]

Dreamworkers are now able to teach basic dream recall, dream appreciation techniques, and dream interpretation skills that can demonstrate and enhance problem solving for people who wish to decode the language of the night. Psychoanalyst Helen Fagin has conducted several dream classes for artists, observing that dreams are less Freud's "royal road" to the unconscious than a river that has been dammed but is ready to flow again in the safety of the dream group.[11]

Edward Storm, a computer scientist, has taught classes in which he and his students explore the association between dream language and computer science. Storm observes that in both instances, important material is coded in a structured and systematic way that can be learned. His classroom experience has convinced him that "These are encouraging times for the dreamer and for the study of dreams. . . . If the same object or situation can mean different things to different dreamers at different times, then the form of a dream is that part that is the 'same'. . . . If we can postulate a mental capacity for organizing this cognitive structure of dreams, and if we can describe the forms generated by this capacity, we will have gained new insight into the formal structural capacities of the mind."[12]

This section opens with psychologist Gayle Delaney's provocative account of personal and professional problem solving in dreams. Literary scholars Kenneth Atchity and Vincent Atchity's astute report of dreams in literature and the arts selects from a vast literary resource that could fill several volumes. Over the years, psychologist Fariba Bogzarin has used her own and her students' dreams to foster painting and drawing. These chapters describe innovative techniques, while at the same time revealing some of the authors' personal experiences and insights. Finally, psychiatrist Montague Ullman, who, in my opinion, has done more than anyone else to provide useful guidelines for lay dream groups, presents an authoritative guide for those who wish to pursue dreamwork.

Gayle Delaney

Personal and
Professional Problem
Solving in Dreams

In this chapter I will discuss the natural problem-solving nature of many spontaneous dreams and introduce a method for eliciting dreams that are helpful in solving specific, targeted problems. During the last two decades, experimental laboratory researchers and clinical psychotherapists have studied the information-processing and problem-solving functions of dreaming. Studies by Pearlman, Greenberg, Horne, Glaubman, and others have demonstrated that depriving animals and people of their REM, or dream, sleep impairs their ability to think creatively and to solve problems.[1] In addition, intensive learning may require increased dreaming. Students who improved their language skills in an intensive language course had more REM sleep than usual, while the students who did not show an improvement had no increase in REM sleep.[2] Greenberg and Pearlman, two innovative psychoanalysts, have shown the direct connection between the manifest content of dreams and the dreamer's current life concerns.[3]

Many scientists and mathematicians have solved problems while asleep and apparently dreaming. After three days and nights of working on his periodic table without sleep, Mendeleyev fell asleep and later said, "In my dream, I saw the Chart where all the elements are placed as they should be. I woke up and immediately wrote it all down on a piece of paper. Eventually there was only one place which needed to be corrected."[4]

Otto Loewi won the 1936 Nobel prize in physiology and medicine for demonstrating the chemical nature of the transmission of nervous impulses, which had previously been thought to be an electrical process. The unlikely design for the experiment that demonstrated this finding came to Loewi in his sleep. He later wrote, ". . . we should sometimes trust a sudden intuition without too much skepticism. If carefully considered in the daytime, I would undoubtedly have rejected the kind of experiment I performed."[5]

Elias Howe dreamed the solution to a design problem that allowed him to invent the lock-stitch sewing machine.[6] Sometimes a dream is not re-called, but the scientist awakes in the middle of the night or in the morning with the solution to the problem clearly in mind. Such was the case for the great German physicist Hermann L. F. von Helmholtz, best known for his statement of the law of conservation of energy, the invention of the ophthal-moscope, and his research in optics, acoustics, hydrodynamics, electrody-namics, and meteorological physics. Helmholtz's original ideas generally occurred to him in the morning after a night of sleep. He said that after hav-ing investigated a problem "in all directions, . . . happy ideas come unex-pectedly without effort like an inspiration. So far as I am concerned, they have never come to me when my mind was fatigued or when I was at my working table."[7]

W. B. Cannon, one of America's greatest physiologists, the first to use X-rays in physiological studies and the first to articulate the theory of homeo-stasis, wrote that awakenings in the middle of the night led to new theories and designs for inventions such as his device for obtaining an automatically written record of the clotting of blood. As a child he would purposely "sleep on" problems in algebra and on how he might repair broken toys. Cannon wrote further that,

> As a matter of routine I have long trusted unconscious processes to serve me— for example, when I have had to prepare a public address. I would gather points for the address and write them down in a rough outline. Within the next few nights I would have sudden spells of awakening, with an onrush of illustrative instances, pertinent phrases, and fresh ideas related to those already listed. Paper and pencil at hand permitted the capture of these fleeting thoughts before they faded into oblivion. The process has been so common and so reliable for me that I have supposed that it was at the service of everyone. But evidence indicates that it is not.[8]

Many contemporary mathematicians who have studied with me or who have written me about their dreams express similar surprise that most people don't seem to know how to use their sleep and dreams to solve problems.

(Since these innovators were not in sleep labs when they awoke with their solutions, we cannot be sure what stage of sleep produced the solutions, especially in cases where no dream was recalled.) In my experience, mathematicians take particular pleasure in the discovery process, and often note that their discoveries made or realized upon awakening are among the most thrilling. Elmer Tory, Professor of Mathematics and Computer Sciences at Mount Allison University, wrote of a solution to a problem in unilateral Gaussian fields with which he awoke at two in the morning while on sabbatical at Harvard. While Tory's solutions usually come to him in "successive revelations," he wrote that

> this case was unusual because the final result was a quantum leap from my previous understanding. All the elements of the complete solution were revealed and my mind leapt intuitively from one result to another. . . . Perhaps because it was so sudden and complete, it was my most exhilarating discovery.[9]

The remarkable Indian mathematician Srinivasa Ramanujan, who, as a young man in relative isolation, reconstructed—and in certain areas surpassed—a rich half-century of European mathematics, claimed that he was regularly inspired with formulae in dreams throughout his life. Friends tried to send the very poor Ramanujan to Cambridge, but his mother refused to give her consent. She changed her mind when she had a dream "in which she saw her son seated in a big hall amidst a group of Europeans, and the goddess Managiri had commanded her not to stand in the way of her son fulfilling his life's purpose."[10]

Like scientists and mathematicians, artists use dreams for inspiration and problem solving. Beethoven, Brahms, Stravinsky, and Wagner are among the best-known musicians to have used their dreams and reveries in their work. August Strindberg insisted that his brain worked sharpest when he was asleep. Milton, Blake, Robert Louis Stevenson, and many other writers have used dreams as inspiration and sometimes instruction in their art.[11] D. H. Lawrence wrote to a friend:

> I can never decide whether my dreams are the result of my thoughts, or my thoughts the result of my dreams. It is very queer but my dreams make conclusions for me. They decide things finally. I dream a decision. Sleep seems to hammer out for me the logical conclusions of my vague days and offer me them as dreams.[12]

PROFESSIONAL AND PERSONAL PROBLEM SOLVING
IN PRIVATE PRACTICE

Among my clients are lawyers who work out touchy contracts in their sleep, corporate managers and executives who identify problems and devise solutions via their dreams, public relations people whose dreams lead them to creating new programs, and journalists who learn how to tap their dreaming minds for ideas on how to approach a new story.

Dreams are perhaps best known for their usefulness in helping us to understand ourselves better and to solve emotional and interpersonal problems. Many therapists today see in dreams the individual's best efforts to cope with and solve emotional problems from waking life. Some dreams serve simply to identify a problem the dreamer ignores while awake. For example, Gina, one of my clients, dreamed that she was being strangled by her new boyfriend. Once awake, she was baffled by the dream. All she was willing to see in her new boyfriend were his dashing, handsome, attentive ways. However, after reflecting upon the possibility that she was hiding from herself a more unflattering assessment of the man, she wondered whether his extreme possessiveness might become a problem that could strangle her.

Gina soon had a dream that went one step further: it revealed some of the dynamics of the problem. She dreamed that she was in bed with her former boyfriend, who was holding a pillow over her face. When she described his personality, she recognized for the first time that he was very much like her current boyfriend: handsome, wealthy, and dashing, but also possessive, overbearing, and suffocating. Gina was reluctant to give up her new beau, and so her dreams hammered away at the same theme for several months.

Gina needed a better understanding of why she could not give up her boyfriend even after she had recognized her pattern of selecting this sort of partner again and again. As often happens, she had a dream that seemed to go to the source of her problem. She dreamed that she was invited on a trip around the world by John Kennedy. She was delighted, but soon discovered that she would have to follow his schedule, do whatever he wanted, and always be on call to meet his needs. She wondered whether she was invited as a companion or as a prisoner. While working with this dream, Gina described Kennedy as a dashing, exciting, powerful male who was ambitious and admirable, but who used women to gratify his needs for sex and dominance. Asked if this description reminded her of anyone in her life, she said, "My father, and most of my boyfriends!" Thus Gina began to understand that she was repeating a pattern of painful relationships that reflected her childhood relationship with her father. Now, as an adult, she would have to learn to make more conscious and more mature choices regarding men.

These dreams brought Gina's attention to a problem she had been denying, and they helped her to understand the dynamics of her problem. More dreams followed that assisted her in her conscious efforts to recognize and appreciate the sort of man who could satisfy her needs.

It is important to emphasize that, except in presenting new ideas or concrete solutions to concrete problems, dreams will not solve your problems *for* you. They *will* open your eyes to information you have failed to appreciate or acknowledge while awake, and this "new" information will help you solve your problem if you are willing to change your attitude or point of view. This is not often easy, and it requires courage in the face of resistance and persistence in the face of frustration.

DREAM INCUBATION

While the spontaneous dreams you have every night will help you to better understand and solve your intellectual, creative, and artistic problems, you also can learn how to elicit dreams on a given night that will help you out with specific problems.[13] Suppose you need a new idea for a creative project, such as a paper you are writing or a picture you are painting. By using a form of "dream incubation" you can target your dreams to help you. If, instead, you want your dreaming mind to work on a problem you are having, such as getting along with a business partner, your spouse, or your child, or if you want to explore a particular problem you have with anger or fear, you can incubate a dream on that. Dream incubation is easily learned. If you carefully follow these instructions, you should be able to dream about the issue you target the first time you incubate a dream.

Six Steps for Incubating Dreams

Choose the Right Night. Choose a night when you are neither intoxicated nor overtired, and one that will allow you to get a full night's sleep followed by enough time in the morning to record a dream or two. As you gain experience in incubating dreams, you will be able to abbreviate the method; but in the beginning, and whenever incubating dreams on very sensitive issues, you will have the best chance of success if you follow every step. The process will take about ten minutes before sleep and enough time to record your dream upon awakening.

Record Your Day Notes. Before going to sleep, write down the highlights of your day in the dream journal, which should be kept beside your bed. Ask yourself what you did during the day and what you felt. Then record in just four or five lines the emotional highlights of the day. If you felt exhausted after a frustrating day at work, write that down. Note anything that stirred your feelings, even if the day's most moving event was a phone call from your brother. By learning to note the emotional news of the day, you will become more aware of thoughts and emotional reactions that trigger your spon-taneous dreams and that may inspire you to incubate a dream. These notes are much more useful in helping you to understand a dream than are those writ-ten upon awakening. If you keep your day notes brief, you will be much more likely to keep them faithfully.

Incubation Discussion. Next, write a few lines about the issue you would like to dream about. Describe the problem, your readiness to take a fresh look at it and to alter your position, and what benefits you might have to give up if you resolved it. Stir up your feelings. Don't write much more than a page, or you may turn the process into a chore. Keep your notes brief.

Incubation Phrase. Now write a one-line phrase that clearly states what you would like to understand about your problem, or on what matter you need a new idea. This is the most important step in the process. Be sure to write out your incubation question or request on a separate line in your journal. Choos-ing your question may be easy, or it might be very difficult. This step will help you to focus your thinking and to clarify your problem and your relation to it, and it will force you to decide upon the next step you are willing to take in its exploration.

A good deal of insight can be gained by struggling to formulate a clear, succinct question, a troublesome issue, and actually writing the question in your journal will insure that you focus thoughtfully and carefully enough. It will also give you the necessary discipline to choose only one issue and to settle on one among many ways of phrasing the question.

Repeat the Phrase as You Fall Asleep. Place your journal beside your bed, turn out the light, and close your eyes. Repeat over and over your incubation phrase as if it were a lullaby or a mantra. Each time your mind wanders, bring it back to your phrase. You will fall asleep quickly, because you are not allowing your-self to ruminate or worry about your problem. As you repeat the phrase, feel the desire to learn something new tonight, to make a shift in your perspective. This is a very comfortable way to fall asleep and is far more productive than counting sheep.

Record Whatever Is on Your Mind When You Awaken. When you awaken, whether in the middle of the night or in the morning, write down whatever is in your mind. Learn to ask yourself, "What was I just thinking?" Frequently, a dream memory will feel like an ordinary thought that you might dismiss if you asked yourself, "What was I just dreaming?" And to the surprise of many, answers to incubation questions sometimes come in the form of ready-made ideas and formulations, or in the form of songs playing through one's mind in the morning.

Most often, however, the answers are embedded in the metaphors of the dream and are easily overlooked by the dreamer until he or she takes the time to explore those metaphors and interpret the dream. If your dream seems to have nothing to do with your question, write it down anyway. Wait a few hours, and then work on understanding the dream without trying to make it answer your question. Remember that whatever your dream is about con-stitutes an important issue in your life, whether your incubation effort was successful or not. Only after you have understood what your dream is about should you ask yourself whether it sheds new light on the incubation issue. This will discourage you from reading into your dream something that is not there, and it will help you to appreciate whatever dream you did have.

A LAWYER'S INCUBATED DREAM

Let's look at an example of a dream incubation. Judith, a lawyer for a major corporation, had grown frustrated with a job that she had once found very ex-citing. Yet the security and status of her job were very good, and she was un-sure whether she could find a better job in the area. Judith did not want to move, and she thought she should be happy with her enviable job. She won-dered whether she might have an attitude problem rather than a job problem. Judith incubated a dream with the question, "What should I do about my job?" That night she had the following dream.

A small group of people from my high school (who are adults in the dream) are meeting for dinner. We wait in the bar for the ones who have yet to arrive. My "pair" is Jim O'Hara, but in the dream, I realize that Jim is really Tom Douglas. Everyone has arrived, and we have trouble finding places for all six of us to fit in, so we put two tables together in the bar.

Jim/Tom takes charge in a sort of pushy-game-playing way. He dictates where we will all sit at the tables and where we will dine. The group takes on the feeling of a group of college drinking buddies with dates. Jim/Tom calls all fraternity brothers to go dine where there is lots of food and booze. I decide to leave. I feel self-confident. This is not where I belong. I have better things to do.

Asked to describe the personalities of Jim and Tom, Judith said that she had seen neither of them since high school, but that Jim was a sweet, nice guy, while Tom was the smooth, glib, good-looking leader of the pack. Asked if there was anyone in her current life who seemed sweet and nice, but who was in fact smooth, glib, and a leader of the pack, she said that her direct counterpart in another department at work, a lawyer named Samuel, was very much like a combination of Jim and Tom. Then Judith noted that just as in high school, a good deal of her discomfort with the job came from her difficulty feeling as though she fit in with the group. She said that her work group was more like a high-school clique or fraternity gang than she had recognized. Judith felt that her dream decision to leave the fraternity scene was a healthy one, and that whether or not she decided to leave her job, she should give up trying to fit in and be fully accepted by a group that simply does not suit her. Her growing self-confidence was liberating her from an exaggerated need to be accepted.

Like most dreams, incubated or spontaneous, this dream, once understood, opened the dreamer's eyes to a dynamic she had failed to adequately appreciate. Also, it did not "tell the dreamer what to do," but showed her what she *was* doing to help her make a more informed decision.

Kenneth Atchity and Vincent Atchity

Dreams, Literature, and the Arts

The arts and dreamwork are synonymous. Film without the dream sequences of Luis Buñuel or Federico Fellini, Stanley Kubrick or Woody Allen, would demonstrate a tediously one-dimensional storytelling grammar. From the nightmarish "Caprices" of Francisco Goya to the droll eccentricities of René Magritte, painting has employed dream material to comment on its own aesthetics. So, too, dreams are woven in and out of the history of music, from Tartini's "Devil's Sonata" to Stravinsky's "The Rite of Spring." The artistic inventiveness of the human brain is at its freest when we dream. "For the poet," said André Gide, "as for God, the word creates the world."

Western literature has been transfused with the blood of dreams from time immemorial, when words reached only as far as a voice could carry them—until now, when the earth hangs suspended in a satellite-spun web of words flying at light speed. Words create images, invoking pictures we perceive and shape into the meaning of our lives, just as Carlos Fuentes' narrator in *The Death of Artemio Cruz* reframes his now-completed inventory of memories into a portrait closer to his heart's desire. Literature's use of dream material reminds us that the most incontestable human reality is that of perception and imagination. The history of literary dreams reveals a consistently adamant uncertainty as to precisely where the boundary lies between life—the objective reality—and life—the subjective dream.

In his play *Life Is a Dream*, Pedro Calderón de la Barca toys with his protagonist's sense of direction by mercilessly shifting the boundary between dream and reality until Sigismundo's uncertainty has been aggravated to the extent that he declares:

What is life? An insanity.
What is life? An illusion,
A shadow, a fiction,
And the greater part of it is very little;
For all of life is a dream,
Even dreams are a dream.[1]

Sigismundo makes no attempt to discern a dividing line between dream and reality. Instead, Calderón's protagonist governs his actions solely in light of the expectation of being ultimately *awakened* by death—and only then, if at all, being *judged*. Perhaps Sigismundo's determined agnosticism about the distinction between dreams and reality is the most natural position for humans to take. If there is judgment in the land of the dead (if indeed there is a land of the dead), it would seem that the highest expression of our humanity should be considered not our ability to draw boundaries but our ability to live more or less sanely despite our recognition that in some cases, any boundaries we might draw are themselves imaginary. Calderón grapples thematically with our uncertainty about the relationship between dreams and reality; he suggests that no clear distinction can be made between them, at least by the living; and he reveals that the more useful focus of concern is not the boundary between reality and dreams, but the boundary between life with all its dreams and that "dreamless sleep," death.

THE CLASSICAL PERIOD

Sigismundo is part of a tradition rooted in the very origins of literature. From China to India to Egypt to Mesopotamia, poetry first arose from dreams and visions. In Homer's *Iliad,* Zeus sends an "evil Dream" to deceive Agamemnon into "believing things in his heart that were not to be accomplished."[2] He awakens to initiate combat with Troy. The dream performs a multipurpose narrative role. It serves through indirect discourse to explain the inexplicable: why did the Achaians allow Agamemnon to lead them without the support of Achilles? Because he had a dream, and dreams were normally considered by mortals to be messages from the gods. In the world depicted by the *Iliad,* the authority of a dream is usually not questioned, even though the intent behind its message may not be entirely discernible to the dreamer.

Moreover, Homer uses the dream to underline the pitfalls resulting from his characters' mortal inability to distinguish between false and true images.

Sigismundo's recognition of his incapacity to discern that boundary enhances his objectivity toward the events he experiences. However, Homer's Zeus cynically channels Agamemnon's lack of discernment through the king's subjectivity. Agamemnon knows he has wronged Achilles. His royal hubris is all too ready to believe a dream that tells him that he can conquer the Trojans without the help of the Achaians' greatest warrior. To distinguish between the *false* dream and the fateful reality of his waking world, Agamemnon's knowledge would have to equal that of Zeus. He would then have had to declare that the "gods must be crazy." Certainly the gods Homer portrayed were untrustworthy. Indeed, his portrait of Zeus' duplicity suggests that Homeric man lived in a world where he remained victim to the gods' intentional confounding of any and all boundaries—a world where the origin of images was always uncertain.

Perhaps nowhere in classical Western literature is the uncertainty about the boundary between dreams and reality, and its use as a narrative strategy of indirect discourse, more clearly seen than in Vergil's *Aeneid*.[3] After visiting the dead in the underworld, Aeneas returns to carry on with his life and destiny. At this juncture, Vergil reworks a famous passage in the *Odyssey* (19.560–70), where Homer has the gates of horn and ivory reflect the complementary natures of Odysseus and Penelope.[4] Vergil's narrator gives us a piece of information that undermines the credibility of his entire narration:

> There are two gates of sleep; of which one is made of horn, by which easy exit is given to true shades, the other of gleaming ivory polished to perfection, but through which the spirits send false dreams skyward. Here, then, Anchises accompanies his son, and the sybil with him, when all was said—and sends him through the ivory gate.[5]

With this passage, the discursive progress of the *Aeneid* is momentarily interrupted by indirect discourse. The description of the Gates is a perturbingly informative digression, and the interruption augments the reader's accelerating sense of uncertainty.

As the first half of the *Aeneid* comes to a close, Aeneas returns to the surface of the world through the gate of false dreams. The chief character of the epic, his substantiality within his heroic world carefully linked to the legendary prehistory of Rome, is with this single stroke severed from the seamless credibility toward which the fictional narrative otherwise, superficially, aspires. As he walks onward toward Tiber, the hero of Vergil's epic is seen as less substantial, less palpably real, than the very shades of the dead he encountered in Hades. What kind of an image is he?

Perhaps Vergil means to suggest by this remarkable indirection that Aeneas is a kind of dream—the false kind—and that the epic myth, created by Vergil at the request of Augustus, is of the same unsubstantial nature as a dream. Of course, he may be telling us at the same time that dreams are as substantial as myths—that ready-made myths, the products of the poetic imagination, can play as meaningful a role in reality as can myths inherited from the remote past, and that they are no more or less yielding than a dream.

Whichever is the case, clearly it is only in Vergil's underworld that all dreams may be seen for what they are, be they true or false. Only in the land of the dead does the boundary between dream and reality become clear. Aeneas issues forth from that land through the ivory gate of false dreams; the gate of horn is reserved for true shades, and Aeneas is not yet a shade. Like a shaman, he returns to the upper world, the land of the living, where he will carry on with his dream life until he, too, finally awakens—and permanently rejoins the authentic, somber company below. Centuries later Calderón was following Vergil when he had Sigismundo declare "that to live is only to dream; / and the experience teaches me / that the living man dreams / what he is until he awakens" into death.

The sudden and immense sense of doubt—the accumulating suspicion of the unsubstantiality of Vergil's hero—that is triggered by this passage accompanies us to the very end of the *Aeneid*. The progressive hiatus of this indirect discourse (the digression about the gates) diminishes our conviction at the same time that the direct discourse seeks to affirm it. The result of Vergil's dreamwork is the acute sense of depth or irony we experience when we read his melancholy masterpiece.

THE MEDIEVAL PERIOD

Macrobius' intriguing *Commentary on the Dream of Scipio* and Boethius' *Consolation of Philosophy* link the dream literature of the classical and medieval periods. The Middle Ages are replete with dream poetry, from Dante's *Commedia*[6] to *Le Roman de la Rose.* No medieval dream poem is more subtle and psychologically persuasive than Chaucer's *Booke of the Duchesse,* in which the dramatic tension between narrator-as-dreamer and dreamer-(awakened)-as-narrator dictates the reader's involvement with and response to the poem's treatment of the relationships among the thematic elements of death, memory, and perfection. Although Chaucer does not depict uncertainty about the boundary between dreaming and waking, he explores the implications of dreaming values being quite different from waking values. The subject of this dream-vision poem is bereavement, and Chaucer's narrative considers the mysterious distinction between life and death even more directly than do the *Aeneid* and *Life Is a Dream*.

Two dreams are described in the *Booke of the Duchesse*. The first occurs in a tale read by the narrator in which a dream comes to "awaken" the bereaved wife of a husband lost at sea and to urge her to "bury" her dead husband and cease her grieving. The second dream is the narrator's own, which forms the largest part of the poem. This second dream also begins with an awakening:

> *Me thoghte thus: that hyt was May,*
> *And in the dawenynge I lay*
> *(Me mette thus) in my bed al naked,*
> *And loked forth, for I was waked*
> *With smale foules a gret hep*
> *That had affrayed me out of my slep,*
> *Throgh noyse and swetnesse of her song.*[7]

This dreamer-(awakened)-as-narrator serves as envoy to the bereaved black knight he discovers in the forest glade. The dreamer/narrator seems to be attempting to convince the knight to cease his grieving, and he seems to be convinced by the knight that the death of his beloved is a loss that he will mourn ceaselessly. In this way, Chaucer uses the narrator's dream to distance his narrator as well as his readers from a sensitive topic in order that it may be seen from a fresh perspective. His repeated use of the image of being awakened within a dream (what contemporary dreamworkers term *lucid dreaming*) suggests that the perspective on death found in the dreams the poet creates may be more enduring than that held by the bereaved reader in the waking state.

In effect, the narrator's seeming naiveté in forcing the black knight to repeat his lady's praises is an indirect way of transforming the knight's objective grief to a subjective, narrated, perfected image of his lady that nothing can ever take away from him. The narrator's questions lead the knight to make art of his memories—to express and, at the same time, to internalize a completed portrait of her in words. Through memorializing his lady the knight transcends his grief, uniting her with Keats' sweeter "unheard melodies" and Yeats' "artifice of eternity." In the knight's recollection, his lady achieves a perfection unattainable in life. We truly become immortals through literature.

Chaucer's sensitive treatment of bereavement through the distancing

device of the two dreams suggests that taking Reason off guard to allow uncertainty about the boundary between dreaming and waking may lead to a
most felicitous uncertainty about the division between life and death.

THE RENAISSANCE PERIOD

From Santa Teresa and Juan de la Cruz to John Bunyan's *Pilgrim's Progress,* the
Renaissance continued to exploit the relationship between dream and poetry
in every way imaginable. Shakespeare, like his contemporaries Calderón,
Quevedo, and Gongora, took dramatic advantage of the analogies between
dream and theater, and made great play of the uncertainty surrounding
dreaming and waking. The thematic family of sleep, dreams, death, ghosts,
memories, illusion, madness, and imagination circulates through Shakespeare's works like a vitalizing current until they proclaim, resoundingly, as
Jorge Luis Borges points out, "the fundamental identity of existing, dreaming, and acting."[8] Both in Hamlet's famous "To be or not to be" soliloquy and
in *The Tempest,* the metaphorical identification of life with dream and drama
with imagination is given natural expression and natural closure:

> *Our revels now are ended. These our actors,*
> *As I foretold you, were all spirits, and*
> *Are melted into air, into thin air;*
> *And, like the baseless fabric of this vision,*
> *The cloud-capp'd towers, the gorgeous palaces,*
> *The solemn temples, the great globe itself,*
> *Yea, all which it inherit, shall dissolve;*
> *And, like this insubstantial pageant faded,*
> *Leave not a rock behind. We are such stuff*
> *As dreams are made on, and our little life*
> *Is rounded with a sleep . . .(5.1)*

Shakespearean characters like Prospero, Richard III, Mercutio, Bottom, and
Caesar stage-manage their dreams and nightmares so that the audience can
and must take part in them.

No one explored the poetic uses of dream as brilliantly as did Cervantes
(who died the same year as Shakespeare). The "Cave of the Montesinos" episode of *Don Quixote* is a marvelous intertextual indirection on the part of the
master strategist of indirect discourse. Whether the hero's account of his descent is a "dream report"—as Sancho suspects and Don Quixote stalwartly

denies—or a dreamlike fabrication matters not at all, because it strays "not one iota" from Don Quixote's sacred and idiosyncratic vision of the truth. The world Don Quixote imagines is the world he perceives; the world he lives in is *imaginary*. Don Quixote's cave is the successor of Vergil's entrance to Hades and a predecessor of Alice's rabbit hole.

Interrupting the primary narrative of his epic novel, Cervantes sends his character to explore the depths of the cave. The character's subsequent report, if we can determine how to receive it, may be of great use to us in exploring this work of Cervantes' imagination as well as the function and products of our own conscious and unconscious processes. The stature of Don Quixote's attitude is mythic. His sacred, priestly, shamanic character is defined in his ability and determination to accept the mission to explore fully and unflinchingly the deepest recesses of the cave and, most importantly, to return skyward and tell us what he found and saw. Will we believe his eyes? His words? Will we live in the world he imagines? Do we believe Aeneas fresh from the ivory gate? Do we believe the dreams of others (as the Achaians did Agamemnon's), or even our own? Dare we live in the world we imagine? Can we dispense with our need for boundaries? Since Don Quixote (and his Merlin, Cervantes) invents worlds as he speaks, how in any world can we know that he isn't, even as he speaks, inventing what he saw in the cave?

Don Quixote says he "traveled into that obscure region below without any certain or determined path";[9] and so we are uncertain, but nonetheless filled with eagerness to *see,* as we descend with his words into the narrative (the indirect dreamlike discourse) of his descent.

"I think," Sancho tells his master after hearing only part of the account, "that Merlin or those enchanters that laid a spell on the whole crowd Your Grace says you've seen and communicated with down there have stuck into your imagination or your memory all this machination that you've been narrating to us, and all that remains to be narrated." Sancho's sweeping dismissal places him in an excessive position that neither we nor he want to maintain. We are almost relieved to hear how easily Don Quixote's imagination rises to Sancho's incredulous challenge: " 'Such a thing could be, Sancho,' replies Don Quixote, 'but it is not so in this case; for I have narrated what I saw with my own eyes and touched with my own hands.' " Calderón's Sigismundo says much the same thing when he asserts, "No, I'm not dreaming, since I both feel and believe what I've been and what I am." Nevertheless, the play goes on to establish how unsubstantial that assertion is and how any boundary drawn between dream and reality is a matter of perspective. The veracity of anyone's visualization is essentially unquestionable.

THE NINETEENTH CENTURY

The Romantics continued the dream tradition, but were influenced more by the emotion of the medieval dream visions than by the intricate metaphysical conceits of the Renaissance. "Was it a vision, or a waking dream?/ Fled is that music:—Do I wake or sleep?" Keats' "Ode to a Nightingale" holds our attention precisely because we don't know where we are in it. The boundary between dreaming and waking vanishes entirely: the poet is led into the dream "on the viewless wings of Poesy" and is as easily summoned back by a word: "Forlorn! the very word is like a bell/To toll me back from thee to my sole self!" Similarly, in "La Belle Dame Sans Merci" (transmuted wonderfully in Yeats' "The Song of the Wandering Aengus") Keats pronounces the interrelatedness of dreams and reality for the hopelessly expectant knight, who is helpless to distinguish between them.

Coleridge's "Kubla Khan" echoes Keats' message that the doorway between dream and reality may be open or shut with a word. The dreamlike "pleasure dome" is not built, but instead is created by the Khan's "decree"— just as in Borges' "Parable of the Palace" the poet destroys the palace with a word: "the real and the dreamed became one, or rather reality was one of dream's configurations."[10] At the end of Coleridge's poem, when the poet/narrator discovers that his vision has slipped away from him, he asserts that if he could but recall the words he had seen so vividly in his dream he would then be able to do much more than simply complete the poem:

> . . . with music loud and long,
> I would build that dome in air,
> That sunny dome! those caves of ice!
> And all who heard should see them there,
> And all should cry, Beware! Beware!
> His flashing eyes, his floating hair!
> Weave a circle round him thrice,
> And close your eyes with holy dread,
> For he on honey-dew hath fed,
> And drunk the milk of Paradise.

Given the necessary words, the poet assumes a mythical, priestly, shamanic role and transcends the indefinite boundary, having "drunk the milk of Paradise" to make reality from dream, and dream of reality.

Edgar Allan Poe, in "Dream-Land," describes a place that "lieth, sublime, Out of *Space*—out of *Time*," where "the traveller meets, aghast, Sheeted memories of the past." The title character of Hawthorne's "Young Goodman Brown" journeys by night to precisely such a locale and returns to find not only that he is unable to determine whether what he witnessed actually occurred or whether he had only "fallen asleep in the forest and only dreamed a wild dream of a witch-meeting," but also that his entire life has been irreversibly altered by the event, to the extent that even his own wife is now under suspicion of devilry. Hawthorne leaves it to the reader to determine the exact nature of young Goodman Brown's experience, with the result that, in light of the concreteness of the change in Goodman Brown, we are forced finally to admit that the distinction between dreaming and waking reality is almost entirely irrelevant.

The Twentieth Century

Among the greatest contemporary examples of the dreamlike strategies is Gabriel García Márquez's *One Hundred Years of Solitude,* which expands Borges' metaphor of the parallel mirrors in the dream of the infinite rooms of José Arcadio Buendia.[11] When the town of Macondo contracts "the illness of insomnia," objective reality disintegrates: "In that state of hallucinated lucidity, not only did they see images of their own dreams, but some saw the images dreamed by others. It was as if the house were full of visitors."[12]

Memory breaks down, then language, until the circular "story of the capon" becomes the narrative microcosm of the living death we would lead if we no longer alternated sleep with waking.

Another masterpiece of the twentieth-century European novel, Stanislaw Lem's *Solaris,* includes within the scope of its narrative every conceivable form of dreamlike phenomena (copies, hallucinations, delirium, drugs, intoxication, daydreams, memories, reveries, meditation, chimeras, trance, mirror images, incubi, mirages, ghosts, and doubles) to suggest how close to being infinite are things imaginable—how many more numerous are the obscure forms than the local shapes of the limited surface world.

Like Keats and Yeats before him, Wallace Stevens examines the dynamic by which dreams become the impetus for human activities and are therefore as fundamentally real as any other objective reality. In "Sunday Morning," Stevens depicts dreams as having a darkening effect on the waking world: "The pungent oranges and bright, green wings/Seem things in some procession of the dead." The otherworldly nature of dreams in primitive religious literature drew humanity's focus outward and away from the natural world, and the results of this were manifested in the development of divinities of "silent shadows": Jove, for instance, who "in the clouds had his inhuman birth."

Stevens portrays the advent of the Christian perspective as the event in which "our blood, commingling, virginal, with heaven" drew dreams back down to the earth, their origin, with the suggestion that the earth is "all of paradise that we shall know." He asserts that there is no dreamlike vision, or myth, or otherworldly rumor

> . . . that has endured
> As April's green endures; or will endure
> Like her remembrance of awakened birds,
> Or her desire for June and evening, tipped
> By the consummation of the swallow's wings.

These constructs of the waking world—the perception and memory of images—are the source of dreams. When we recognize this continuum, our need to distinguish between dreaming and waking diminishes. More disturbing is the boundary between life and death. Stevens' poem suggests that the need we feel for "some imperishable bliss" will not be satisfied in some inaccessible and divine dreamland. The mystery of dreams lies in ourselves; it is a human mystery. As the beautiful, living earth is the mother of our dreams, so, then, Stevens' poem concludes:

> Death is the mother of beauty; hence from her,
> Alone, shall come fulfillment to our dream
> And our desires.

The foreknowledge of its own demise makes our imagination produce and applaud its waking and sleeping dramas, the dramas that immortalize.

In the ordinary waking world, most people have a fair sense of where dream has ended and where reality begins. The uncertainty takes hold at the extraordinary moments when we ask, "Am I awake, or am I dreaming?" Literature always has given us freedom to resist our strong natural drive to define boundaries and to recognize that that very drive is itself an image of our desire for order. The poetic narrator—from Dante and Chaucer to Calderón and Shakespeare; from Keats and Shelley to Yeats and Stevens; from Cervantes to Hawthorne, García Márquez, and Fuentes—finds ways to introduce the shadows that lurk in a world where all the boundaries are of our own imagining. In its interweaving of *true* and *false* dreams, of sleep and waking, life and death, the art of words achieves what Aristotle called imitation, the imaginative encapsulation of reality—as it shows us not merely "the thing that has been," but, what we most want to celebrate, "a kind of thing that might be."[13]

Fariba Bogzaran

Painting Dream Images

. . . every night, while replenishing our energy, for the
next day, in deep sleep, we visit the Great Spaces of the
mind; but, on waking up, they are forgotten. The Great
Spaces, though they exist, probably can not be observed
objectively, but they can be expressed in painting.
GORDON ONSLOW-FORD

Our nightly journeys to the world of dreams offer a unique path
to the discovery of our creative potential. Our dreams appear to be
created spontaneously and we have an abundance of these creations in our lifetime. Each dream is unique, like each sunrise, with different
feelings, textures, and colors.

The expression of dreams through visual arts has been recorded cross-
culturally in paleolithic cave painting, Navajo sandpainting, and Egyptian,
Indian, and Renaissance painting. If we look at the development of dream art
in the Western world, we observe that in the seventeenth and eighteenth centuries, art moved from the static Renaissance to the Baroque to Neoclassicism
and Romanticism.

During that transitional time, John Henry Fuseli became a recognized
artist after exhibiting a painting entitled *The Nightmare* at the Royal Academy
in London in 1782. Although he was not the first artist to paint from dreams,
his painting captured a wide audience by inviting viewers into the mysterious
world of the unconscious.

The Nightmare, second version, 1790–91, by John Henry Fuseli.

I chose Fuseli's painting as an example of one of the artworks in the western world that brought an awareness of expressing dreams through visual arts. However, the composition of *The Nightmare* was not unique at the time; many artists prior to Fuseli had attempted similar compositions, such as Marcantonio Raimondi in *The Dream of Raphael* (1506–10), Giulio Romano in *Hecuba's Dream* (1538–39), Lodovico Carracci in *Jacob's Dream,* (1605–08), and others.[1]

In *The Nightmare* and similar compositions, the artists painted a waking environment that is familiar to us. They typically depict a sleeping person dreaming or visioning, while at the same time we observe their dream or vision. Because during the seventeenth and eighteenth centuries paintings were mostly the representations of waking life, this theme affected the awareness of the observer by shifting attention from the external reality (or waking state) to the internal reality (or dream state).

It was not surprising that Fuseli encountered strong reactions to his creation. Not only was his subject matter disturbing to the observer, but he also combined different styles of art to create his compositions.

Art historian H. W. Janson comments on this integrative style: "In *The Nightmare,* the sleeping woman (more Mannerist than Michelangelesque) is Neoclassic; the grinning devil and the luminescent horse come from the demon-ridden world of medieval folklore. The Rembrandtesque lighting, on the other hand, reminds us of Reynolds."[2]

Simultaneously, Fuseli's friend, William Blake, a visionary poet and painter, captured his mystical experiences in both painting and poetry. As Blake expressed his visions in painting, his style diverged markedly from the art of his time. In *Fearful Symmetry,* Northrop Frye writes about Blake's work: "He is an interruption in cultural history, a separable phenomenon. The historian of painting has to abandon all narrative continuity when the time comes to turn aside and devote a few words to Blake's unique output."[3]

The works of Blake and the paintings of Fuseli were truly an interruption for that era; the full exploration of the unconscious did not gain popularity until two centuries later when the art world witnessed the gradual birth of futurism, cubism, and surrealism. With the surrealist movement, artists attempted to bridge the world of dreams and that of wakefulness through various styles of paintings.

The art historians Horst De la Croix and Richard Tansey have commented on the progression of style from cubism (abstract, reasoned, and cool) to surrealism (dreamlike, intuitive, and expressive): "The artist's free imagination now draws upon materials lying deep in his consciousness and his act

Conscious Dreaming, 1982, by Fariba Bogzaran.

of expression is the proclamation of new realities, not less real because they are psychic."[4] Indeed, we no longer observe the painting of a person dreaming *about* a dream image; the painting *is* the dream image.

This expression is clearly shown in the art of Italian painter Giorgio de Chirico. His art contained a definite invitation to enter a dreamlike atmosphere, with familiar images distorted through different perspectives, shadows, and spaces. Although Italian art historians place de Chirico in a school called Pittura Metafisica, he can be considered one of the early inspirations of the surrealism movement. Salvador Dali is another surrealist artist who utilized unconscious material to create his work.[5]

André Breton defined surrealism as "Pure psychic automatism . . . thought dictation in the absence of all control exercised by reason and outside all moral and aesthetic."[6]

Automatism was a technique used by surrealists to paint without stopping to analyze. Gordon Onslow-Ford, who was actively involved with the surrealist movement in the 1930s, defines this technique: "Automatism was associated with dreams, and it was hoped that there would be a rapprochement between the dream and the waking state."[7]

Before surrealism, art was the representation of our waking world; at the height of surrealism and after, much of it became the representation of our dream world. Paintings that represented the waking world together with dream images were gradually replaced by a world beyond dream imagery.[7]

Since surrealism, painting dream images has become a source of self-expression for many contemporary artists, some well-known and others obscure. The following examples illustrate different ways in which the dream world is expressed.

As in Fuseli's *The Nightmare,* in *Conscious Dreaming* the artist shows dream images as they appeared in her dream.[8] This painting became a representation of the dream world; however, the images changed slightly as they were painted. To manifest dream images exactly as they appear in dreams is to evoke a pure expression of the unconscious, which in many ways is an impossible task. As soon as we recreate the dream in any art medium, the dream is no longer exactly as it was experienced. In reproducing the image, we call upon all our expertise to find the appropriate composition, medium, colors, and so forth to re-create the dream.

When the artist starts a painting, the process of recreating the dream becomes a lucid integration of the conscious and the unconscious. The artist may have had a preconceived notion of how to represent the dream, but once the actual process begins, the initial image may slowly evolve into a surprising form.

The Gift of the Dolphin, 1984, by Dorothy Rossi.

In her painting *The Gift of the Dolphin,* San Francisco artist Dorothy Rossi re-created a scene from her dream. She writes:

> At first I tried to paint that wonderful lace-like design of the dolphin's skeletal structure, but everything in me fought this. Although the two dreams fit to-gether as a concept, and esthetically I was attracted to the skeletal figure, artis-tically I knew it didn't work. The skeletal image is too vague for the rest of the composition. That is when I got the idea to paint the complete dolphin.[9]

This process of changing the dream image is common among artists who express their dreams through paintings. The painting itself becomes like a dream journey in which the dreamer/artist imbues a new experience with the information from the dream. It becomes the expression of the invisible world, and therefore the artist becomes the bridge between the visible and the invisible.

There are various ways in which dreams are expressed through visual art forms, which can be regarded as different categories of manifesting the dream world.

The first category is the bridge from the dream reality (invisible) to wak-ing reality (visible). The painting by Fuseli, *The Nightmare,* is an example of such a bridge. In it, we see waking reality: a sleeping woman, the familiar bed, familiar curtain. At the same time, we see the dream reality: the incubus, the horrified horse, the nightmarish mood.

The second category is the integration of the invisible with the visible without any information about the waking environment. De Chirico's and Rossi's paintings are examples of artwork that contains no information about who is dreaming. The observer is taken straight into a dream scene filled with images that are recognizable and representational but somehow disjointed, distorted, or placed in a different perspective.

In the third category, the artist expresses the invisible. The painting does not show any elements of wakefulness or dream images but is an expression of a new dimension with its own forms, structures, and colors unlike anything seen while awake. The painting might be familiar to us, but as something ex-perienced during waking vision, mystical experience, lucid dreaming, or other altered states.

Gordon Onslow-Ford captures these moments, calling them the expres-sion of the inner-world. He writes:

> Some dreams are messages from the depths in symbolic language, but how rare it is in dreams to catch an inkling of what the inner-worlds are really like! But I

Depths Unspoken, 1928, by Yves Tanguy.

am sure that I visit the inner-worlds every night while asleep—as I recognize what appears spontaneously in my paintings, and am led on with a sure sense of direction.[10]

As an expressive dream artist, I realize that dream art reveals the artist's own process of exploring the dreamscape. For example, when we observe the nature of Salvador Dali's paintings, it is obvious that he must have experienced hypnagogic imagery; much of his art represents the vivid, colorful, and disjointed images that occur in this creative "twilight" state of consciousness.

In the work of De Chirico, one can move into the archetypal imagery of the Greek and Roman sculptures, which reveals various mythological themes. From the world of De Chirico we may move to the world of Yves Tanguy, where structure collapses into spontaneous movement, creating a new world of images, the seed of lucid awakening in the dream state.

The work of Onslow-Ford take us to the world of lucidity, where the conscious and unconscious meet. In fact, the images in his paintings represent that state of lucidity in which one image moves into another, as colors lose their boundaries and shift hue. Onslow-Ford calls this stage Involution. He writes:

> Involution refers to the worlds within worlds that move from the surface between the conscious and the unconscious toward the depths of the unconscious. . . . Unconscious material becomes conscious, conscious material stirs the depths. There is a cross-fertilization between the conscious and the unconscious.[11]

In my own process of re-creating dreams while painting, I first brought dream images into a familiar waking composition (such as *Conscious Dreaming*). When my dreams had an archetypal theme, I expressed them in archetypal images. As I started to have more lucid dreams, I discovered forms, structures, and images that I had never seen or experienced in the waking state; I then needed to change my art medium to express those images.

After a lucid dream of making paper marbling, I adapted that medium to express my nocturnal dreams. Marbling is painting on the surface of water, and while painting I become close to the essence of lucidity as similarly experienced in my dreams. The energy, movement, flexibility, and impermanence belong to the nature of both lucid dreaming and marbling.

Painting my dreams through marbling became a novel expression of a

Space Travel, 1971, by Gordon Onslow-Ford.

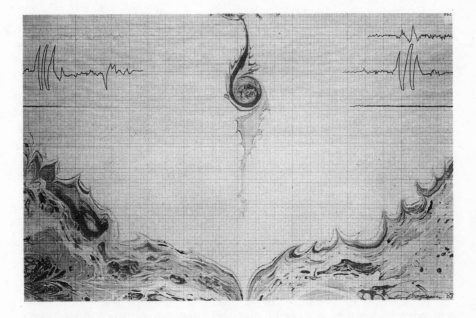

Lucid Dream, 1988, by Fariba Bogzaran.

new dimension in which the familiar is no longer the external representation, but the opening to an inner experience where the familiar is no longer separated from who we are.

In re-creating dreams through painting, the artist becomes a conscious traveler to the world of the unconscious and brings messages from this mystery land. Through painting, this mystery can be unveiled.

Montague Ullman

Guidelines for Teaching Dreamwork

In recent years, a great many books about dreams have appeared that are addressed to the layman and that offer a diverse array of viewpoints and strategies describing how to work with dreams. Their number seem to be growing exponentially. My goal is to provide readers with what I think they will need if they are to make an informed judgment on a particular book.

Two preliminary questions have to be raised first, if only to dispose of them. Should dreamwork be taught to the general public? The answer is an unequivocal "yes" as far as I am concerned, although I can hear dissenting voices among my psychoanalytic colleagues. Freud certainly felt that, while dreams were of interest to the public, interpretive activity was best left in the hands of the psychoanalyst. Jung released this stricture a bit but still felt that a guide knowledgeable in the ways of the unconscious (personal and collective) was needed.

The next question is, can it be taught? Again, the answer is "yes," but with a caveat or two. Teaching implies learning and learning implies commitment, the mastery of certain skills, experience, and, in the case of dreams, a bit of risk-taking.[1] It is not possible to explore that deeply personal domain where our dreaming self resides without on occasion coming across material difficult or painful to handle.

With the growing interest in dreams and in working with dreams by the general public, the question arises as to what extent the public is prepared to pursue this interest. For those of us who write books about dreams for the public, how well are we succeeding in getting across the principles of dreamwork and how successful are we in teaching safe and effective strategies necessary to carry them out? At least two serious problems can be anticipated. There is the danger that dreamwork may be pursued in a cultlike fashion, with one or another approach that promises more than it can produce being sold to the public. The public is often gullible when it comes to whatever promises instant relief, instant solutions, or instant healing. Then there are those who may be swept up in the dream movement who need more than dreamwork alone can give them. These people are in need of therapy, but have not or do not wish to face up to that need and seek a compromise solution through dreamwork.

In what follows, I have formulated a number of questions readers might keep in mind as they pursue their reading about dreams.

How well does the book provide information about the nature of dreaming and the nature of the dream? The first need of the newcomer to dreamwork is to have some understanding of the basic phenomenon that is dreaming and of its connection to the recalled dream. The distinction is important. Dreaming is a biologically instigated phase of sleep that recurs periodically—approximately every ninety minutes throughout the sleep cycle. It is the way we think while asleep. This thinking takes place predominantly in the form of uniquely crafted imagery that is related symbolically to feelings and experiences in our waking life. In most instances, they can be regarded as potential visual metaphors in which the metaphorical meaning becomes obvious when the link between image and feeling residues from waking experience comes to life. Dreaming may occur at other stages of sleep, but it most characteristically occurs during the rapid-eye-movement, (or REM), phase of sleep. Meaning is expressed in dreaming in the form of puns, play on words, double entendres, and symbolic imagery.

What are the specific features of dreaming that make it worthwhile to work with the remembered dream? There are three essential features that account for the potential healing power of the imagery. The first important feature of dreaming is its relevance to our current life. Freud provided the clue to this feature when he identified the dreamer's day residue as the starting point of what occupies the dreaming psyche. The feeling residues of recent experiences surface when our brain gets the signal to start dreaming. Those residues continue to linger because of their connection to earlier emotional residues from our past.

The second important feature is our ability to gather more information relevant to a current issue than we can readily do while awake. We bring a historical perspective to our thought processes while dreaming and seek out residues of experience from our past that, in a feeling way, are related to whatever the current issue may be.

The third important feature of the dreaming psyche is the profoundly honest way in which it reflects our subjective state. There is an honesty to our dreaming psyche, as if, in its naiveté and innocence, it had no choice but to tell us the truth about our life, regardless of our waking interest in knowing that truth.

The dream is what we bring back to the waking state from this repetitive dreaming phase. It is not identical with the dreaming state, because it is no longer being experienced in that immediate, spontaneous, involuntary way. In the recall, it is exposed to the vicissitudes of the waking ego doing the recall. We now engage with the memory of the dreaming episode through language. This, in turn, transforms what originally was experienced in a sensory form (predominantly visual), often in a disjointed fashion, into a narrative form, with some attempt to smooth out the illogical and ambiguous wrinkles.

The combination of these three features of our dreaming psyche endows the remembered dream with its potential for healing. Dreamwork, by capturing the felt relations of the image to our life, present and past, brings us in touch with more of the determinants of our behavior and does so in a way that has the ring of truth.

Does the book emphasize the fact that most dreams do not yield their secret easily and that real work is involved in the pursuit of that secret? We use a different language when asleep and dreaming than we do while awake, and we say different things about ourselves. For both these reasons, the dreamer awake may have a difficult time distinguishing what the dream is saying. One must become familiar with a new language, that of the visual metaphor. Our dreams may accentuate the positive or expose the problematic. In either event, their language and their message strike an unfamiliar note. It is not always easy for us to lower our guard and let what is new and unfamiliar upset a pre-existing equilibrium. All of us approach unknown truths about ourselves, good or bad, cautiously. Awake, we often are working against certain built-in resistances. It takes motivation and commitment to do the work necessary to retrieve the information we invested in those images while asleep.

Does the book clarify the nature of the work that must be done by the dreamer and the extent to which the dreamer can do it alone? On awakening, a dream may seem obvious, somewhat apparent, or completely obscure. There are a number of steps for a dreamer to take to bring life and feeling to the imagery. One generally speaks of freely associating to the images in the dream. This is certainly a basic instrument, but it is not a sufficient one in addressing the dream. In order to fit the dream into one's life one must zero in on the recent emotional soil on which the dream took root; explore the full range of associations that come to mind in connection with each image in the dream; and then work with the information now available to capture the metaphorical quality of the dream, with the images as one pole of the metaphor and the associative data unearthed as the other.

The Search for the Recent Context

Dreams start with the tensions and preoccupations we bring to bed with us at night. To what extent can we reconstruct the recent past to shed light on these emotional currents? What aspects of our recent past left us with emotional residues? What feelings or thoughts surfaced in our mind just prior to falling asleep? The dream is a continuation at night of feelings stirred up during the day. Any technique that professes to work with a dream without stressing the importance of identifying the recent emotional context will fall short of embedding the imagery in the concrete life situation of the dreamer and will run the risk of superimposing theoretical or speculative ideas on the dream to fill in the gap.

The Search for the Associative Context

The next step involves bringing to each image in the dream, and to each detail of each image, whatever associations occur to the dreamer. What contact, past or present, has the dreamer had with that image? What might that image mean?

The important thing about the work at this stage is that it be done systematically. The goal of the dreamer is to recover information first and, in so doing, lay the basis for linking the dream to his or her life. The most effective way to do this is to begin by breaking the dream down into its various scenes, consider each scene first as a unit, and then work with the individual elements in that scene.

Consider the first scene as a whole. Are there more things you can say about it? Are there more things you can say about the individual images or elements (such as numbers and colors) that appear in that scene? Play back your thoughts about the scene against what you have noted about the recent emotional context of your life. Do any further associations occur as to why you chose those particular images that night? Do this with each succeeding scene. The work you do on each scene enables you to bring a richer network of associations to the next one and often sheds light on why one scene follows another.

IN PURSUIT OF THE METAPHORICAL MESSAGE

In most instances, as more and more associations are brought to light, the dreamer will begin to make the connections between image and reality and catch on to the way the image reflects metaphorically a certain feeling, trend, or life situation. For a dreamer working alone, this may not be an easy matter even after doing one's best to elaborate the associative matrix. There are many helpful hints in the literature to overcome this block. One is for the dreamer to take an objective point of view about a particular image that remains puzzling, without regard to this particular dream. Sometimes in doing this, the dreamer will come across a message that suddenly feels right in its application to the dream.

Having done this work, it can sometimes help to let some time elapse; then, on coming back to the dream, the dreamer may be surprised to find some meanings emerge that escaped him or her the first time around. This is most likely to happen if enough groundwork has been done at the time the dream occurred. It can't be overstressed that dreams have a current meaning. Although they engage with our past, they start in the present.

There remains an intrinsic reason why a dreamer working alone may have difficulty in grasping fully all that the dream has to say. This can, perhaps, be best understood by viewing dreamwork as involving a series of steps designed to socialize the dream. In effect, dreamwork is the socialization of a part of the psyche that has not yet been socialized, a part that has had a kind of underground existence. "Socializing" it is making it a felt and viable part of our waking social existence. We are introducing a relative stranger to our inner circle of friends (all that goes into perpetuating our self-concept). At the outset, we can never be quite sure how the stranger will fit in.

The preceding outlined the first two stages in the socialization process that any teaching technique has to address. The first has to do with the transformation of the dreaming experience into the dream. On awakening, we are once again active social creatures, and the remembered dream now becomes an item on our waking social agenda. Most books outline some of the many helpful techniques to aid recall.

The next step in the socialization of the dream is to use the instruments of waking consciousness, such as language, associations, feelings, and memories, to explore the basis for the dream's connection to our lives. As we do this, the dream becomes more deeply embedded in our ongoing social existence. The orientation of many current books is focused on the dreamer working alone and stops at that point.

It has been my experience, based on the work I have done on my own dreams as well as my work with patients for thirty years and with groups for fifteen years, that sharing and working on dreams in a supportive and stimulating group setting is the most natural and effective method. It is as if our dreams require this level of socialization to bring out their full healing potential. Nor should that be surprising. Confronting the message of the dream alone, regardless of one's degree of sophistication, is to do so with all one's defensive apparatus ready to spring into operation should one get too close to an unpleasant truth. One is more apt to risk that confrontation in a supportive social context where trust has been established and where, through the sharing that has taken place, our human frailties have become known to each other. Our dreams cry out for this level of socialization.

Many books do encourage a group approach. There are certain minimum requirements for such an approach if it is to be effective. The atmosphere has to be that of a learning experience in which dreamers have the freedom to learn at their own rate and to the extent they feel ready. A leader should be there to teach whatever process is being used, not to confront the dreamer as the expert on his or her dream. The basics of group dreamwork should stress the following factors:

The safety of the dreamer. The dreamer who shares a dream should be in control of the process. The dreamer has the responsibility to set his or her own limits and is never to be pushed beyond that. In its effort to provide assistance, the group should always follow the associative track offered by the dreamer and never lead him or her. Leading questions take the control away from the dreamer. They arise from a concern with issues in the mind of the questioner that have not been opened up by the dreamer.

To maintain the dreamer's control, certain constraints on the group are necessary. In addition to avoiding leading questions, the group must respect the privacy of the dreamer at all times. That means, in effect, that however one conducts the dialogue between dreamer and group member, the questioning is never intrusive—that it never goes beyond areas opened up by the dreamer.

Respect for the authority of dreamers over their dreams. This entails never superimposing an interpretation on the dreamer. All interpretive ideas, be they right or wrong, should be considered as projections on the part of the person offering them unless they are accepted as meaningful by the dreamer. In my opinion, group work with dreams is best carried out in the absence of a single ideological metapsychological system. Working within the framework of any one system will constrain the imagination of both dreamer and group members to what is consistent with that system.

Both Freud and Jung endowed us with very powerful metaphors that are often, but not necessarily always, applicable to particular dream images. One should be free to draw upon them when indicated but, at the same time, remain aware that a dreamer may use any image in a highly idiosyncratic way. This accords true respect for the dreamer's individuality.

An atmosphere where all the participants, including the leader, share their dreams. This flattens the structure, lessens dependency on the leader, and diminishes his or her role as an authority. The only authority is that of someone teaching the particular process being used. In all other respects, the leader should be a fully participating member of the group.

The time factor. It takes a good deal of time to work through a dream in its entirety. It is not always possible to capture the meaning of every element of a dream, but there should be time to work on each element. If the dream is not treated with the thoroughness and care it deserves, it is best left alone.

All of the above can be summarized by saying that group work is best carried out in an atmosphere that generates safety and trust and that respects the dreamer's privacy, authority over the dream, and control over the work being done with it. The dreamer is left to manage his or her own defensive structure. The safer one feels, the more open one will be to explore the message of the dream.

IV

Women, Sex, and Dreams

In dreams we see ourselves naked and acting out our real characters, even more clearly than we see others awake.
HENRY DAVID THOREAU

Freud admitted that the number of potential dream symbols is immense. However, he insisted that the number of items symbolized "is not large," because "those pertaining to sexual life are the overwhelming majority."[1] Despite this early emphasis by Freud, remarkably few dream studies have focused on sexuality, gender differences, or the unique nature of women's dreams.

The articles in this section attempt to redress this neglect. Kenneth Rubinstein's knowledgeable chapter illustrates the use of content analysis for the study of gender differences in dreams and how these differences have changed over the years, at least in the United States. It is followed by chapters by two psychologists: Patricia Maybruck's skillful account of dreams during pregnancy, and Patricia Garfield's elegant description of how women's body-images are revealed by their dreams. Part Four ends with social worker Karen Surman Paley's sprightly rendering of sexual content in dreams.

Do dreams bear the unmistakable stamp of gender? Or are they flexible enough to reflect cultural differences in gender roles, as well as the social changes that influence male and female roles and self-images over time? Milton Kramer remarks, "If one accepts the dream as a reflector of inner processes . . . , the sexual revolution may have indeed contributed to meaningful internal change."[2]

I believe that the interface between the individual's inner and outer world was revealed in our 1974 study of transsexual dream content. When I directed the Dream Laboratory at Maimonides Medical Center, we made seventy-two comparisons of male-to-female transsexual dream reports with those also collected in dream notebooks by a standard male comparison group, along with seventy-two comparisons to a standard female comparison group.[3] The results were provocative: in twelve areas, transsexuals dreamed *less* about a given content than the typical man, while in eight areas they dreamed *more* about a topic. In eleven content areas, male transsexuals dreamed *less* about a topic than the typical woman, whereas in seven areas they dreamed *more* about a topic.[4]

For example, the transsexuals' dream reports contained more references to witnessing friendly interactions than did typical male dreams but to participating in fewer friendly interactions that did the male group. This may reflect an identification of the participants with the female cultural stereotype (of that time) as the recipient or observer of social interactions rather than the initiator. As Harry Benjamin, a physician and psychotherapist who pioneered work with transsexuals, observed, "It is my considered opinion, based on many years' experience, that transsexuals are mostly . . . non-aggressive and therefore no threat to society."[5] Only two sexual interactions were reported in the thirty dreams examined. If the dreams were honestly reported, this observation supports Benjamin's observation that the desire for direct sexual gratification rarely plays a significant part in the stated reasons for gender reassignment. Rather, the conviction that "I am a women in a man's body" is the intolerable dilemma that, for better or for worse, puts the preoperative transsexual on the surgery trail.

The similarities of these dreams with those of the two normative groups are also illlustrative. The transsexuals resembled the male group in that they rarely dreamed about household items, but they resembled the female group (of that era) in that they rarely dreamed about money.

In some cases, transsexuals' dream reports differed from those of both normative groups. The subject of clothes appeared more often in transsexuals' dreams than it did in either the male or female comparison group. One merely needs to recall that cross-sex dressing is an important activity for male transsexuals who typically feel better when dressed as women. For those transsexuals preparing for gender-conversion surgery, most physicians and psychotherapists insist on a lengthy "trial period" in which their clients dress as women and attempt to "pass" in their desired gender role.

On the other hand, transsexuals' dream reports contained fewer references to other adults than did either typical male or female dreams. But in the course of their daily life, transsexuals often display a lack of social interaction, especially before surgery.[6] When they did mention other people, transsexuals' dream reports contained more references to characters of indefinite sex than those of either comparison group, but fewer references to male characters. The participants often dreamed about themselves as female; one remarked, "Since childhood, I have dreamed about myself as a girl; that is why I know that I was meant to be a female." In addition, they dreamed about children and adolescents more often than did the typical man or woman.

Transsexuals used significantly more positive evaluative remarks ("pretty," "handsome," "beautiful," "good") than both normative groups and fewer negative remarks ("ugly," "bad"). We asked ourselves whether this could reflect "positive thinking," a defense against depression, or a reference to their hoped-for new bodies and lifestyles. Despite the plethora of positive adjectives, there was only one "cognitive" dream containing a deliberate continued mental effort or thought.

We did not need to look far to find support for Freud's notion of sexual symbolism in the transsexuals' dreams. In one, a doorknob is taken from a door. In another, a chimney falls off a house. In a third, an interior decorator removes unsightly light fixtures and other protuberances from a room. If, indeed, these are symbols and metaphors for the prospective operation, they might be less a disguise than the best way in which an individual who had never experienced (or even seen) such an operation could present an omnipresent concern in a dream.

This investigation of preoperative transsexuals' dream reports strongly supports the position of Alfred Adler and others who have maintained that dream life mirrors waking life. That is not to say that unconscious, inaccessible, and forgotten material is absent from dreams, but it does impel dreamworkers to consider the most obvious explanation of a puzzling dream before wildly conjecturing a psychodynamic that may reveal more about the therapist than it does about the dreamer. Gender-reassignment surgery is a high-risk procedure; moderate long-term improvement in psychological functioning has been reported *if* candidates for the operation are carefully selected.[7] However, some clients do not "live happily ever after" once the "desired" body is a reality. Perhaps the dream reports of this desperate group contain clues as to the outcome of their quest.

Kenneth Rubinstein

How Men and Women Dream Differently

We can learn a lot about people from their dreams: we can get a good idea about what concerns them, what they wish for, and what scares them. This chapter will examine research on men's and women's dreams and what it has to say about the differences between men and women. It will also consider whether these differences are related to cultural factors and to what extent they might be changing.

RESEARCH FINDINGS CONCERNING GENDER DIFFERENCES

In their review of the literature, Winget and Kramer[1] report that the first study to examine gender differences in dreams was that of Jersild, Markey, and Jersild in 1933.[2] The dreams of 400 boys and girls were studied, and it was found that the boys' dreams included more instances of mutilation, as well as feelings of powerlessness in the face of kidnappers and robbers. Girls had more unpleasant dreams in which they were anxious, and the themes they dreamed about often involved the loss of relatives. In a similar study six years later, Witty and Kopel found that girls were more likely to dream of being chased, while boys dreamed more frequently of accidents, injury, and being punished.[3] In early studies that looked at themes of sexuality, both Gahagan and DeMartino found that among college students, male dreams included more nudity and sexual feelings than those of females.[4]

In 1966, Hall and Van de Castle published *The Content Analysis of Dreams*, a comprehensive look at a sample of 1,000 dreams that were collected from college students at Case Western Reserve between 1947 and 1952. They compared males and females and found a number of striking gender differences in dream content. Men's dreams included more male characters, more unfamiliar characters, more sexual incidents, more incidents of physical aggression, more references to weapons, and more outdoor scenes. They also included fewer emotional experiences, fewer family members, fewer children and babies, less social interaction, and fewer references to clothing than dreams reported by women.[5]

The following is an example of a typical male dream that Hall and Van de Castle included in their book:

The first part of the dream I can remember started in a monstrous hunting lodge which, for some reason, had live deer walking around. This did not seem to excite me or the others who were walking around (all male and only one I knew in real life—a man I used to hunt with). The deer were mostly doe, but there were a few buck. Only spike horns, however. Later, I went outside and saw two hunters and told them about the deer. Then a doe came out and one of the hunters shot it, but only I could see this since it went behind a tree right after he shot. I heard him say "I missed," and the next thing I knew, he had hit me in the ankle, but only with a couple of pieces of buckshot. I went into a hunting store to get a first aid kit, but ran into a Spanish speaking saleslady who couldn't understand me. Finally, I got the kit and fixed myself up.

A number of aspects of this dream fit the typical model that Hall and Van de Castle found among males. The scene takes place outdoors, the characters are mostly male and unfamiliar, there is physical aggression (the shooting of the deer), and a weapon is used.

The following is an example that fits the model they found for female dreamers:

I walk into a cedar wood house, the room is long and narrow. I see Ned, a psychiatrist friend of mine, holding a baby. The baby can speak quite well (beyond his years) but has the physical strength of a baby. Ned is the father. He cares for the baby but is swinging him around, and the baby keeps falling down and off its chair. One time I catch the baby.

It's Thanksgiving and many people are due to arrive for dinner. The table is set with dishes for everyone. It is discovered that there are not enough placemats and someone goes to find more. She returns saying that she could not find any placemats. I look down and find large black spots over the table. I feel disturbed. Then dinner is served quickly.

The last scene is seeing my aunt and another female in the back of a car. My aunt is eating a plate of food hastily. They're waiting for my dad, who is saying goodbye to the other guests. I comment to myself how soon they are leaving after the meal.

One obvious difference between this dream and the previous one is that here we are told about a stereotypically female activity (setting the table) as opposed to a traditionally male one (hunting for deer). In addition, the setting is indoors, the characters are familiar, and many are relatives. The presence of a baby is also a feature that is far more common in female dreams than in male dreams.

Studies by DeMartino and Paolino both confirmed Hall and Van de Castle's finding that male dreams include more aggression,[6] and Griffith, Miyagi, and Tago found that men dream about money more than women do.[7] Hall found that in male dreams, misfortunes occur to the dreamer more often than to other characters, while female dreamers do not experience misfortunes to themselves any more than to the other characters in their dreams.[8]

DIFFERENT INTERPRETATIONS OF RESEARCH FINDINGS

While a number of these results seem to point to important differences between men's and women's dreams, the meaning that one draws from these gender differences is open to interpretation. For example, one clear difference found in practically every study is that men's dreams include more male characters than women's dreams. In 1984, Hall wrote an article entitled "A Ubiquitous Sex Difference in Dreams Revisited," in which he surveyed thirty-five different studies that compare male and female dreams. In twenty-nine of these, men's dreams included more male characters than women's dreams; in the remaining six there were no significant differences. Hall interprets this as an indication that men are more preoccupied with other men than women are and suggests that this may be related to Freud's theory of the male and female Oedipus complex.[9]

According to Freud, a young boy sees his father as a rival for his mother's love and unconsciously fears that his father will castrate him.[10] As he grows older, he transfers his fear of his father to other men, leading to conflicted feelings with men in general. Girls, in contrast, turn their attention from their mothers to their fathers at an early age (according to Freudian theory, due to their mother's lack of a penis) and end up feeling equally ambivalent toward both sexes.

Urbina and Grey offer a different explanation for this frequently observed gender difference.[11] They argue that the difference in the number of male characters does not reflect differences in preoccupations, but rather differences in the amount of actual contact that each gender has with the other in daily life. To support this, they cite Grey and Kalsched's study in which the amount of heterosexual contact for each dreamer was determined and was shown to be strongly related to the ratio of men and women within his or her dreams.[12]

Wood, Sebba, and Griswold have suggested that the common gender difference in male versus female characters is related to differences in the dreamers' interest in sex-typed activity. They found that subjects who were interested in stereotypically masculine activities were more likely to dream of male characters, whether or not the dreamer was male or female.[13]

As Hall and Van de Castle's sample included dreams that were reported forty years ago, one might wonder whether their results reflected the societal values of their time rather than any innate difference between men and women. Many of the gender differences they found conform to our stereotypes—men are more concerned with sex and aggression, while women are more emotional and interpersonally oriented—yet these stereotypes have changed considerably over the last generation. With the coming of the feminist movement and the "sexual revolution," society has become more accepting of assertive behavior on the part of women, and men are being encouraged to express their emotions to a greater degree than they were forty years ago. Recent studies that measure cognitive skills have found that many gender differences that were thought to be "natural" are no longer present. Feingold studied performance level on standardized tests and reported that gender differences have declined sharply between 1947 and 1980.[14]

MORE RECENT FINDINGS

About a decade ago, two studies were undertaken to examine this question of cultural change using large samples of dreams from both men and women. In 1979, Hall, Domhoff, Blick, and Weesner collected 600 dreams from undergraduates at the University of Richmond and found a striking similarity between the Richmond sample and the Case Western Reserve sample from thirty years earlier.[15] Aside from a decrease in the number of friendly interactions and friendly characters in dreams, there were not significant differences between the two samples taken as a whole. And, most importantly, the gender differences in the more recent sample were identical to those found in the original one. Reflecting on the fact that the gender differences in the two samples were exactly the same, the authors concluded that either dreams reflect basic human nature and are therefore relatively unaffected by social change, society did not change significantly between 1950 and 1980, or social changes take a long time to manifest themselves in dreams.

However, in 1980, Kramer, Kinney, and Scharf studied the dreams of university students in Cincinnati and did not find a number of the gender differences that were reported in earlier samples. They did not find differences in aggression, misfortunes, or social interactions, though men still dreamed of male characters and strangers more frequently and women's dreams still included more emotions. They concluded that the "sexual revolution" has had some effect on the traditional differences between men and women.[16]

Cramer studied the daytime fantasies of twenty-one college men in 1986 and found that they were significantly different from male fantasies reported twenty and fifty years earlier. In the 1986 study, males were more often depicted as psychologically isolated and threatened by outside forces that were beyond their control, and females were less often portrayed as helpless victims. When the dreams of these men were compared to the Hall and Van de Castle 1950 data, it was found that in the recent sample, men dreamed equally of male and female characters, in contrast to the usually higher number of male characters mentioned above. There was also a significant decrease in the amount of physical aggression and an increase in the amount of misfortune experienced by the male dreamer.[17]

In 1985, Lortie-Lussier, Schwab, and DeKonnick compared the dreams of fifteen working mothers and fifteen nonworking mothers to see whether the changing roles of women have had an effect on dream content. They found that working mothers experienced more unpleasant emotions and that their dreams included more male characters and fewer indoor settings than those of nonworking mothers.[18] They argue that Hall and others may have failed to find any evidence of cultural changes because they looked only at the dreams of college students, while the impact of these changes is more apparent in the post-college years. In addition, they cite their data as support for Urbina and Grey's notion that the commonly found gender difference in male characters has more to do with daily experience than with the Oedipus complex.

In 1988, Krippner and Rubinstein studied the dreams of 220 men and women who had sent in dream reports in response to an advertisement on a nationally televised talk show. By using a sample that included both men and women of all ages and from every part of the country, they hoped to obtain results that were more generalizable than those of previous studies, which either examined only one sex or used a sample composed entirely of university students. Within their sample, they did not find a number of gender differences that had been reported in previous studies. There was no difference between men's and women's dreams in the amount of aggression, friendliness, male characters, sexuality, weapons, or clothes. However, women still had a higher number of family members, babies, children, and indoor settings in their dreams than men did.[19]

These results were seen as reflecting the fact that some aspects of women's lives have remained the same. On the one hand, there has been an increasing liberalization in society's attitudes about sex-appropriate behavior, and women have entered the traditionally male-dominated workplace; yet at the same time, women are still primarily responsible for raising children and keeping the family together, and they still spend more time in the home than men do.

Krippner and Rubenstein also looked at differences between dreamers from different geographic regions in the country and found that while patterns of aggression no longer distinguish men from women, they do distinguish residents of different areas. In dreams in which the dreamer was either the aggressor or victim, dreamers from the East Coast were more likely to be the aggressor (40 percent of the time) than those from the Midwest (10 percent of the time) and West Coast (22 percent of the time).

Other studies have looked at differences in aggression among people of entirely different cultures. In his study of the Mehinaku Indians of Brazil, Gregor found a much higher amount of aggression than did Hall and Van de Castle for both men and women, but he noted that men's dreams still contained more aggression than women's and that the degree of gender difference was identical to that found in the American sample.[20] However, Munroe and others who studied the dreams of students among the Gusli, Kipsigis, and Logoli tribes of East Africa found a different pattern. East African women's dreams contained as much physical aggression as, and more nonphysical aggression than, men's dreams.[21] This finding helps to highlight the important role that is played by culture, and it raises questions about the extent to which some gender differences are biologically determined.

LIMITATIONS OF DREAM RESEARCH

When we say that researchers study dreams, what we mean is that they study verbal reports in which subjects relate or write down what they remember from their dreams. The distinction between the dream and the dream report is important, because this kind of dream research is limited by the fact that we are studying a verbal report of an essentially visual experience, as well as a waking report of an experience that occurred during sleep. In addition, some people question the validity of this kind of work, arguing that the real meaning of dreams can be found only through psychotherapy or some other uncovering process.

Freud distinguished between the manifest dream content (the dream as it is remembered) and the latent dream content (the underlying meaning of the symbols in the dream), and he believed that a reliance on the former led to only a superficial understanding of dreams.[22] In contrast, others—among them Alfred Adler, Walter Bonime, and Montague Ullman—have argued in favor of the "continuity hypothesis," believing that there is a basic continuity between the characteristics of the manifest dream and the waking emotional concerns and cognitive style of the individual. In support of the continuity hypothesis, Hendricks and Cartwright report a high correspondence between subjects' cognitive style during dreaming and during waking activity,[23] and Foulkes has found that the cognitive development of children is mirrored in their dreams.[24]

Researchers generally study dream reports using "content analysis," in which a number of very specific aspects of each dream, such as the number of characters or the number of physically aggressive interactions, are calculated. While this is a fairly reliable and objective method and has been successfully used to analyze large numbers of dreams, some argue that the unique meaning of each dream is lost when a study is conducted in this manner.

PSYCHOLOGICAL RESEARCH AND THE ISSUE OF SEXISM

Because our main topic is differences between men and women's dreams, it is important to point out that the subject of gender differences recently has been a controversial one in psychological circles. In an effort to combat the masculine focus within psychological research, McHugh, Koeske, and Frieze have argued that all psychological researchers should keep track of whether subjects are male or female and be aware of how this affects their results. They caution against reporting gender differences, however, unless they are replicated or are of theoretical interest, noting that the overreporting of small gender differences and the underreporting of gender similarities has led to a bias in the literature.[25] Eagly has argued that one of the best ways to fight sexism in research is to have all psychological researchers report gender differences and similarities, whether or not they are relevant to the theoretical purpose of their study.[26] She reasons that placing limitations on the reporting of these differences would result in less accuracy and a greater reliance on current theoretical assumptions about what is relevant. However, Baumeister has responded that Eagly's approach might increase sexism, since any highlighting of the differences between the sexes could lead to the perpetuation of stereotypes and discrimination. He also points out that gender differences are often greatly confounded by other variables, including "social oppression, physical stature, past exposure to role models, personal ideas, flirtation with the experimenter, and so on."[27]

In looking specifically at gender differences in dreams, we need to ask to what extent they reflect "natural" male-female differences and to what extent they are the result of the different societal conditions that men and women find themselves in. While we cannot answer this question conclusively, the most recent evidence supports the idea that society has played a strong role in determining a number of gender differences that have been reported. These differences appear to be less evident today than in the past, which seems to coincide with an expansion of our notions of what kinds of behaviors are appropriate for men and women and an increased sense of our possibilities.

Patricia Maybruck

Pregnancy and Dreams

For decades, dream researchers have known that pregnant women's dreams are remarkably different from those of nonpregnant women. The earliest research was conducted in 1968 by Robert Van de Castle and Peggy Kinder.[1] Since then, there have been at least twelve investigations of this phenomenon. My own 1986 doctoral study of more than a thousand dreams from sixty-seven pregnant women, one of the largest investigations in this field, was probably the most in-depth study.[2] Additionally, popular books have described the topic in detail. These include *The Secret Life of the Unborn Child,* by Thomas Verny and Jack Kelly, published in 1981;[3] *The Dream Worlds of Pregnancy,* by Eileen Stukane, 1985;[4] *Women's Bodies, Women's Dreams,* by Patricia Garfield, 1988;[5] and my own *Pregnancy and Dreams,* 1989.[6]

As will be discussed later, expectant mothers report more dreams than most nonpregnant women, probably because they are able to recall their dreams more easily than was the case before they conceived. The content of dreams in this group is also unusual in that it is frequently vivid and rich in detail, bizarre, and often nightmarish.

Further, the themes and symbols of pregnant women's dreams appear to have certain common traits, in that these dreamers report similar associations to many of the same dream characters, settings, and motifs. Although a variety of these dream elements may reflect cultural changes, in each decade of research, expectant mothers have consistently assigned the same meanings to specific images.

For example, in Van de Castle and Kinder's 1968 study of fourteen pregnant women, small animals in their dreams were said to represent the unborn child. Kittens, puppies, bunnies, and other small creatures were also typical fetal symbols in investigations conducted by Stanley Krippner and others, with eleven subjects, in 1974;[7] by Cecelia Jones, with thirteen subjects, in

1978;[8] and in my own 1986 and 1989 studies, which investigated a composite total of 2086 dreams.

This same similarity of dream symbols, at least for dreamers in the United States and Canada, holds true for water (as a symbol of the pregnancy or the amniotic waters in which the baby is suspended); architectural references (the dreamer's body—her uterus, the fetal "home"); threatening dream elements such as robbers, intruders, or disasters such as funerals, fires, and earthquakes (the dreamer's fears of pregnancy complications); and references to the past (unresolved adolescent conflicts).

This chapter will provide an example of a typical pregnant woman's dream and will explore possible reasons for the unique qualities of these dreams, as well as the benefits expectant parents can receive from the findings of dream researchers' investigations. Although these theories and applications of research findings are so recent that they have not yet "stood the test of time," it is my hope that obstetrical professionals will pay more serious attention to pregnant women's dreams as valid diagnostic tools.

WHY DREAMS DURING PREGNANCY ARE DIFFERENT

Most of the studies cited above noted that pregnant women recalled their dreams more frequently than nonpregnant women, yet we still do not know exactly *why* expectant women are able to remember their dreams more easily than any other group. Moreover, as yet we can only theorize about the reasons these dreams are usually so intense and extraordinary in content. Several theories that might explain the unusual traits of pregnancy dreams include:

1. Extreme hormonal changes of pregnancy are directly related to certain biochemical levels that are present in the body during dreaming.

2. Because most pregnant women's sleep patterns are irregular, it is probable that they recall more dreams simply because they sleep more and awaken more frequently.

3. Since pregnancy and childbirth are major transitions, the dreams of expectant mothers reflect the emotional turmoil typical of critical life changes.

My own investigation convinced me that all three of these concepts may work together at various times during pregnancy. However, these observations do not constitute what the scientific community would accept as solid data. Similar observations would have to be duplicated and documented by other researchers before my belief that all three theories account for these unusual dreams could be scientifically supported.

The first theory, that hormonal changes affect pregnancy dreams, has not yet been confirmed. Neurophysiologists are still investigating the nature of the biochemical changes that occur during dreaming. In the future, these scientists may be able to offer data that the increased levels of certain hormones during pregnancy are also present in smaller amounts when nonpregnant people are dreaming. However, since the precise nature of hormone levels during dreaming has not yet been established, a relationship between the increased hormone levels of pregnancy and dreaming cannot be substantiated.

We do know that these hormonal upsurges contribute to the greater variety and intensity of the pregnant woman's emotions during her waking state. The Columbia University College of Physicians and Surgeons' *Complete Guide to Pregnancy* reports that pregnant women's rapidly changing hormonal levels can cause bouts of depression and euphoria, crying jags, and mood swings, especially in the first trimester of pregnancy.[9]

According to Tracy Hotchner, a childbirth educator,[10] pregnant women's levels of estrogen and progesterone remain high until delivery, even though their bodies achieve a balance by the second trimester. This causes expectant mothers' emotions to be stronger and less stable throughout pregnancy. This high degree of emotionality is likely to be mirrored in their dreams and may account for the vivid richness of dream images during pregnancy.

The second theory, that frequent awakenings may aid dream recall, does not provide much new information. It is true that expectant women's sleep patterns are quite different from those of most other women. In 1968 and 1969, Ivan Karacan and a group of other prominent sleep researchers and dream psychologists conducted two carefully monitored investigations of sleep patterns during pregnancy,[11] which provided evidence most pregnant women already knew—that an uninterrupted night's sleep during pregnancy is rare. (This is especially so during the last trimester, when the pressure of the enlarged uterus on the bladder necessitates frequent trips to the bathroom.) It seems logical that these awakenings would help anyone recall her dreams more easily.

Karacan and his colleagues also found that pregnant women sleep more than other groups of women. Garfield comments that increased hormone levels may act as sedatives. People who sleep more may have more opportunities for the rapid-eye-movement sleep in which dreaming typically occurs.

However, this theory does not explain the unusual *content* of pregnancy dreams. There is a remarkable consistency in the actual components of most expectant women's dreams. An experienced dream psychologist can identify certain dreams as being the creations of a pregnant woman's mind— sometimes when physicians do not even know she is pregnant.

The third supposition, which suggests that any transition of life-crisis proportions will be reflected in one's dreams, appears to come closest to explaining the unusual nature of pregnant women's dreams. Ernest Harmann found that most people have remarkably different dreams while going through any type of transition or life-crisis, such as marriage, divorce, or even such comparatively minor changes as a new job or moving.[12] In *Dreamworking,* Stanley Krippner and Joseph Dillard explain that one theory about dreams in general, which has stood the tests of time and repeated investigations, is that most dreams tend to reflect the dreamer's personality and concerns during waking life.[13] Obviously, pregnant women's dreams are a mirror of one of the most important events in their lives, that of the growth of a new life within their bodies.

This third explanation also accounts for the frequently different dreams pregnant women experience during each trimester, differences that most of the above-cited studies of pregnancy dreams have observed. Since each trimester is accompanied by different physical changes both in the fetus and in the mother's body, it makes sense that these concerns would be mirrored in consistently similar dreams.

DREAM THEMES IN PREGNANCY

Carrying this reasoning further, the transition theory might explain the remarkable fact that pregnant women's dreams contain the same or similar elements. For instance, the high percentage of pregnancy dreams with references to water, animals, architecture, and past events is illustrated in this dream reported by Robyn in the fourth month of her first pregnancy.

I am swimming in the ocean, trying to get to the shore. There's a strong undertow that keeps me from going very far but I'm not worried. The water feels pleasantly warm and I'm only a few yards from a house which is built right out into the water. Somehow I know I'll get to the house eventually. It's a big two story shingled house, and I can see every detail—even the nail heads in the shingles. Then I notice my mother (who I haven't actually seen for several years) looking out one of the windows. She's smiling and waving to me. Next I notice the water around me is full of turtles of all kinds! Most are huge and they're swimming right along beside me. Then I woke up, feeling quite puzzled about this weird dream.

Robyn's dream took place in an ocean setting and is typical of second- and third-trimester dreams. It is interesting that this dream gives almost no clues as to other facts about Robyn, a secretary who worked part-time as an aerobics instructor, yet her dream indicates a more important aspect of her life, her impending motherhood.

A number of pregnancy dreams depict amphibians, such as lizards or the turtles in Robyn's dream. Numerous others portray small animals—furry, cuddly bunnies, kittens, or puppies. All these small life forms appear to represent the fetus. Van de Castle speculates that new mothers may dream about baby animals because they cannot visualize themselves capable of caring for a tiny, newborn human infant.[14]

Another reason for these distinct fetal symbols may be that the dreamers are imagining the actual shape and appearance of the fetus. For instance, when a childbirth instructor showed pictures of the developing fetus, a number of her pregnant students commented that the embryo resembled a lizard in the early stages and a small, four-legged animal in a later stage. The day after this class, six women in their second trimester reported dreams of lizards. Three others, in their third trimester, submitted dreams about kittens and rabbits.

Pregnant women also dream frequently about their mothers. This may be a symbol of themselves as mothers, or it may be a reminder that the dreamer has some unresolved conflicts with her own mother that need to be addressed before she can make the transition to motherhood herself. While Robyn's dream portrays her mother looking out the window, it doesn't seem to indicate any such conflict. Rather, the mother figure is smiling and waving in a supportive, encouraging manner. Robyn thought the mother-figure represented herself. "When I reach my goal of delivery, the beach house of my dream," she said, "I'll be a happy mother waving to everyone with my good news."

Many dreams during pregnancy depict some type of architecture—believed to represent the dreamer's body or the uterus, the space within—such as the large house in Robyn's dream. Had I not known Robyn personally, I might have guessed from this dream that she was in her second trimester. She mentions that the house she's swimming toward is big, with two stories. If Robyn were still in the first three months of her pregnancy, it's more likely that her dream's setting would be a smaller, more confined space. Note that the mention of a *two*-story house might also indicate the second trimester.

These dream images may change in size and appearance as the pregnancy progresses, probably because they are the dreaming self's way of depicting either the growing fetus or the dreamer's enlarging body. Yet the same general category of images continues to appear in each trimester as important clues to the dream's meaning.

For example, the small kittens that characterize dreams during the first three to five months may become panthers or lions in later stages of pregnancy. Robyn dreamed of tiny lizards and mice in her first trimester. Note that in the dream quoted, these fetal symbols had changed into huge turtles. The small rooms depicted in first-trimester dreams often give way to larger buildings (such as Robyn's big two-story house) and even skyscrapers by the last trimester. Again, these architectural references may symbolize the dreamer's enlarging body. Although the details and size may be different, they usually continue to appear as the dreamer's perception of her body.

NIGHTMARES IN PREGNANCY

The results of my studies show that expectant mothers' dreams consistently reflect more anxiety and fear than the dreams of other groups. The pregnant women I've studied had many more disturbing dreams than they did pleasant, positive ones. In my 1986 doctoral study, 40 percent of all the dreams I analyzed were nightmares from which the dreamers awoke feeling terrified and upset. Another 30 percent contained anxiety-provoking elements such as hostile or threatening characters, environmental disasters such as storms, fires, or earthquakes, and catastrophes such as deaths or funerals. Thus, 70 percent of the 1048 dreams collected for my study were unpleasant and indicated anxiety on the part of the dreamers.

This is a startling statistic. Ernest Hartmann, author of *The Nightmare,* says that not more than one in every 200 adults has nightmares on a regular basis.[15] In order to study nightmare sufferers, he had to select people he characterized as an extreme group. However, Hartmann's investigation did not include the dreams of pregnant women.

In 1978, Cecelia Jones[16] and Judith Ballou[17] investigated pregnant women's dreams in two separate studies. Both these researchers noted the similarity of their subjects' dreams as to images and themes, yet neither study indicated the unusually high percentage of negative dreams that my doctoral research revealed. However, in 1980, Myra Leifer, after closely following nineteen women throughout their first pregnancies, concluded that childbirth in the United States has become an experience of anxiety and pain.[18]

Dream researchers already have established that dreams usually reflect the concerns and experiences of waking life. If pregnant women's unpleasant dreams are reflecting their actual waking state, then it seems logical to conclude that many such women are currently experiencing much more anxiety than mothers-to-be did a generation ago.

More mothers are working today than ever before, a larger number are older as a result of having postponed pregnancy to pursue careers, and many suffer from what has been called the "Superwoman Syndrome"—an often unrealistic drive to excel simultaneously in careers, homemaking, and parenting. All these cultural changes have contributed to the anxieties today's pregnant women undergo. They worry about being able to balance careers and motherhood, about possible physical complications for themselves and their babies when they're in their thirties, and about being unable to meet the high expectations of their mates, their peers, and society at large.

When these contemporary concerns are added to the normal emotional turmoil most pregnant women experience, it is small wonder that their dreams are nightmarish. However, there is some indication that such frightening dreams may be beneficial.

The notion that frequent nightmares may help the pregnant woman resolve issues that contribute to stress and tension, thereby helping her to be more relaxed during labor, was explored by Carolyn Winget and Frederick Kapp in 1972.[19] Although these investigators studied seventy pregnant women's reports to counselors about sleep disturbances, these dreams were not individually examined or analyzed.

Winget and Kapp found that those women in their study who had more nightmares had labor of shorter duration than did those who had fewer nightmares. They cited studies indicating that deep relaxation without sedation during labor promotes uterine motility, thereby decreasing the duration of labor. These researchers speculated that frequent nightmares about waking fears relieved anxiety to the extent that the subjects were able to relax during labor.

In an attempt to replicate Winget and Kapp's study, I compared the frequency of nightmares with labor duration of the sixty-seven volunteers in my 1986 study and found no relationship. However, when I examined the *content* of the nightmares, I discovered that those women who were assertive in their nightmares had significantly shorter labors than did those who were consistently victimized in such dreams.

This finding suggests that merely dreaming about an anxiety-provoking issue does not promote the deep relaxation necessary for the facilitation of uterine motility during labor. Rather, it may be that those dreamers were able to relax deeply during labor because they had taken assertive action to resolve their fears.

More research is needed to ascertain the best ways this finding can be used to help childbearing women. We do not know whether those women who are assertive in their nightmares are also assertive in waking life, nor do we know whether teaching pregnant women to be assertive in their dreams would have the same relationship to labor duration as do the spontaneous dreams of this type. Thus, the most beneficial type of intervention that would utilize this information to promote an easier delivery cannot yet be precisely determined.

DREAMS DURING PREGNANCY

Although many topics remain to be investigated, there is already an abundance of data that points to the importance of dream research and dream therapy with pregnant women. These include identifying and resolving waking fears with dreams and the use of dreams as diagnostic tools for predicting possible physiological complications.

In 1983, E. S. Bassoff pointed out that the expectant mother tends to become withdrawn and to refrain from communicating her inner feelings.[20] This normal reluctance to reveal herself is compounded by societal pressures on the modern woman to succeed, so that she is even more unlikely to admit to any anxiety, lest she be thought too immature or incompetent.

DREAM THERAPY

Using dreamwork as a therapeutic process, health professionals can lead the pregnant woman to discuss her fears in a nonthreatening manner. The mothers-to-be in my dream-study classes, seminars, and workshops become so deeply involved in the fascinating task of dream interpretation that even those who initially claim they have no anxiety admit to secret fears that their babies might have defects, that delivery may be frighteningly difficult, or that they feel inadequate in their impending roles as parents.

Once these fears are confronted, most of my clients report less stress and fewer nightmares. The ability to relax deeply does not guarantee an easier labor, since many physiological factors may have an even greater influence on pregnancy outcome. Nevertheless, when the mother is able to release muscle tension to the fullest without sedation, the outcome is more favorable even if there are physiological complications. For this reason alone, continuing the study of pregnant women's dreams can promote easier childbirth.

DIAGNOSTIC AND PREDICTIVE DREAMS

Although many new mothers insist they dreamed correctly about their babies' sex, appearance, and personality, no quantitative evidence has been presented in this area. When I performed statistical tests on dream predictions of gender, my subjects' dreams were correct only 50 percent of the time, which could have occurred by chance.

However, while there is little quantitative evidence that pregnant women's dreams predict pregnancy outcome, the anecdotal evidence is quite impressive. Medard Boss,[21] Robert Van de Castle,[22] and Patricia Garfield[23] have reported dreams symbolic of conception on the same night the dreamer had intercourse and was convinced she had conceived. David Cheek reported an apparent relationship between nightmares and miscarriages, although he did not cite the number or types of nightmares his patients had just prior to these complications.[24]

Subjects in my own studies have reported dreams which appeared symbolic of stillbirths and other complications that had not yet been detected by their physicians. At least 5 percent of all the pregnant women I've studied have reported dreams they believed were predictive of complications during labor and delivery. For example, three women who had stillbirths reported nightmares that clearly depicted the baby as being born dead. Two women reported dreams of unexpected complications, and in both cases these abnormalities did arise, causing attending physicians to feel compelled to perform C-sections. Since all these women reported their seemingly predictive dreams to me after the tragic outcomes, there is no absolutely valid data showing that their dreams were, in fact, predictive.

Nevertheless, in view of this array of ancedotal data, I believe the wise approach would be for health professionals to be alert for possible complications when women report such dreams. As dream research advances, it is to be hoped that more satisfactory explanations of these puzzling, perhaps predictive dreams during pregnancy will be discovered.

Patricia Garfield

Women's Body Images Revealed in Dreams

 Women gaze into the looking-glass of their dreams every night of their lives. Their reflected images are expressions of their physical sensations, emotions, or thoughts about their bodies. Of course, dreams depict states of mind as well as feelings about the body, yet dreams offer a portrait of the woman's body image that is often overlooked.

Because their bodies undergo rhythmically recurring change during menstruation and pregnancy, these principles are more observable in women's dreams than in men's, although the same principles presumably operate in the latter. A portion of the following material is excerpted from the author's study in *Women's Bodies, Women's Dreams*; for more information, see this work.[1]

Definition of Body Image

A person's body image refers to the mental notion of what his or her body is, or should be, like.[2] In healthy individuals, this concept of the body is fairly close to its actual condition. In cases of mental imbalance, the body image may be widely divergent from the physical body. Women suffering from anorexia nervosa, for example, often perceive their bodies as being fat, while in fact they exhibit life-threatening thinness.

The Body Image in Dreams

Since it is the nature of dreams to dramatize, a woman's body image is almost always exaggerated in her dreams. The body image in dreams is depicted as a distortion or extension of the dream body, or a dream object or animal that symbolizes the body. An example of the former is the dream of a woman in early pregnancy who saw herself driving a car while she literally wore a spare tire around her waist. The image of the tire in her dream was a pun on the common expression that refers to an expanding midsection. The sensation of bloatedness she felt as her fetus expanded was pictured as a spare tire—a distortion of her dream body.

The sensations and feelings a woman has about her body are sometimes depicted not as objects on her dream body, but as symbolic dream images, such as clothing, architectural structures, animals, food, machines, or elements in nature. For instance, women who are sexually aroused often choose to dream of a building on fire, the structure of the building being likened by the dreaming mind to the woman's body. The fire in her dream becomes a metaphor for "being hot," experiencing a bodily heat or passion that consumes her.

By becoming familiar with the typical images women use to express the condition of their bodies, dreamers will understand better the language of their dreams and clinicians will be better able to assess and guide their clients.

DREAMS DURING NORMAL DEVELOPMENT

As a woman's body transforms from childhood to adolescence, from menstrual cycle to menstrual cycle, from maidenhood to sexually activity, from conception to giving birth, and from nursing to old age; these changes pass over the mirror of her dreams.[3] Any traumas inflicted on her body by accident or disease are likewise depicted in her dreams. Transformations in the size, shape, sensation, or functioning of the woman's body, as well as her emotions about these changes, are revealed by the images she creates in her dreams.

Dreams During Menarche

The hormonal upheaval in the young woman's body as she approaches puberty is well known. Sometime between the ages of eight and sixteen, she is physically transformed. She has a growth spurt, growing taller by about four inches in one year; she becomes heavier and rounder; breast buds appear and pubic hair sprouts almost two years prior to her menarche—the average menarche occurring between twelve and thirteen years in the United States.[4] At puberty, she becomes increasingly sleepy, especially prior to her menses.[5]

These bodily changes produce changes in young women's dreams that, so far, are less well documented. One of these shifts is an emerging breast consciousness. Characteristic dreams included:

My round jewelled sweater pin was flat. Puffy pins were for sale.
I saw a popular girl wearing falsies.
I insisted on a larger-sized blouse.
All the mothers compared their daughter's figures.

Actual sensations in the growing breasts may help stimulate such dreams.

At puberty, the increased oiliness of the skin causes many adolescents to suffer acne. One young woman dreamed of being a soldier with a bullet in his cheek; she awoke to find a new acne pustule in the same location as the dream bullet.

Feelings of being too tall, too short, too skinny, too fat are also themes in the adolescent's dreams and may sporadically appear throughout her life.

Around the time her menses begin, the young woman's dreams include menstrual blood, sanitary equipment, and fear of leaking, spotting, or showing pads. Young women who experience premenstrual tension reflect it in their dream imagery: water retention is sometimes depicted as ripe, juicy fruit about to burst; menstrual cramps sometimes appear as images of being bitten. Ovulation may be marked by dreams of eggs, jewels, or precious, fragile objects.[6] The womb full of blood was depicted by one dreamer as a giant red purse, so heavy it had to be carried on a pole by two men.

The color red is more frequent in the dreams of women during menses,[7] as are anatomical and room references;[8] images of flooding, dirty water, or disintegrating buildings often represent the menstrual debris. One dreamer, who was bleeding heavily during her menses, dreamed of a sink overflowing with water; the image of the sink was a receptacle like her womb; the water represented her flowing blood. Such topics continue to appear throughout the woman's menstrual years.

Dreams After Sexual Intercourse

Any sexual experience is quickly depicted in the young woman's dreams. Depending upon the nature of her encounters, these images vary. Early sexual experience often leads to physical pain, conflict, or guilt, producing such dreams as:

My house was broken into.
My bedroom window was smashed by a burglar.
A red tick crawled across my bedcovers.
My locker was ransacked and my things ruined.
A wedding dress was soiled.

First sexual encounters that are more loving and tender lead to dreams with romantic overtones:

I was gliding across a ballroom floor with my boyfriend.
My boyfriend filled my arms with flowers.
I ate a delicious hot-fudge sundae.

In general, the woman's body image in adolescent dreams depicts her feelings about her changing and growing body; she also expresses her emotional reactions to any sexual experiences as her body is entered for the first time.

As the woman becomes more sexually experienced, she may dream directly of sexual encounters and even experience orgasms. Kinsey found that a woman's peak sexual responsiveness was during her forties.[9] This height of arousability was paralleled by the highest average reporting of erotic dreams accompanied by orgasm. By the age of forty-five, about 37 percent of the women in Kinsey's study had had dreams with orgasm; among men of the same age, 83 percent had had such dreams. On average, men are more sexually experienced and sexually responsive at an earlier age in their dreams as well as their waking life. Dreams echo life experience.

Women, like men, are undergoing sexual arousal during the dream state; there is increased blood flow to the vagina, lubrication of the vaginal walls, and erection of the clitoris.[10] These physiological changes are a natural part of dreaming and may account in part for the predominance of sexual imagery in dreams.

Women often represent their womb and vagina as a container or enclosure in dreams, as psychoanalysts since Freud have observed. This fact was demonstrated poignantly by a recent widow who dreamed of a precious crystal vase she had received from her mother becoming shattered. Her waking sexual life, represented by the image of the vase, had been shattered along with the life of her husband.

Dreams During Pregnancy

The stimulus of being pregnant produces dramatic changes in a woman's dream life.[11] Her dreams of animals increase and the type of animal changes:

in early pregnancy she often dreams of aquatic creatures like tadpoles or lizards; in middle pregnancy, of cute, cuddly animals such as kittens, puppies, bunnies, or chicks; and in late pregnancy, about apelike animals or other big creatures.[12] These dream animals are thought to symbolize her fetus, since they get larger as pregnancy progresses.

In the same way, some researchers find that the architectural structures in the woman's dreams express the woman's enlarging body, with miniature buildings occurring in dreams of early pregnancy and large ones appearing in those of later pregnancy.[13] Weight gain during pregnancy frequently leads to dreams of carrying heavy objects, such as suitcases, the "excess baggage" of weight.

Lush growth of plants, flowers, and gardens is often observed in the pregnant woman's dreams; these images are thought to symbolize her fertility.[14] Likewise, dreams of water often increase as the woman's uterine waters are gathering. Movements of the fetus may stimulate dreams of the baby itself.

As a woman's uterus prepares itself for the task of delivery, she has Braxton-Hicks contractions (sometimes called "false labor") during her sleep as well as in her waking hours. These sensations become magnified during the dream state and probably produce the dreams of labor that occur near term.

Dreams During Menopause

As the woman's reproductive years draw to a close, another grand hormonal shift takes place in her body. During the seven years prior to cessation of her menses, there is a gradual lowering in her estrogen level;[15] eventually her eggs no longer ripen and erupt. This reduction in estrogen frequently imbalances the woman's body "thermostat," resulting in rapid changes of internal temperature.

The sudden flooding of warmth, often accompanied by sweating and dizziness, is termed a "hot flash." The menopausal woman may have several hot flashes a day, and she may find herself awakened from sleep sweating profusely, a phenomenon called a "night sweat."

Hot flashes and night sweats are directly linked to low estrogen. Sleep becomes shallower and less refreshing, and the amount of dreaming decreases. Researchers who administered replacement-estrogen therapy to menopausal women observed increased dreaming and smoother sleep.[16]

The sensations of heat the menopausal woman experiences during sleep appear in her dreams in the form of fire or heat. Typical dream images include:

> I was in a house with problems when a fire alarm rings.
> I saw dry neglected grass and plants.
> I was in a barren, rocky landscape.
> There was overripe fruit too close to a heater.

Depending upon her attitudes toward her life situation, the woman may interpret the dream image of heat as destructive or constructive. One menopausal woman cited dreams of a burnt-out barn and charred bodies of babies. She associated the scorched barn with her unproductive womb and the dead babies with the miscarriages she had had.[17] Yet another woman who dreamt of a burnt-out garden saw a gardener who assured her that the debris was making mulch for the best garden ever. The same physical sensations of heat were depicted differently according to the dreamer's emotional attitude.

Dreams During Older Years

In general, the older woman is sleeping less and having shorter dream time than when she was younger. At sixty-five, her deep sleep is about half of what it had been in her twenties. Yet older women exceed older men in the amount of deep sleep they get, and they often dream more.[18]

Naturally, the older woman's body is becoming frailer and more liable to breakage, disease, illness, and death. These physical realities become subjects in her dreams. Although the older woman still has pleasurable romantic and erotic dreams, imagery of loss is often observed.[19] Characteristic dream images include:

> I was lost in the hospital.
> Somebody stole my purse.
> A small boy stole all my handkerchiefs.
> An old man sat in a rocker on a porch with rotting floorboards.

It is important to remember that a woman's dreams can remain supportive throughout her life. One older woman with a positive attitude dreamed of a barn being reconstructed; another found her lost purse. Damaged, destroyed, or stolen objects in an older woman's dreams often symbolize her sense of deteriorating body and loss of powers. However, many older persons can be helped to draw on dream resources.

Dream themes about approaching death are common. Some older women dream that they are taking a journey or see themselves in coffins or attending their own funeral. Here, dreams can help prepare the elderly woman for her eventual demise. Many older women reported dreams of white birds, colorful celebrations, or beautiful flower-filled villages. Such visions may express the dreamer's hopes for heavenly afterlife and may comfort her passage.

DREAMS DURING PHYSICAL CHANGE OR TRAUMA

When a woman experiences a change in her body, this change is registered in her dreams. Her emotions about such change are depicted by the type of imagery she chooses to portray them.

Dreams During Weight Loss or Gain

Women undergoing restrictive diets respond in their dreams. One dieting woman dreamed she was eating cardboard, a comment on the bland food she was ingesting. Many women on restrictive diets dream of binging on their favorite dishes and feeling guilty about it. One woman who had been dieting less than a week dreamed she was so slim her trousers were falling off. By envisioning herself the way she wished to be, she encouraged herself to go forward in her program.

Likewise, women who are rapidly gaining weight respond in their dreams. After overindulging in several rich meals, one woman dreamed she saw dozens of pigs, a comment on the piggishness she judged her behavior to be, as well as a warning.

Dreams After Abortion

Women's dreams following an abortion tend toward violence and destruction. There is often imagery of a building being damaged. One woman, a few days after an abortion, had a nightmare that her garage door had been torn off and her car stolen. Furthermore, a gang of "mad lesbians" were tearing up her yard with bulldozers. This dream dramatized her sense of destructive intrusion. Her dreaming mind likened her womb to a garage that was forcibly opened; the destroyed fetus was symbolized by the stolen car; the chaotic overturning of earth by the "mad lesbians" suggests she felt that her feminity was threatened.

Women who undergo abortions by choice or for medical necessity sometimes dream about the lost child for years afterward.

Dreams After Sexual Abuse or Rape

Women who have been sexually abused often dream directly about their molester. Inevitably, the imagery involves severe damage to the dreamer's body. In one study, the most common theme was being attacked, usually resulting in death.[20] Characteristic dream imagery reported by abused girls and teenagers included:

> The steam roller drove over me and crushed me flat (the driver was her abuser.)
> I was lying on a hospital bed paralyzed while all my sisters and brothers were dying.
> I was in the bathtub when a shark bit off my arm.
> I was shot out of a cannon (operated by the molester) and killed.

A woman who was raped by a gang when she was seven described dreaming that night of choking on white glue. The unfortunate child had been forcibly subjected to oral copulation; the white glue in her dream symbolized semen. Any physical sensations experienced during abuse—being unable to breathe or feeling crushed—are often replicated in the dream imagery. Feelings of helplessness and terror are typical.[21]

Dreams After Injury or During Disease

Imagery during illness or injury varies widely depending upon the area of the body that is traumatized. A woman who was still in the hospital recovering from a hysterectomy twice dreamed that she had been raped. Her dreaming mind likened the intrusion of the surgical knife into her body to the brutal invasion of rape. A woman whose hand had been crushed in a metal-shaping machine had nightmares that several larger machines were attacking her; her sense of increased vulnerability was being portrayed. A woman whose treatment for cancer involved medication that produced heavy sweating dreamed she was drowning in a lake that had her name. Injured dreamers sometimes see themselves dressed in rags or defective clothing; they dream of objects that break or malfunction.[22]

As the body undergoes repair and healing, dreams often include images of wearing or buying new and attractive clothing, which seems to symbolize the dreamer's reintegrating body image.[23] Surgical scars became integrated into one woman's body image when she dreamed of a beautiful wedding dress with an attractive design of "V cuts" where her scars actually were.

During normal developmental stages, most women's bodies undergo a sequence of orderly transformations. Menarche, sexual intercourse, pregnancy, menopause, and aging are depicted in her dreams by structures that change in size, expand or contract, function well or malfunction, overflow or empty, are constructed or destroyed, flourish or die, and are flexible or rigid. These may be organic structures, such as people, animals, or plants, or inorganic ones, such as buildings, objects, or things.

In normal development, the structures representing the woman's body image are often growing or expanding, as with the images of wanting a larger blouse or seeing ripe fruit, cuddly baby animals, or big buildings. Even in the elder years, images may be expansive, as with dreams of journeys to paradisal settings that express hopes for a future beyond physical death.

In abnormal change or physical trauma, the woman's body image in dreams often tends to be of structures that are disintegrating or destroyed. When a woman's body is invaded roughly by sexual intercourse, sexual abuse, rape, accident, or surgery, its integrity is threatened. The structures in her dreams are often violently torn apart, emptied, malfunctioning, rigidly contracted, broken, or dying. We saw examples of these in dreams of stolen goods, decaying floorboards, a torn-off garage door, being paralyzed while others die, being crushed, drowning in glue, and other images.

The clinician who works with a woman's body image will find it useful to observe the form of structures in the woman's dreams, the condition and functioning of these structures, and the forces impacting them. To heal the woman who has been traumatized requires guiding her to move from restrictive and destructive imagery toward the opposite pole, to expansion and construction. The woman whose dreams exhibit healthy imagery should be helped to recognize, emphasize, and honor these pictures of her inner growth.

Karen Surman Paley

Dreamers Do It in Their Sleep

Erotic dreams make people uncomfortable. Upon awakening from one, many people feel embarrassed and guilty with emotional hangovers that pose the question, "Did I or didn't I?" In this moment of truth, the dreamer may forget that, asleep or awake, sexual feelings are simply feelings, not facts or events that must be acted upon in real life.[1]

Dreams have many purposes, and erotic ones are no exception. Conflicts may be highlighted and warnings issued. On the other hand, these nocturnal interludes can be a highly pleasurable form of the safest sex imaginable. For an individual trying to get some sleep, a simple wish-fulfilling fantasy may dispose of the libidinous drive that comes to the surface in the absence of one's usual self-restraint.[2] The point is that sexual desire exists whether or not we allow it expression in waking life.

PURPOSES OF EROTIC DREAMS

Those who have no routine sexual outlets may have particularly powerful sexual dreams as compensation for waking-life deprivation. John Money's study reported in the *Archives of General Psychiatry* described twenty-one paraplegic men and women whose vertebral nerve fibers were severed. Despite complete genital paralysis, these fourteen men and seven women experienced "phantom orgasms." They had dreams with vivid orgasm imagery in spite of the absence of physical sensation and paralysis of the genital area.[3] The sleeping brain is capable of achieving these "dry dreams" or mental orgasms, hallucinations that feel like real orgasms, devoid of ejaculation. Clearly, whether sexually abstinent by choice or by accident, no one has to forego sexual pleasure.

While release of sexual tension may be the purpose of erotic dreams for some, for others the need is less physiological and more psychological. It is not uncommon in waking life to find oneself attracted to someone who, for whatever reason, is not appropriate. Dealing with these impulses by pretending they do not exist or trying to restrain oneself with rigid, white-knuckled self-determination may temporarily keep one's hands "where they belong," but the unconscious mind will not tolerate this predicament for long. Constantly trying to control one's behavior only intensifies the underlying problem.[4]

Usually, and thankfully, such restraint is overcome during sleep. I say thankfully because it is when one is able to acknowledge impulses in the form of a dream that the danger of acting them out in waking life is reduced. In her book *The Dream Game,* Ann Faraday says that by becoming "aware of one's own feelings, [a person can] avoid the danger of the repressed impulses seeking expression in some devious way, perhaps by outbursts of anger against one's partner or by 'accidentally' finding oneself in some compromising situation with the dream lover in waking life."[5]

Sexual dreams whose primary purpose is the prevention of sexual acting out in real life can be precognitive in the sense of providing a dress rehearsal for an upcoming temptation as yet outside of waking consciousness. A client of mine was discussing his attraction to a woman with whom he was working. The woman always had worn "power suits" in his presence but the night before a scheduled meeting, he dreamt that he was with her at a party at which she was clad in an especially skimpy bikini. The next day, she arrived at the appointed hour apologizing for her unprofessional appearance. She was wearing shorts! My client commented, "If I hadn't 'seen' her the night before in practically nothing, I don't think it would have been business as usual. As it was, the shorts were a relief!"

DREAMUS INTERRUPTUS

Sexual dreams also unfold when one is well aware of the feelings but ambivalent about acting upon them. In this case the dream can become a laboratory for testing one's desires. One married bisexual woman utilized this technique to maintain monogamy.

I dreamt I was holding Phyllis all night long. At one point I French kissed her and, at the same time, almost superimposed, I was eating corn with my teeth. It didn't feel comfortable. She said it was a little strange having that kind of relationship with me.

This dream is a Socratic dialogue, a direct communication between the unconscious and the conscious, providing an answer to the question, "What would it feel like to sexualize my relationship with Phyllis?" The answer is that it would be unpalatable. The dream enabled this woman to avoid jeopardizing her marriage for what might have proven to be "a little indiscretion."

The kissing/eating dream made its point through what looks like a photographic blunder, a double exposure creating a composite image. Erotic dreams, in general, seem to be especially rich in metaphor, puns, and double-entendre, and many turn out to be about something quite different than the imagery would lead one to believe. Tom, a writer, was having a problem completing a project on human sexuality because he could not stop himself from reviewing the literature in order to begin writing. During this time he had the following dream.

I was with a woman who seemed to be forcing herself on me and I couldn't shake her off, so I thought I'd try to satisfy her. I was rubbing her crotch to give her a quick orgasm. Then I was on top of her and I was unbuttoning her blouse and her breasts were soft and beautiful. I said, "I can't go on with this. I'm married and I feel too guilty."

Tom was able to interpret this dream to his own satisfaction. Just as the woman was forcing herself on him, he had been feeling imposed upon by forcing himself to continue exploring other people's ideas way beyond what was necessary. "The scene in which I suddenly got into the sex and was opening the woman's blouse and enjoying myself was literally telling *me* to open up. In order to begin writing I had to stop obsessing, let myself go, and bring out some of my own thoughts on the subject. The dream helped me begin to write."

As a writer myself, I have had my share of sexual dreams that served as humorous carriers of the message from within. Recently I was writing a story about a local theater company directed by an internationally renowned playwright. The public relations director was not following through on her commitment to send me a copy of a play that I needed to do the article. I was feeling quite frustrated and helpless at the time I had the following dream.

I was alone with the playwright in his cottage. At dinner, when his wife and some other women were there, he kept trying to get me to put my hand on his erect penis. I clearly rejected it.

I was surprised by this dream because I had not wanted him, only his play. But when I thought about the words, I laughed to myself as I realized, "That publicity director has really been giving me *a hard time* and I have been putting *up with it*." I immediately picked up the phone and left a message for all to hear on the theater's answering machine that if the publicity director did not get me the material I needed, I would not be able to do the piece. Two days later it came in the mail.

These last examples were of the category of "dreamus interruptus," where the sexual act is cut off. One school of thought, which calls itself "Senoi," after a tribe that at one time was thought to have organized communal life around dreamwork, urges dreamers to pursue pleasurable sexual contact to orgasm.[6] The belief is that releasing sexual tension in dreams has a very direct impact on real life: "By allowing open sexual expression in dreams, . . . we may actually be freeing creative thinking on all levels of consciousness."[7] In spite of the fact that Tom stopped before the achievement of sexual gratification, the dream relieved his inhibition about writing.

Furthermore, according to Senoi thinkers, Tom's dream ought not to merely come to an end in orgasm. The dreamer needs to extract a gift from his dream lover, one that expresses beauty, so that "no dream man or woman can take the love which belongs to human beings."[8] In his book *The Mystique of Dreams,* Domhoff offers another suggestion for the dreamer who awakes feeling ill at ease: "The best thing to do is tell your spouse or lover about it so the alien dream soul will be too embarrassed to return."[9]

What of this theory of pursuing pleasurable sexual dreams to climax? Is this a dangerous way to encourage promiscuity in real life? In an article entitled "The Night Residue," Alan Leveton talks about drives that arise in sleep and persist into waking life as not necessarily being harmful. In cultures that attach importance to dreams and provide the dreamer with a good deal of external support, these drives can be sublimated to enrich society in the form of new myths and uplifting ideas. For example, the concept of transmigration of souls is believed to have been expressed first in dreams. The benefit to the individual of such external support is the elimination of waking feelings of self-condemnation and guilt.[10]

When cultural validation takes the form of discussing the dream liaison with a trusted friend or therapist, dream sharing with a knowledgeable person is clearly advisable with any highly charged material. In fact, some people casually share dreams with no cognizance that the dream is pointing to pathology that needs addressing. In answer to a query I placed in a newsletter, one gentleman wrote to say he had been having dreams of sex with his mother most of his adult life. The problem, as he saw it, was that the sex was always being interrupted and he wanted to learn how to prolong it. Rather than dream counseling, this man needs support from the self-help program Survivors of Incest Anonymous.

It is not unusual for repressed incest memories to surface in dreams. One woman had the following dream during her treatment as an incest survivor.

Three men were on an elevator going down and, referring to me, one said, "You take care of her. She knows too much." We were lying crosswise on a bed and having sex. He wasn't being too gentle. He put his penis inside me and it kept getting longer and longer until it was up to my throat and I was choking.

The dream indicates this woman's fear of being punished for revealing what had been perpetrated upon her as a child. Fear had held a stranglehold over her up until this point. She later made an association: "His penis kept getting longer and longer like Pinocchio's nose. It came up to my throat and I was choking, but the lies are starting to come up and out." The dream enabled her to get in touch with the fear of exposing long-time secrets that might otherwise have short-circuited her therapy.

RECOVERY DREAMS

Sexual dreams can do more than simply unveil old trauma. In my research on dreams of recovering sex offenders and sex addicts, what has become apparent is the healing power and self-validation inherent in what I call *recovery dreams.* Don, incarcerated on a rape conviction, had the following dream during the course of his rehabilitation program.

It seemed that I had recently been released from prison. I was at a kind of party and talking to a woman. She had a sexy sensualism that attracted me greatly. I was telling her my life experiences, about my crimes, prison, etc. She said out of all the men present she wanted to go to bed with me because my story was more tender.

I was sitting on a couch and this woman approached and straddled me in a sexual position. However, instead of attempting to have sex immediately I said to her, 'Just hold me.' She embraced me and I lay my head on her breast and began to cry. At that moment I had an awesome feeling of peace, joy, relief, and emotional release. We held each other for a long while and then I entered her with my penis. It was a fantastic sexual feeling; I was totally engulfed by it and in it. The most powerful factor was not the intercourse per se but the embrace.

In this dream Don was being granted a sneak preview, in which he made the personality change he was working on in therapy during imprisonment. "The dream shows that I'm finally getting a correct concept of 'caring' as opposed to just seeking sexual gratification. I'm learning how to properly relate to women, sex, love and relationships, and *I have no desire* to return to my old ideas."

While providing the much-needed sexual gratification, the sexual experience is a tender one now that Don has been able to admit his past. He is a man who wants to be held, and the fact that he can receive this kind of nurturance in a dream is indicative of his own burgeoning self-love. As he expressed it, "I'm becoming aware of and accepting the 'woman' in me, my nurturing faculties."

Dick, a dream educator in his professional life, also had an erotic dream that he believes to be about self-love.

We are rolling around on the floor, this blonde woman and I. I don't know her very well, but this is fun. As we play, it gets more sexual. I wonder just how far the sexual play can go, so I get more sexually aggressive and she is very responsive and willing. It seems clear that we are now about to "do it," when I get this strong feeling that I should produce some condoms or at least initiate a discussion of safe sex.

Oh, what a hassle. This moment feels so good, so spontaneous and nonverbal. I say the heck with all that. We keep making love, I have an orgasm, and it feels great. But now I'm sure I made a big mistake. This is not like me. I hardly know this woman and I'm certain I've contracted AIDS now. I used to be so certain I couldn't have AIDS, but no more. It was enjoyable at the time, but I feel sick now, like I need to leave and be alone.

The woman turns to me. She looks more familiar now. Oh, this is an ex-lover. She says she really enjoyed our lovemaking, particularly that she was able to take her own time. I assure her that next time we meet, we can do so again, and I will spend whatever time she likes.

Dick believed himself to be responsible about his sexual practices in real life but the dream had a profound impact on him, suggesting that he might be on the verge of losing self-control. However, the gentle voice of the female dream character, coming as it does after he begins to feel angry and afraid, represents the part of himself that is self-accepting of mistakes.[11] The movement from shame to self-love is crucial, for self-hatred feeds on itself. The person filled with self-loathing will continually sabotage plans for safe sex, which, in turn, provides a reason for more self-hatred followed by more self-destructive behavior. Those who cannot break out of the cycle of acting out and remorse, who are powerless to curtail sexually compulsive and dangerous behavior, are truly addicted to sex.

Thousands of persons so affected have gotten involved in twelve-step programs modeled after Alcoholics Anonymous. Part of recovery in these programs is getting in touch with a "Higher Power" or "God of one's own understanding." Some feel that this Higher Power makes contact in the dreaming state. One theological dreamworker believes that erotic imagery can indicate a desire to connect with divine energy. "Dreams with pleasant, enjoyable, and rapturous sexual images are often associated with solving spiritual and moral problems, while dreams with frightening and repugnant sexuality are often associated with the repression of spiritual and ethical concerns and the inadequate resolution of religious and philosophical problems."[12]

Craig, now in his third year of recovery in Sexaholics Anonymous, provides a good example of this kind of experience. Once known as one of the "Bible club kids," he studied theology as an adult and was very active in his religious practices. On the other hand, he led a totally separate private life that included compulsive masturbation, use of prostitutes, extramarital affairs, and thousands of obscene phone calls. About six years before he sought help, Craig had the following dream.

God was a man and he had a wife. They were trying to tame wild dogs and foxes. The father never went out to get these animals himself, rather he would explain to this other person—who became myself—how to reach each individual dog or fox. I would then go out and in various ways, appropriate for that fox, try to get them to be willing to follow me back. I remember one instruction was not to say anything but to just reach out my arms to them and beckon them to come. This one ran and hid and I ran after it. It went down into a hole and I gently reached down my hand and touched its head and began to plead for it to follow me home.

I was surprised by the mundaneness of the old man's place. It was very natural and not very "celestial." His wife hurt her foot at one point. At the end of the dream I was on another errand and found myself jogging and was suddenly gripped by love of God and shame at my own sin. I began to sob way down deep.

Back to where the foxes were coming to the old man's place—God's place— there was a powerful jet of water that went in spurts up into the sky. Each spurt began slow and speeded up; some came down. This old man was a very gentle, down to earth, humorous, wise, omniscient fellow. I was surprised that he was God.

The dream persona is rounding up wild dogs and foxes. Is it for the work of God or in the interest of sexual gratification? Trying to get them to be willing to follow him sounds a bit like sexual intrigue. The images of putting a hand down a hole and the ejaculatory spurts do not bode well for the work of God, either.

The dream occurred during a time in Craig's life when he was very active in both fundamentalist religion and sexual addiction. What he was hearing from his evangelist congregation intensified the shame he already felt around his covert behavior. When I reminded Craig of the dream recently, he was totally surprised and said, "I would never have conceived of God in this way as a fundamentalist." Yet, in the midst of the chaos of his life, he possessed the dream power to conceive of a gentle, nonpunitive divine being. Although unable to experience the spiritual healing at the time, Craig's dream God was trying to forgive him in spite of rigid superego forces both within and without that were subjecting him to ruthless condemnation.

Compare this dream to one Craig had six years later, after only two months of sobriety in Sexaholics Anonymous.

I am in an apartment with some women. I am tempted to have sex with one of them. We begin and I am dismayed because I know I am breaking my sobriety. I wake up, realize it is a dream, and feel immense relief.

Later I dream that my wife and I move and go to an Alliance church. It has a good Sunday School and is plush, but I am not interested. Then we go into an Anglican church that is charismatic. We can't follow all the liturgy but then there is a healing service. My wife goes forward for our daughter's dry skin and for my back. (My back is fine.) I say I want to go deeper into God and I have a shovel in my hand. I am weeping. He lays hands on me and I feel power coming in, surging through me. I begin to laugh and cry simultaneously, deeply.

In these two dream fragments from the same night, Craig has separated the sexual activity from the spiritual. "This dream reveals the two extremes of my inner longings, which are basically spiritual: erotic/genital contact and transcendent mystical experience" He wants to go deeply into a woman and deeply into God. The God is as warm and friendly as in the other dream but far less distant. In sexual sobriety, Craig weeps as he feels the power of God rushing through him. The divine surges are the watery spurts of the previous dream made spiritual. The dreaming Craig may feel dismay at his loss of sobriety, but he no longer needs to feel shame. He is able to receive the love of God directly without having to give what he himself did not possess to others.

Sexual dreams obviously appear with all levels of intensity. One can feel free to express libidinous desires in a dreamer's romp. If one does not want to act on the feelings, it is best not to keep them secret.

Medieval dreamers had a great deal of trouble taking responsibility for their own sexual desires. Erotic dreams were thought to be instigated by succubi and incubi, evil demons who had intercourse with men and women when they slept. If this remains true for the dreamer on an emotional level, dream sharing becomes exorcism and release.

V

Dreams in Different Times and Places

The dream is a little hidden door in the innermost and most secret recesses of the psyche.

CARL JUNG

The people called "Senoi" by dream researchers are actually two groups, the Temiar and the Semai, neighbors in the jungles of the Malay peninsula. Anthropologist Kilton Stewart claimed that, prior to the Second World War when he investigated them, the Senoi were a "dream culture" and that the Senoi families' early-morning dream discussions laid the basis for a society so calm and peaceful that murder, robbery, and mental illness were unknown.[1] Later investigators did not support the existence of this utopian ideal; in fact, a Senoi native killed a colleague of Stewart's in a pique of jealousy because of a love triangle. Evidently, Senoi shamans did work with the tribe's dreams, but the family rituals and parent-to-child dream instruction claimed by Stewart were not substantiated.[2]

There are reports of other societies around the world where dreams play an important role. The Mapuche Indians of Chile share their dreams daily within the family unit, especially in times of physical and emotional stress. The communal interpretation and sharing of dreams provides individuals with another level of communication to alleviate problems. Anthropologist Lydia Degarrod studied the Mapuche from 1985 to 1987. She was accepted as a family member, sharing their dreams as well as other daily tasks.[3] Among the Mapuche, the *machis* (shamans) are in charge of religious rituals, healing, and contacting spirits. However, they work only with the dreams that family members cannot decipher themselves.

Among the Mapuche, dreams are viewed as voyages of the soul. Degarrod observed that group dream interpretation serves several functions. It allows an indisposed individual to dispel fears, gaining reassurance that the dream's negative prediction can be aborted by the proper ceremonies. In addition, it assists family cohesiveness by enabling people to share their dreams and obtain interpretations from other group members. Mapuche dream analysis is fairly sophisticated, as it focuses not only on specific dream imagery, but also on the dreamer's emotional reaction to the dream and on its connections to dreams previously reported by that individual. Furthermore, the dreamer examines the events following the dream to further explore its meaning.

One day, an elderly Mapuche woman shared a troubling dream with Degarrod.

A young girl went to a nearby hut to warm up, but there wasn't any fire there. She left the place. She was very cold. She came to our place and she sat at the fire and warmed herself.

The old woman was upset because to dream of fire is considered a negative omen, and the young girl was seen as a messenger of death. A week later, she became ill and was certain that death was near. But her son recalled that the fire in the dream was a "small fire"; hence it predicted illness, not death. This interpretation reassured the old woman, and she recovered. Degarrod was struck by the unique manner in which dream reports enhanced communication in the family and served to bring family members closer together.

In this section, psychologist Wilse W. Webb succinctly traces the history of dreams in Western culture. Next, I describe the role that dreamworking has played in shamanic traditions. Anthropologist and psychoanalyst Benjamin Kilbourne places dreamworking in a comprehensive cross-cultural perspective.

Dreams are mentioned in any number of ancient texts and scripts. Clay tablets have been found, dating to about 3000 B.C., containing interpretive material about the dreams of Babylonian and Assyrian dreamers. Negative dream content was attributed to spirits of the dead and malevolent demons. Flying dreams indicated disaster and imbibing wine forecast a short life, but drinking water foretold a long one. This "dictionary" approach to dream content provided the same meanings for everyone, regardless of the dreams' context and circumstances. Unfortunately, the dictionary approach is still with us today.

The Egyptians were less concerned with demonology, interpreting dreams as messages from the gods. The Papyrus of Deral-Madineh of about 2000 B.C. gives instructions on how to obtain a dream message from a deity. Serapis was the Egyptian god of dreams, and there were dozens of *serapims,* or dream temples, throughout the land. Incubation, the deliberate attempt to induce dreams while sleeping in these temples, was widely practiced. "Stand-in" dreamers were even sent to the *serapims* to incubate a dream for someone who could not make the journey.[4] The dreams of royalty were given special attention; a dream of Thutmose IV is recorded on a stela (a stone pillar) in front of the Sphinx.

The sacred *Vedas* of India contain lists of favorable and unfavorable dreams. This literature, probably written sometime between 1500 and 1000 B.C., contains specific interpretations of dream images. Dreams from different periods of the night were given different interpretations, and the dreamer's temperament was considered before an interpretation was made. Early philosophers in India conjectured that there are four states of the "soul": waking, dreamless sleep, dreaming, and mystical unity.

The earliest Chinese work on dreams is the *Meno Shu,* dating to about A.D. 640. The Chinese classified dreams according to their source, which revealed physical and mental changes taking place in the dreamers. They believed that a dream was internally generated by the "soul" but that external physical stimuli could also be important. Sleeping on a belt, for example, was believed to induce dreams about snakes.

Of all the pioneering psychotherapists and dreamworkers, it was Carl Jung who delved most deeply into dreams in different times and places. His theoretical formulations came from an impressive galaxy of sources: mythology, comparative religion, alchemy, esoteric texts, his own dreams, and the dreams of clients who came from around the world.[5] Jung used the term *archetypes* to describe universal mythic symbols and metaphors.[6] Among them were dream characters such as wise old men and women, magical children, heroes, and charlatans, and dream activities such as journeys, initiations, and transformations. For Jung, the universality of archetypes was based on the existence of innate neuropsychic centers that have the capacity to initiate, control, and mediate similar behavior among all people, regardless of race, culture, and creed.[7]

However, this commonality of powerful dream images—if it exists—can be demystified. Psychiatrist Anthony Stevens points out that all cultures, whatever their geographical location or historical era, display a large number of social traits due to the fact that human beings share a common genetic code. No human culture has ever existed that lacked

> Laws about the ownership, inheritance, and disposal of property, procedures for settling disputes, rules governing courtship, marriage, adultery, and the adornment of women, taboos relating to food and incest, ceremonies of initiation for

young men, associations of men which exclude women, gambling, athletic sports, co-operative labour, trade, the manufacture of tools and weapons, rules of etiquette prescribing forms of greeting, modes of address, use of personal names, visiting, feasting, hospitality, gift-giving, and the performance of funeral rites, status differentiation on the basis of a hierarchical social structure, superstition, belief in the supernatural, religious rituals, soul concepts, myths and legends, dancing, homicide, suicide, homosexuality, mental illness, faith healing, dream interpretation, medicine, surgery, obstetrics, and meteorology.[8]

So rather than posit an unknown universal mental structure, we need merely acknowledge that certain beings and activities achieve salience in the dreams of dreamers worldwide because they share a common humanity.

Even so, the ways in which these archetypes take specific form will vary from culture to culture because of historical and social differences. Most early societies venerated an "Earth Mother" who gave birth to plants and creatures, but in ancient Egypt, the world's vegetation sprouted from Geb the Earth God, as he lay prone on his stomach. In Scandinavia, Njord, another male god, personified the earth, while the Incas of Peru worshipped Lord Pilcomayo, Lord of the Earth.

The marital archetype appears to be universal, but it takes different forms around the world. In nonindustrialized countries, 68 percent of people practice monogamy, 31 percent polygamy (multiple wives), and 11 percent polyandry (multiple husbands), and half of the "monogamous" societies practice occasional polygyny (plurality of wives and/or mistresses).[9]

Some dreamworkers do quite well without recourse to the term *archetype*, but those who use it need to consider the wide variation in human behavior; many life themes are the same, but the way in which those themes shine in the galaxy of experience resembles a variegated rainbow rather than a narrow spotlight.

Wilse B. Webb

Historical Perspectives:
From Aristotle
to Calvin Hall

For this historical perspective on dream theory, I have chosen to emphasize the writings of Aristotle, Cicero, and Freud for several reasons. First, they are among the most famous, systematic, and comprehensive writers of their times. Secondly, each presented a theory of dreams that was unique to and beyond his time; in other words, they did not simply reflect their historical periods. Therefore, the unique outlooks of these three writers—the naturalism of Aristotle, the sociophilosophical orientation of Cicero, and the psychoanalytic stance of Freud—may help us to understand how dream theories have changed as intellecutal belief systems have changed. Recent changes in world views have influenced Western culture in many ways; today's dream perspectives reflect those shifts.

ARISTOTLE ON DREAMS

Although Aristotle and Cicero lived and wrote about dreams some 300 years apart (ca. 340 B.C. and 40 A.D.), there was a pervasive idea about dreams across their time span. The notion that dreams were messages from the gods, or from some other extraordinary source, extended temporally from the fragments of the earlier writings of the Egyptians and Sumerians through the literature exemplified by Homer, the Old Testament, the Grecian plays, and the histories of Heroditus into Artemedorus' collection in the later Roman period of the second century A.D.

As can be seen from these sources, even with minor geographic variations there was a common theme throughout the known Western world.[1] Underlying the premise that dreams originated outside the dreamer was a general set of of beliefs: the future is fated, and there is a "higher order" involved
in that fate that includes human beings. In addition, it was believed that the
future could most readily be accessed during sleep and that this was typically
mediated by divine intervention.

Examples of the crucial role of dreams in the lives of earlier prominent
people are plentiful: dreams of the Pharaohs and of the leading characters of
the *Iliad* and *Odyssey;* the Old Testament dreams of Jacob and David; the an-
nals of Cyrus' dreams; Hannibal's responses to dreams; the divination dreams
of Sophocles and Socrates; and the dreams of Joseph in the New Testament.
Perhaps the clearest concrete evidence of this idea of the dream can be found
in the hundreds of "sleep temples" scattered throughout Greece.

In *On Divination by Dreams,* Aristotle writes that dreams are perceptions
of sensory-based occurrences:[2] "The objects of sense-perceptions corresponding to each sensory organ produce sense-perceptions in us, and the affection
due to this operation is present . . . even when they have departed.[3] These residual impressions constitute dreams. The unusual quality of dreams stems
from three primary sources: (1) we receive dreams but do not exercise reason
or opinion during sleep; (2) residual impressions may have particular impact
on dreams because they are not "extended or obscured" by "the intellect and
the senses working together"; and (3) dreams are uncontrolled, like "little eddies formed in rivers . . . often running what they were like when they first
started out, but often, too, broken into other forms."[4]

Given this position, it is not surprising to find Aristotle rejecting the
dominant theme of divine dreams: "It may be concluded that dreams are not
sent by God. . . . Nor are they designed [to reveal the future]. . . . They have
a divine aspect, however, for Nature [their cause] is divinely planned."[5] By rejecting extraordinary sources for dreams, Aristotle reflected a change among
intellectuals of his era. Literal belief systems about the gods were breaking
down, and philosophers were explaining the world in ways that were natural
rather than supernatural.

Aristotle's examination of the issue of divination is also naturalistic.
Dreams may be related to the future as tokens, causes, or coincidences. Physicians may attend to dreams as tokens: "Movements which occur in the
daytime are, unless very great and violent, lost sight of. . . . In sleep the
opposite takes place, for then even trifling movements seem considerable. . . . The beginnings of all events are small, so, it is clear, are those also of

diseases and other affectations." Indeed, some dreams may be "causes" of the future in the sense that "Movements set up first in sleep [may] prove to be starting points of actions to be performed in the daytime." However, Aristotle regarded most dreams about future events as coincidences, not prophecies: "The probability is that many such things should happen. . . . The dream is . . . neither token nor cause of its fulfillment, but a mere coincidence."[6]

Aristotle leaves us with some wise words about dream interpretation: "The most skillful interpreter of dreams is he who has the faculty of observing resemblances—dream presentations are analogous to forms reflected in water. . . . If the motion in the water be great, the reflection has no resemblance to its original. . . . In a similar way, some such thing is a troubled dream . . . for the internal movement effaces the clearness of the dream."[7] In other words, the greater the emotional turmoil of the dreamer, the more disguised is the dream; the more tranquil the dreamer, the greater the resemblance of the dream to waking life.

CICERO ON DREAMS

Cicero, the famous Roman orator, considered the question of divination in dreams (presenting his arguments in classic rhetorical form). First, he makes the case for divination: (1) The human soul is an emanation of the Divine Soul and hence they are in contact. (2) This contact is enhanced when the soul is unencumbered by the senses and flesh. (3) Fate is an orderly succession of causes and thus is predictable.

Cicero then argues against this position, first focusing on "artificial" divination: (1) The presumed connections between portents and predicted events; for example, a prediction based on the dream of a kidney and the outcome of a naval battle in a kidney-shaped sea are "unnatural" and make little sense. (2) While the observations of our senses often yield correct predictions, this is not divination but skilled performance. (3) Some events occur by chance and are not predictable.

Cicero argues that whatever theory one holds about dreams, they are "phantoms and apparitions." We place faith in our waking delusions and hallucinations but certainly not in those of the insane or drunk. Why then value the prophetic power of dreams? If one wishes to solve a problem in geometry, physics, or logic, or wants to learn flute-playing, he or she should consult the "peculiar knowledge of the related art or science. . . . If I want to sail a boat, I would not pilot it as I might have dreamed I should." The dreamer cannot learn a skill in his or her dreams, and using dreams for divination purposes is a waste of time.

Clearly, argues Cicero, dreams are not the work of God: (1) Most dreams are ignored; thus God is either ignorant or vain. (2) If God were "consulting for our own good," he would send us clear visions while we were waking rather than unintelligible ones while we sleep. (3) Because at least some dreams are not true, why would he send false dreams with no distinguishing marks? He summarizes, "Do the immortal gods, who are of surprising excellence in all things, constantly flit about, not only the beds, but even the lowly pallets of mortals . . . and when they find him snoring, throw at him dark and twisted visions. . . . Or does Nature bring it to pass that the very active soul sees in sleep phantoms of what it saw when the body was awake?"[8]

Unlike Aristotle, in the end Cicero did not find the time of sleep propitious for wisdom or divination: "When the soul is supported by the bodily members and by the five senses, its powers of perception, thought, and apprehension are more trustworthy. When the soul itself [is] weakened in sleep, . . . many sights and sounds . . . are seen and heard in all manner of confusion and diversity."[9] He refutes the argument that by "long continuing observations . . . and recording of the results [of dreams] an art has been evolved." After arguing that he can see no possible connection between a "phantom" dream and a future physical event, Cicero further denies the possibility of establishing such connections: "For [dreams] are of infinite variety and there is no imaginable thing too absurd, too involved, or too abnormal for us to dream about. How then is it possible for us either to remember the countless and ever-changing mass of visions or to observe and record the subsequent results? . . . As a rule we do not believe a liar even when he tells the truth . . . [yet] if one dream turns out true . . . [there are] countless others that are false."[10]

The naturalism of Aristotle and the rhetoric of Cicero did not stem the prophetic interpretation of dreams. The popularity of this approach was crowned by the five volumes of the Greek scholar Artemedorus of Daldis in the second century. These volumes make up an exhaustive review of the dream interpretations in the classical world in combination with Artemedorus' own interpretations of more than 3,000 dreams. While giving prototypical indexings of particular dreams and their meanings, Artemedorus emphasized the individual dream and the context of its time. These volumes were republished in 1518 under the title *Oneicritica* and were published in English in 1606. The continued popularity of this approach to dreams is attested to by a volume by Thomas Hall imprinted in London in

1576, entitled *The Most Pleasaunte Art of the Interpretation of Dreams, Where-unto is Annexed Sundry Problems with Apte Aunsweares Neare Agreeing to the Matter, and Very Rare Examples, not the Like Extant in the English Tongue.*

There is, however, a landmark in the history of dreams that dramatically entered the course of philosophy in the seventeenth century and today continues to reverberate within it. In his *First Meditation,* René Descartes cites his dream experiences as a central source of skepticism concerning the senses. He reports, "For example, there is the fact that I am here, seated by the fire, attired in a dressing gown, having the paper in my hands, and other similar matters. . . . At the same time I must remember that I am a man and consequently in the habit of sleeping, and in my dreams representing to myself the same things."

The ongoing puzzle of the status of dreams as sensory data clearly contributed to Descartes' central theme of doubt. Moreover, this puzzle continued to be a lively issue throughout subsequent philosophical inquiries.[11] However, Descartes attributed the development of his philosophy and his life to three "revelatory dreams."[12]

In the meantime, Christian writers originally agreed with the ancient Greeks and Romans that dreams were of divine origin. Cyprian, bishop of Carthage in 250 A.D., asserted that the very councils of the church were guided by God through dreams and visions. St. Augustine described dreams of the dead as "gifts" from God. "Dreams, more than any other thing, entice us toward hope," wrote Cynesius of Cyrene, a fifth-century bishop of Ptolemais.[13]

In a book relating dreams and theology, Morton T. Kelsey, after a lengthy review of dreams in the Bible, cites the extensive writings of the early Christian church founders. However, in preparing a Latin translation of the Bible during the fifth century, St. Jerome consistently mistranslated a Hebrew word in order to include prohibitions against dreamwork in the sacred text.[14] As a result, dreams were categorized with witchcraft for more than a thousand years. Kelsey notes that the present absence of theological considerations about dreams is a relatively recent development.

FREUD ON DREAMS

By the dawning of the twentieth century, the dream had lost its potency as a popular force for mediating between human and divine realms. Theologians no longer regarded dreams as bona-fide revelations, philosophers were concerned primarily with their metaphysical implications, and literary critics emphasized only their frequently inaccurate portrayal in literature.[15] There is little evidence that the leaders of society sought guidance from their dreams. In poetry, the dream was more typically a literary device, as in William Wordsworth's "Dream of a Slave" (in which the slave dreamed of his years of freedom) or in Edgar Allan Poe's elaborate fantasies of a dream world. The dream dictionaries were still sold, but they were ragtags of Artemedorus' work.

Historian and psychologist Hendrika Vande Kemp has reviewed the place of dreams in American and British periodicals, both popular and professional, between 1860 and 1910. She discovered a steady increase in articles about dreams from 1860 to 1870. Thereafter, articles in popular periodicals declined, while those in professional journals increased. By 1910 the dream literature was almost exclusively contained in professional journals.

Vande Kemp found four general areas in which dreams were cited: the reporting of dreams, dreams and memory, dreams and reality, and the consciousness of dreams. The first section is a particularly striking reminder of the vanished tradition "when the famous were not at all disinclined to share their dreams," these including Dickens, Coleridge, Goethe, Wordsworth, Robert Louis Stevenson, and Havelock Ellis. Within these areas, particularly in the popular literature, a strong interest in the paranormal and an interest in the epistemology and metaphysics of the dream were apparent.

The nineteenth-century literature may be viewed as a transitional period between the oneirological tradition of the classical and biblical periods and the interpretive/investigative traditions of the twentieth century. In the earlier traditions, dreams were viewed as messages assuming a *transpersonal* significance. During the nineteenth century, they were viewed either as *interpersonal* messages from one person to another or as *extrapersonal* epiphenomena of physiological processes devoid of deep meaning. Twentieth-century theorists added aspects of messages from the person to the self—the *intrapersonal* dimension.

Freud's contribution was to place the dream squarely within the scientific domain while emphasizing its clinical interpretation. According to Vande Kemp, Freud downplayed those dreams that had obvious transpersonal implications and derided dream theories that were metaphysical in nature. As a result, the post-Freudian tradition failed to incorporate earlier popular interest in "parapsychological dreams and the philosophical interest in the epistemology and metaphysics of dreaming."[16]

Contrary to many writers' opinions, Freud did not inaugurate scientific interest in dreams. In *The Interpretation of Dreams,* he cited 214 references prior to 1900.[17] However, in 1893, Mary Calkins had described the status of the dream literature of the 1890s as follows:

> The phenomenon of dreaming has rarely been discussed or investigated in a thorough and in an experimental manner: of description, of theory, of discussion, of poetical analogy and illustration there has been no end; of accurate observation almost nothing. . . . The most scientific books . . . have been wholly and chiefly the results of the observations of abnormal subjects and in the interest more or less distinctly of pathology. . . . The fullest discussion[s] of the subject . . . are largely compilations of the recorded dreams of other people.[18]

Freud's evaluation of the literature was succinctly stated: "Many stimulating observations are to be found and a quantity of interesting materials bearing upon our theme, but little or nothing that touches upon the essential nature of dreams or that offers a final solution of any of their enigmas."[19] In writing *The Interpretation of Dreams,* Freud's purposes, as stated in the preface, were twofold: "to give an account of the interpretations of dreams," and to establish "their theoretical value as a paradigm."

Freud concluded that dreams emerge from the dynamically repressed unconscious, but many of his predecessors had taken a more organic point of view. Philosopher Arthur Schopenhauer, in 1862, stated that while someone is awake, external stimuli impinge upon the mind and cause it to erect models of time, space, and causality in relation to the realities of the external world. During sleep, by contrast, the sources of external stimulation decrease markedly, allowing internal stimuli to be remodeled into forms occupying space and time by rules unique to the brain itself. Freud criticized this viewpoint, arguing that dream interpretation would be rendered practically impossible if the analyst had to trace dream content back to an obscure organic stimulus.[20]

Peretz Lavie and J. Allan Hobson have reviewed other dream literature of the late seventeenth, eighteenth, and nineteenth centuries on the issue of the internal production of the dream by brain activity.[21] The British philosopher Locke, in his 1690 *Essay Concerning Human Understanding,* argued for sensory determinants of dreams. This position was criticized by German philosopher Leibnitz, who argued that ideas are not caused by sensations but exist independently of the senses and of consciousness. Thus dreams may exist within sleep as expressions of ideas in the absence of sensation or awareness.

In England, the Lockean notion of sensory determinants of dreams became centered as opposed to the Leibnitzian position, which was popular in intellectual circles in Edinburgh, Scotland. The supporters of Locke held that consciousness depended on sensations, even in sleep—albeit at a lower and sometimes even imperceptible level. Wilhelm Wundt, founder of the world's first psychological laboratory in Germany, echoed Locke, holding that the content of dreams arose mainly in response to sensory stimuli. The French scientist Alfred Maury was the first to attempt a systematization of self-observation experiments on external stimulation and its effects on dreaming. In France, the Marquis d'Hervey de Saint-Denis filled twenty-two volumes with his self-observations and hypotheses. The Spanish neuroanatomist Santiago Ramon y Cajal discovered that the nervous system is a collection of independent but interdependent neurons and saw the unconscious as an intrinsic part of the brain/mind system.

Wundt believed that the visual images in dreams arise through the stimulation of the visual system itself. Even though Freud rejected this hypothesis, it has been demonstrated that the visual system is indeed activated in rapid-eye-movement sleep, although the source is the brain rather than the retina.[22] Freud objected to a physiological approach to dreams, stating that "in this view a dream is not a mental act at all, but a somatic process signalizing the occurrence of indications registered in the mental apparatus."[23] Indeed, in *The Interpretation of Dreams,* Freud moved away from the reductionistic neurophysiological predispositions of his earlier book *Project for a Scientific Psychology* to a less reductionistic psychological approach.[24]

DREAM THEORY TODAY

In the twentieth century, dream theorists have based their ideas on clinical and experimental data rather than on anecdotes, theological dogma, or logically reasoned assumptions. Tore Neilsen has provided us with a valuable overview of the dream literature by compiling the number of citations under "Dreams" in the *Index Medicus* from 1880 to 1985.[25] He considers the publication figures relative to two key reference points: Freud's *The Interpretation of Dreams* in 1900, and Eugene Aserinsky and Nathaniel Kleitman's paper on the relationship between dream recall and rapid-eye-movement (REM) activity during sleep in 1953.[26] Publications on dreams peaked fourteen years after Freud's book was published and sixteen years after Aserinsky and Kleitman's article appeared. These two important breakthroughs in dream theory and research were take-off points for other dream investigators.

A closer look at the flow and dynamics of the systematic research regarding dream content appears in Carol Winget and Milton Kramer's book, *Dimensions of Dreams.*[27] The extensive literature reviews of Freud, Vande Kemp,

Lavie, and Hobson provide a strikingly similar picture. In the midst of the speculative notions and anecdotes of philosophers, theologians, physicians, and laypersons about dreams, there was an increasing emergence of information about physiology and neurology. The data provided new grounds for further speculations about the dreaming process; however, few, if any, were systematically related to dream content.

The dream literature after Freud is full of arguments and conceptual clashes; however, the basis of these differences tended to be clinical case histories. The Winget and Kramer literature review of dream content serves to remind us of the explosive effect on dream-content research resulting from the REM/dream discovery. Winget and Kramer divided their extensive review of dream-content research into nonlaboratory and laboratory studies. The former uses free recall (such as dreams recorded at home and questionnaires about dreams), while the latter category refers to dreams recovered in the laboratory from EEG-identified states. Extensive content analysis could have been attempted earlier, but the demonstration that dreaming was a near-universal human activity rather than an exotic eccentricity provoked curiosity as to how dream content differed across the life span and between groups of different gender and culture.

CALVIN HALL ON DREAMS

This review also revealed the limited impact of the Freudian school on the systematic study of dream content. On the other hand, there were two sharp increases in dream-content studies, one in the 1950s and one in the 1960s. It is possible to attribute the first increase to the remarkable work of Calvin Hall. His first published paper on dream content appeared in 1948, and his book *The Meaning of Dreams* was published in 1953.[28] The Winget and Kramer citations include twenty-six papers by Hall as the senior author and fifteen additional papers by his students William Domhoff and Robert L. Van de Castle. Hall is an often-neglected giant among dream explorers. He objected to "physiologizing the dream out of existence"[29] and developed a number of research procedures to study gender, age, and personality differences in dream reports through content analysis.

It seems likely that the second increase was a parallel effect associated with the REM/dream studies, which had started to accelerate in the 1960s. It is interesting to note that the laboratory-based studies increased rather than eclipsed the nonlaboratory studies. A more disturbing note, however, must be added to this picture. A review of the annually published sleep bibliography for the years 1978 through 1982 reveals that the average of laboratory and non-laboratory studies of dream content has declined to a yearly average of 4.6 and 4.0 papers, respectively.[30] Perhaps researchers believe that their present theories have taken them as far as they can go. If so, the time may be ripe for another major laboratory discovery or theoretical advance.

THE BIG PICTURE

History does not repeat itself but, as Mark Twain said, it surely rhymes. As such, although it may not predict the future, it may help us to understand and endure it. Properly used, it can inspire us or lend us appropriate humility and protect us from overresponding to the fads and follies of our times. But more importantly, history, like paintings, poems, philosophy, and dreams, can enrich our research enterprises.

This review has demonstrated how major figures or movements, such as Aristotle, Cicero, church dogma, and psychoanalysis, have dominated and directed attitudes toward dreams in their time and for years thereafter. It also has shown the importance of laboratory work in stimulating dream research. In the great flow of time, we can see the watersheds, the eddies and backwaters, and the immovable crags that rise and fall—and rise again. Like tourists, we can view, on the shores, those castles and dwellings of abandoned glory, comfort, or neglect. And what a mighty and awesome flow it is that we can view in the long and mysterious story of the dream![31]

Stanley Krippner

Tribal Shamans and Their Travels into Dreamtime

Shamans were the first dreamworkers. As practitioners of religion and magic, they emerged in tribal hunting, gathering, and fishing societies. When tribes settled down and developed agriculture, many of the shaman's roles were assumed by other practitioners such as priests, sorcerers, diviners, and healers.[1] However, shamanic influences can still be found in traditional native medicine as it is practiced today.

Shamans are men and women who use altered states of consciousness to travel into dreamtime, obtaining power and knowledge to help and heal members of their society.

Shamans are able to self-regulate many bodily functions and achieve a degree of concentration that surpasses the ability of their peers. They master a complex body of knowledge through instruction and direct experience, and they are able to apply this wisdom to individual situations in appropriate ways. Dreamwork is an integral part of most shamanic traditions. An Arctic explorer once inquired of an Eskimo acquaintance if he were a shaman. The man responded that he had never been ill and had not recalled dreams; therefore he could not possibly be a shaman.[2] This sentiment is echoed in one way or another by inhabitants of many other tribal societies, as is another key concept in shamanic dreamworking: that if someone could imagine or dream an event, that action was considered to be, in some sense, real.[3]

Accounts of dreamtime date back to the cultural myths of many tribal societies in which events occur in three zones: the Upper, Middle, and Lower Worlds. In these societies' Golden Ages, people traveled between the three worlds with ease; there was no rigid division between wakefulness and dreams. Many of these cultural myths held that a Fall took place, triggered by a sin or an arrogant act. The bridge connecting the three zones collapsed, and travel between the Upper, Middle, and Lower Worlds became the near-exclusive privilege of deities, spirits, and shamans.[4]

Other cultural myths tell of an original Great Shaman who was selected by the gods and was the holder of incredible powers. The Great Shaman was supposed to have been capable of levitation, flying, and bodily transformation. These feats were rarely repeated by later shamans, again because human behavior had evoked divine displeasure.[5] Using illusion and sleight of hand, many later shamans attempted to duplicate the feats of the Great Shaman; therefore, shamans became the first magicians as well as the first healers, dream interpreters, weather forecasters, performing artists, and storytellers.

RECEIVING THE CALL

Shamans enter their vocations in several ways: through heredity, unusual birth conditions or markings, spirit-mediated recovery from illness, vision quests and other rituals, or buying or stealing shamanic power, or by means of an initiatory dream. In Okinawa, spirits notify the future shaman through visions and dreams; many of the recipients who are *called* try to ignore their summons, but eventually succumb to the spirits' directives. Most shamanic traditions take the position that refusal to follow the call will result in a terrible accident, a life-threatening sickness, or insanity.

Common themes in initiatory dreams are dismemberment, death, and rebirth. In one instance, an Eskimo candidate for shamanism went into the hills to sleep, dreaming that he was swallowed by a monstrous bear, chewed up, and spat out. Eskimo tradition held that this was a call to shamanize. The initiation of a shaman in Western Australia consists of being swallowed by a serpent, vomited, cut into pieces by older shamans, and revived by their songs. Anthropologist Joan Halifax has observed the recurring theme of death and rebirth in shamanic art, as in the X-ray-style cave paintings of Paleolithic France, the mutilated bodies in contemporary Mexican Huichol yarn paintings, and the death figures on Tibetan shamanic costumes.[6]

Fred Swinney, a Canadian psychotherapist, was camping in an Ontario forest when he dreamed about animal predators emerging from the woods and devouring him. Awakening in terror, Swinney cast his gaze toward the coals of the campfire; just beyond, he discerned two piercing eyes and the large gray form of a wolf. Surprisingly, fear gave way to total surrender, just as if Swinney had been transformed into a wolf himself. Initially resisting the call, Swinney eventually took the name Graywolf and began working with his clients from a shamanic perspective.[7]

Among several Native American tribes, initiatory dreams contain such birds and animals as bears, deer, eagles, and owls. The dream creature (who often becomes the shaman's power animal or totem) typically enables the dreamer to incorporate its wisdom and to begin shamanic training. Among the Inuit Eskimos, a shaman is called by dreaming about an animal spirit who then possesses the dreamer. Upon awakening, the dreamer withdraws from society and wanders naked through the land. Eventually, the initiate gains control over the spirit, celebrating this victory by making a drum. Dreams about deceased relatives are said to mark one's call among the Wintu and Shasta tribes of California. Among the Australian Wirdadthuri, the call to heal frequently comes through the dreams of the neophyte's father or grandfather.

Among California's Diegueno and Luisano tribes, future shamans can be selected in childhood on the basis of their dreams. Choctaw Indians believe that sick children's dreams should be observed for signs of shamanic calling. Spirits will often seize the souls of these children in the dreams and take them to caves, offering them a knife, a bundle of noxious herbs, or a bundle of medicinal herbs. If the child selects the medicinal herbs, this is an indication that the child has been called to heal.

In 1984 I interviewed an Indonesian shaman, Rohanna Ler, at her home in Ujung Pandang on the island of Sulawesi. In 1973, when she was about thirty, Ler's son became ill with an eye infection and the local physicians were unable to help him. According to Ler, an elderly man appeared in a dream, gave her a stone, and told her to apply it to her son's eyes. Upon awakening, Ler found a stone in her bed and her son recovered shortly after she applied it to his eyes. Ler also interpreted the event as a call to become a *dukun,* or shaman, but her husband, a devout Moslem and a successful automobile mechanic, refused to permit his wife to pursue this activity.

A year later, a young couple appeared to Ler in a daytime vision, asking her why she had not become a *dukun.* They took Ler outside her house and showed her a fire that threatened her husband's garage. They also gave her a ring that purportedly contained healing powers. Upon awakening, Ler shared the dream with her husband as well as her concern that his garage might be in danger if she did not heed the call. Ler's husband reluctantly agreed to allow her to see clients on two conditions: that she not call herself a *dukun* and that she not keep the money. Within a few years, Ler had become the best-known shamanic healer on the island of Sulawesi and was donating her income to charity. She used the ring for healing, claiming it was a gift from the two spirits.

SHAMANIC APPRENTICES

The training program for apprentice shamans varies from one part of the world to another, but it typically lasts for several years. Usually the apprentices will learn their skills from master shamans who teach them nomenclature, such as the names and functions of deities, spirits, and power animals; history, including the tribe's genealogy; technology, such as rituals, music, and dances; herbology, for example, the difference between plants used medicinally and those used for sacred purposes; the location of power places; the identification of power objects; tribal mythology; and dream interpretation procedures.

The apprentice also may obtain knowledge from his or her guiding spirits. Anthropologist Ruth Benedict observed that these spirit guides often take the form of a bird or an animal, protecting the shamans as they enter potentially dangerous altered states of consciousness and as they visit the Upper and Lower Worlds.[8] The Mohave Indians believe that power and knowledge can be imparted by spirits to the initiate in dreamtime, often in the form of songs. Sometimes a dream will repeat what the embryo supposedly dreamed in the womb or a dream that his father had dreamed years earlier. The Yuma Indians take the position that power animals can bestow power songs to dreamers.

Mastery of drumming, dancing, chanting, and singing often is an important aspect of a shaman's training. While in Panama City in 1985, I conducted several interviews with Fernando Fernandez, a Cuna Indian shaman who lives on Ustopo, the most heavily populated of the San Blas Islands off the Panamanian coast. Don Fernando explained that he was an *abisua,* or singer. Other types of shamans included the *inaduledi,* or herbalist, and the *nele,* a diagnostician who obtains knowledge from his travels to the Lower World. All three practitioners work with guardian spirits and power animals.

Don Fernando's training program focused on learning the complex Cuna healing songs, the shortest lasting about one hour and the longest ("The Song of the Dead") about fourteen hours. He stated that he has mastered fifteen songs, including those used to combat fevers, treat headaches, fight alcoholism, chase away ghosts, overcome fears, and ease the difficulties of childbirth. This last song is used in combination with the ministrations of the grandmothers who serve as midwives. Don Fernando also learned how to utilize his dreams to seek advice from Nushu, the most important Cuna healing spirit.

Among the Araucan Indians of southern Chile, the initiate uses dancing and drumming to enter the altered state required to scale the Upper World and performs as a singer and an instrumentalist immediately after initiation. Among Siberian shamans, in contrast, full mastery of the drum is not achieved until a certain amount of time has elapsed.[9] The Tungus initiate makes a stick for his future drum, then practices the shamanic chants. In one case, it took two years before the initiate had a dream about the reindeer whose skin would cover his drum, and it was only after the completion of the drum that he was allowed to shamanize.

Sometimes the training period is quite brief. In the Washo tribe of Nevada and California, the initiate receives power in dreamtime, then is awakened by a whistle. The initiate follows the whistle, which changes to a whisper that dictates instructions. For example, it might give the command to bathe on four successive mornings and treat a sick person on four successive nights. If the client recovers from the illness, the initiate's status as a shaman is confirmed.

DREAMS AND ILLNESS

Among the Naskapi, a group of Algonquin Indians in Labrador, dreams are actively sought by the entire tribe through fasting, dancing, singing, drumming, rattling, sweating, and drugtaking. The Cashinahua Indian shamans of eastern Peru also pursue dreams, believing that the more dreams they have each night, the greater the power they will accrue. Other members of the tribe, however, attempt to reduce the frequency of their dreams, because it is held that dreaming interferes with skill in hunting. As a result, the hunters may request an herbal preparation that will "calm the dream spirits."

In Africa, Zambian shamans believe that they can derive powers of diagnosis in dreams, obtaining accurate information about an illness without examining the client. The Siberian Chuckchee, who incorporate spirits during altered states of consciousness, also consider dreams to be a useful way to communicate with spirits. Spirit incorporation and out-of-body experience are the two major shamanic states of consciousness,[10] the latter of which is more closely linked with dreams. Australian Unambal shamans believe that their bodies can acquire crystals during a dream and that the resulting *luminosity* can aid their diagnostic abilities.

The North American Navajo Indians have a set of standard procedures they use in the treatment of distressing dreams. Navajo shamans believe that unremembered dreams are unimportant but that those that are recalled represent the traveling of the dreamer's spirit outside the body. The spirit can travel through both space and time, sometimes encountering good fortune. In such an event, no intervention by the shaman is necessary. But if a future event is potentially dangerous, or if a past action has negatively affected the dreamer's relationship with the spirit world, dreamtime will take the form of a nightmare. In this instance, the dreamer should reveal the nightmare to a shaman as soon as possible. The shaman will explain the dream's meaning and will prescribe either a major ceremony or a protection prayer. Because the misfortune might involve other members of the tribe as well as the dreamer, there is considerable pressure placed upon the dreamer to perform the recommended prayer or prepare for the ceremony.[11]

Native American Iroquois Indians posit that dreams contain symbols that can be interpreted by shamans through a technique resembling free association. The Iroquois believe that the "unfulfilled natural desires" of the soul (i.e., the unconscious) are expressed through dreams, but that frustration of these dream wishes can result in illness.[12]

Such dreams provide clues to the Iroquois shaman as to what can be done to restore a client's health. Sometimes the client is encouraged to act upon these desires and society-at-large supports what would otherwise be disruptive behavior. These activities are formalized in a dream festival held annually for three or four days. Geza Roheim has presented a vivid description of this festival:

> Men, women, and children would rush about almost naked. Sometimes they would have masks or paint. In a state of frenzy they ran from hut to hut smashing and upsetting everything and pouring hot water or cold ashes on the people. Each of them had dreamed of something and he would not leave the house till somebody had guessed his dream and carried it out in practice. The person in question was bound to present the dreamer with the thing he had dreamed of for his life depended on obtaining it. But he would not state it in simple words, he would hint at it or indicate it by gestures.[13]

The dream festival also encourages children to ascertain their guiding spirits; a man or woman is appointed by each clan to hear children's dreams. These dreams are then related to tribal practitioners whose duty it is to determine the guardian spirits for each dreamer. Similar dream festivals are held by the Hurons and the Eskimos, who also believe that dreams can be influenced by the conflicts and wishes of waking life.

There are other shamanic theories that represent sophisticated attempts to understand dreams. In Barbados, shamans hold that the source of dreams can be found in the memories the dreamer dwells on as he or she goes to sleep. As a result, the dreamer's unfulfilled desires and unsolved problems both may appear in dreams. In the Brazilian Amazon, the Parintinin tribe considers dreams so important that they have devised a special grammatical form for narrating them. The dream is seen as essential to shamanism and, according to Parintinin tradition, everyone who dreams partakes in shamanic power.[14]

For some tribes, dreamtime is held to reduce vitality rather than enhance it. Among the Maricopa Indians, unpleasant dreams are the most common source of illness, bringing on pains, colds, and diarrhea. Dreams also are held to be a primary cause of illness among the Paviotso Indians of western North America. Chidren can become ill if their parents' dreams are unfavorable or if bad dreams are experienced by visitors. In either event, shamanic assistance is called for to terminate the course of the sickness.

In many societies, an important function of the shaman is dream interpretation. The Taulipang shamans of the Caribbean are considered to be experts in explaining their own dreams and dreams of others. Australian aborigine shamans move into dreamtime with great facility to assist tribal hunting activities. Shamans among the Northern Yakuts in Siberia conduct an evening ceremony using the shoulder blade of a deer, then ask group members to pay attention to their dreams. The next morning, the shaman uses these dreams for divinatory purposes, not only for the dreamer but for other members of the tribe. Diegueno Indian shamans make frequent use of dream interpretation to treat their clients; dreams concerning incest are seen as especially critical. These shamans chew Jimson weed to enhance their dreams; if they dream of putting their hands around the world, this is felt to signify all-embracing knowledge, the highest degree of wisdom that a dream can symbolize.

TREATING SOUL LOSS

Shamans exert more control over their altered states (and over the spirit entities they report meeting there) than other magico-religious practitioners. Mundurucu Indian shamans, for example, are careful when pursuing the soul of a dying client not to venture too far, *i.e.,* not to overstep the boundary of death.[15] Many tribes hold that dreams represent the soul's nocturnal voyage, and some believe that the soul is vulnerable to abduction by a sorcerer or an evil spirit during nighttime dreaming. In such cases, it is necessary for the shaman to search for the soul and retrieve it, often engaging in fierce spiritual battles along the way. Among the Kiwai of Papua New Guinea, the souls of sick people are in danger of being abducted by malevolent spirits or otherwise leaving the body during dreams. Sick people are roused at short intervals at night so that they do not oversleep, because it is feared that they might never awaken. If the soul does escape during sleep, the shaman turns into a bird and attempts to bring it back; failure could mean death. Mota shamans in the Banks Islands often are called upon to treat soul theft by ghosts. They make a potion of leaves, drink it before falling asleep, and—in their dreams—leave their body to attempt to retrieve the lost soul. No one dares disturb the shaman, because a premature awakening might cause him to release his grasp of the sick person's soul. The Siberian Tungus assume that only one aspect of the soul is absent during sleep; the absence of the total soul would be unduly hazardous. Nevertheless, malevolent spirits may enter the body during sleep and overpower the remaining aspect of the soul, producing sleepwalking or sleeptalking. Like the Tungus, other Siberian groups, such as the Birarcea, the Manchus, and the Nanais, have pluralistic concepts of the soul, enabling one aspect to be away from the body during dreaming.

Among some competing Siberian tribes, shamanic rivalries are quite intense. One shaman might try to capture the soul of another during a trip to the Upper or Lower World or while the shaman is dreaming or engaging in soul retrieval. Battles between shamans often take place in dreams; these may take the benign form of artistic competitions or may become duels to the death. Siberian Yakut shamans climb a Tree of Life to the Upper World during their dreams; perched on the top of the tree is a two-headed eagle, lord of all the birds. But the treetop is guarded by the souls of unborn infants, who must be pacified. Kung shamans of southeast Africa often encounter malevolent spirits in dreams that must be fought or even killed if the shamans are to fulfill their mission.

THE SHAMANIC IMAGINATION

Because of shamans' involvement in fantasy and imagination, some scholars have concluded that they must suffer from some type of neurosis or psychosis.[16] L. B. Boyer, however, conducted in-depth interviews with Apache shamans and administered them the Rorschach Inkblot Technique, concluding that "shamans are healthier than their societal co-members." He added,

"This finding argues against [the] stand that the shaman is severely neurotic or psychotic, at least insofar as the Apaches are concerned.[17] Richard Noll compared shamans' experiences in altered states of consciousness with symptoms of mental illness found in the third edition of the American Psychiatric Association's *Diagnostic and Statistical Manual.*[18] On the basis of this comparison, Noll concluded that the "schizophrenic metapor" of shamanism was untenable; any similarities that appeared were superficial, while the contradictions were basic, indicating quite different processes to be at work.[19]

I suspect that shamans, in general, fall into the category of "fantasy-prone personalities" identified by S. C. Wilson and T. X. Barber, who reported that about 4 percent of the general American population sees visions, hears voices, and touches imaginary companions. Dreams play an important role in the lives of fantasy-prone individuals; they claim to receive guidance in their dreams and even talk to dead relatives or spirits while dreaming.[20]

The characteristics of Wilson and Barber's fantasy-prone individuals are also the characteristics of many shamans, including their finding that subjects with a propensity for fantasy are as well adjusted as the average person. Wilson and Barber indicated that the life experiences and skill developments that underlie the ability for fantasy are more or less independent of the kinds of life experiences that lead to psychopathology.

Michael Harner, an anthropologist who has written extensively on shamanism, warns against taking a reductionistic approach to the dreams and visions of shamans. Fantasy productions are nearly limitless in the potential scenarios they present, yet the belief systems and techniques of shamans are "similar in different parts of the world."[21] It appears that shamans have tapped into an important human capacity that was especially useful in the evolution of societies, one that still is of value for shamanic communities where the shaman is more knowledgeable, more adept, and more potent in dealing with unseen powers than anyone else.[22] It is likely that the private dreams and visions of shamans not only direct the healing processes of their clients but enrich the cultural myths of the community in ways that are socially adaptive.

Shamans have achieved a degree of concentration beyond the ability of the average person. They can sustain exhaustive efforts during healing rites that sometimes last for several days. They manifest physical prowess and are able to self-regulate many bodily functions. Shamans have mastered a complex body of knowledge through instruction and direct experience; they are able to apply this wisdom to individual situations in appropriate ways. Therefore, it appears that shamans represent not only the oldest profession, but are the original professional practitioners endowed by society with the responsibility of understanding dreams.[23]

Benjamin Kilborne

Ancient and Native Peoples' Dreams

Like myths, dreams express our inner states of mind. Also like myths, they serve both the individual and society. Because dreams are fashioned from our wishes and memories, they are particularly responsive to a culture's values and dynamics. At innumerable points along the way from the nighttime experience to the story of the dream we tell another person, a dream can change. The ways in which these changes take place provide fascinating glimpses into the ways in which we internalize cultural priorities and patterns.[1]

Dreams—however they are related—are extremely important in what anthropologist A. I. Hallowell called the "behavioral environment" in which individuals acquire their basic sense of orientation to the world.[2] In this chapter, I shall explore the meanings of dreams in various cultural settings.

THE DREAM, THE FOREIGNER, AND THE STORY

The missionary W. B. Grubb, working among the Lengua Indians of South America's Gran Chaco, was roused from a peaceful slumber by a great commotion. Grubb awakened to find Indians standing accusingly over him. Breathless, one of them gesticulated to the headman, who then explained to Grubb that the breathless man had run over fifty miles to accuse the missionary of stealing a pumpkin from his garden. When Grubb protested that he had never set foot in his accuser's village, the runner said that he had seen Grubb steal the pumpkin in a dream, and therefore demanded that Grubb duly compensate him for the stolen property.

We can presume that as a missionary Grubb wished to be known for his generosity, one of the virtues he may well have hoped to teach by example to these Brazilians tribespeople. If there had been no hope of being compensated, would the native have dreamed of Grubb and run the fifty miles in order to be paid? Had Grubb not been a European missionary, would the native have dreamed that he stole a pumpkin? And if he did, would he have run fifty miles? Whatever the meanings of the dream, Grubb, by paying for the pumpkin, was forced to behave as though the dream of the runner had not been imaginary. We can only wonder what effect Grubb's payment might have had on the beliefs in dreams in the village and what happened to subsequent missionaries and fieldworkers in the area.

This anecdote illustrates some key problems in understanding dreams in other cultures. First, the foreigner can change the usual context of dream-telling by his or her very presence. Also the presence of a foreigner can contribute to the dream. I do not know of any anthropologist who has collected the dreams that have been about him or her, but such a study would be provocative.

Furthermore, our usual ideas about what dreams can and cannot do simply do not hold up to scrutiny in other cultural contexts. Finally, the telling of dreams is affected by the specific context of teller, listener, and—where appropriate—audience. If we lost sight of the fact that a dream, no less than a play or a musical performance, is never the same twice, we miss much of the wonderment of dreams. As George Devereux and other psychoanalysts have observed, fieldworkers inevitably disrupt the field they study.[3] That which social scientists might consider unwanted interference, psychoanalysts have forced into an instrument of understanding and therapeutic healing: the transference. Because they provide insight into the psychodynamics of informants and of those one is seeking to know, the feelings and initially incomprehensible reactions of the fieldworker as a partner in a relationship are indispensable for knowledge of the field situation. They constitute sources of understanding for anthropological work just as they do for psychoanalytic work.

DREAMS AS RELIGIOUS EXPERIENCES

Nighttime dreams and daytime visions are frequently prized as religious experiences. As such, they confer special powers upon the dreamers, providing solace to the injured and good fortune to those who believe. Father LeJeune, an eighteenth-century Jesuit missionary, writes that for the Iroquois the dream is divinely inspired.[4] Another missionary of that era commented that "Dreams are to savages what the Bible is to us, the source of Divine revelation—with this important difference that they can produce this revelation at will by the medium of dreams."[5]

In the anthropological literature of North American Indians, there are countless examples of dreams that impelled the dreamer to take action. Father LeJeune writes:

> A warrior, having dreamed that he had been taken prisoner in battle, anxious to avert the fatal consequences of such a dream, called all his friends together and implored them to help him in this misfortune. He begged them to prove themselves true friends by treating him as if he were an enemy. They therefore rushed upon him, stripped him naked, fettered him, and dragged him through the streets with the usual shouts and insults, and even made him mount the scaffold. . . . He thanked them warmly, believing that this imaginary captivity would insure him against being made prisoner in reality.

In another example, Father LeJeune tells of a man who dreamed he saw his hut on fire and hounded his neighbors until they obligingly burned it down for him.[6]

Many ethnographic accounts of North American Indian tribes show that wishes expressed in dreams were acted out in some way by the dreamer upon awakening—or acted out by others. If, for example, an Iroquois dreams of giving a feast, he will arrange to give one when he awakens. This the Iroquois called *Ondinok,* a secret wish of the soul that is expressed in a dream. Indeed, Sigmund Freud also maintained that dreams are the expressions of unconscious wishes!

Several other North American tribes held similar beliefs about the relation between wishes and dreams. The Yuma believed that a child can only be conceived if a man has recently dreamed of some guardian spirit or other symbol of potency. Women, for their part, could resist conception by refusing to desire a child. The Cherokee believed that if a man dreams he has been bitten by a snake, upon awakening he must follow the same treatment as if he had really been bitten, for if the snake bite in the dream had been caused by sorcerers, it could become inflamed and even cause death if proper measures were not taken upon awakening.[7]

Such Indian tribes as those of the Plains and Eastern Woodlands, the lower Colorado River, Central California, and the Northwest Coast believed in guardian spirits. These religious beliefs were largely sustained by dreams. The guardian spirits who appeared in dreams granted individuals special powers: prowess in war, skill in hunting, and facility in lovemaking.[8]

These dreams or visions were regarded as among life's most important experiences. The beliefs in dreams afforded the Indians protection and guidance; as part of their behavioral environment, dreams affected behavior. As religious experiences, dreams were allowed to have powerful consequences for both tribal and personal identity, as well as for the inculcation of cultural values. Cultural attitudes toward dreams, like religious beliefs, are patterned. Among some tribes, both past and present, dreamed snake bites are treated in reality just as they would have been had they actually occurred. As sociologist Emile Durkheim has argued, what has real effects cannot be summarily dismissed as simply illusion.[9]

THE VISION QUEST

One of the clearest expressions of the patterning of dreams is the vision quest.[10] Anthropologist J. S. Lincoln tells of one Menonmini Indian who, after fasting for eight days, dreamed of

> a tall man with a big red mouth [who] appeared from the east. The solid earth bent under his steps as though it was a marsh. He said, I have pity on you. You shall never live to see your own grey hairs, and those of your children. You shall never be in danger if you make yourself a war club such as I have and always carry it with you wherever you go. When you are in trouble, pray to me and offer me tobacco. Tobacco is what pleases me. Having said this, the dream visitor disappeared.[11]

Such a report is typical of visitation dreams and visions sought by adolescents who, in order to become adults, were required to dream. Among the Plains Indians, adolescents went out in search of a dream or vision promising the protection of a guardian spirit for the remainder of their lives. They sometimes had to dream a protective song and return to sing it. In contrast, Cheyenne men waited until they were adults before seeking visions; if they failed, they would fast and inflict wounds on themselves.

As Wallace notes, for the Mohave "all special abilities of funds of knowledge were to be had by dreaming and by dreaming alone."[12] When European explorers and settlers appeared with rifles, these new weapons had to be dreamed into the creation myth, the source of all knowledge of their world.[13] Dreams were the one topic of which the nearby Yuman tribes of the Gila River constantly talked, the most significant aspect of their life.[14] As Last Star succinctly said, "Everyone who is prosperous or successful must have dreamed of something. It is not because he is a good worker that he is prosperous, but because he has dreamed."[15] All powers—whether leadership, physical strength and courage, or skill in conceiving children, singing songs, and obtaining information clairvoyantly—could only be obtained through dreams.

SHAMANIC INITIATION DREAMS

The English work *shaman* is derived from the Tungus term *saman,* meaning "inner heat," perhaps referring to the internalized magical and spiritual powers of these Siberian "masters of ecstasy."[16] Because of the similarities between shamanism in those areas and in the Americas, the Pacific, and elsewhere, the term *shamanism* is now used to designate these practices wherever they may occur.

Shamans rarely select themselves; they are called into the profession in ways that are culturally determined. Dreams are a common form of the call. Often, the dreamer is reluctant to acquiesce but becomes convinced that there is no alternative, as an account from the Paviotso tribe indicates:

> When Rosie's father had been dead about eighteen months, she started to dream about him. She dreamed that he came to her and told her to be a shaman. Then a rattlesnake came to her in dreams and told her to get eagle feathers, white paint, wild tobacco. The snake gave her songs that she sings when she is curing. . . . Now she dreams about the rattlesnake quite frequently and she learns new songs and is told how to cure sick people in this way.[17]

In Siberia, shamans have initiation dreams that follow clear patterns. Often, exhibiting symptoms of odd behavior or illness, they dream of being whisked off to the sky. In their sleep, their body is carried off to faraway places, then torn from limb to limb. Their bones may be torn from their joints and their eyes from their sockets, and the fluids may be drained from their bodies. Then all the parts are reassembled and the new shaman, to whom this dismemberment is explained by spiritual beings, is reborn.[18]

The Buriats of Siberia pattern their shamanic visions in a similar way but maintain that the initiate is cooked as well as dismembered. Teleut women become shamans only after dreaming that their bodies are cut up by unknown men and boiled in a large pot. According to a Yakut informant, the shamanic initiate dreams of being mutilated by a black devil, after which a lance is thrust through the head and the jawbone is cut off. An Avam Samoyed initiate claims he was carried to the underworld. Coming to a mountain pass, he encountered a man tending a kettle on a blazing fire. The man grabbed him with a hook, cut off his head, minced his body, and put the entire mass into a pot to boil for three years. Finally, the man fished out what he could find, forged an iron head for the new body, found bones floating in a river and pieced them together, covering it all with new flesh, then sent the new shaman on his way. During his journey back, he met spiritual beings who taught him curing techniques. Then he awakened, and shortly thereafter he began shamanizing.[19]

Similar dreams and visions of dismemberment followed by rebirth or renewal are common in various parts of South America and the Pacific. Among the Dyak of Borneo, the *manangs* (Dyak shamans) report dreams of their heads being cut off and their brains being removed and washed so that they can think clearly. Similarly, Australian aborigine shamanic initiates envision their bodies being cut up and their viscera replaced.

In many shamanic calls, dreams play a central role, and the telling of the dream becomes the form in which the community hears of the call and evaluates it. For Australian aborigines, The Dreaming, or dreamtime, constitutes an eternally present life principle, a mythic source of life that must be sustained and renewed by human activities. Rituals and ceremonies allow the dreamtime to be present in religious belief and daily practice. Knowledge of one's world thus depends on dreamtime, somewhat like Plato's world of ideal forms. As with the Mohave, dreams are a source of knowledge; but in Australia there are even more links between time, dreams, and the mythic ancestors. The Australian aborigines believe that dreamtime is a historical principle that organizes time and space, that it was created by the mythical ancestors at the beginning of things and can be tapped through dreaming.[20]

GATES OF IVORY AND GATES OF HORN

For my purposes, I am considering as dreams nighttime dreams, hypnagogic imagery, drug-evoked visions, waking reveries, and anything else that gets told as a dream.[21] Among native people, dreams often are a kind of shorthand for experiences in which contact with spiritual beings is made; thus they are a potentially religious experience. They become techniques of ecstasy forged into a narrative by the individual who experiences them, are told to others, and are acted upon. Dreaming is among those techniques by which mortals enter into relations with superhuman beings. The word *ecstasy* is derived from the Greek root *ekstasis,* meaning "to stand outside oneself." This is precisely what the dreamer often is believed to do in a dream, particularly when the body stays behind and the soul wanders.[22]

Visions, I have argued, can be conveniently considered as truthful dreams, a category found in many cultures.[23] Dreams raise precisely the same questions concerning their truth and falsehood as do the data from sense impressions. And since truth and falsehood are cultural categories, the preoccupation with truthful dreams has strong cultural roots. In the Western tradition, it reaches back to the ancient Greeks, who expressed the wish that certain dreams be clear, God-sent, and responsive to human suffering and supplications. Truthful dreams, by their very nature, involve divine responses to human needs, even when the dreams reveal sickness or misfortune.

For the Greeks of the Homeric period, dreams passing through the Gates of Ivory were "true," in contrast to the "false" dreams that passed through the Gates of Horn. Gates remind us of the best-known gatekeepers of them all: St. Peter, who screens aspiring souls waiting to be admitted to Heaven, and the Greek deity Chiron, who ferries the souls of the dead across the River Styx and keeps track of admissions into the lands of the dead.

In all societies of which we have any knowledge, ideas about the dead have been profoundly influenced by the cultural notions of dreams and what happens during sleep. Generally speaking, there are two kinds of belief: either the dead come to visit, or the living wander to the other side. Such beliefs mirror those about dreams: either the soul goes wandering in sleep, leaving the body behind, or spirits come to visit the soul in the sleeping body.

Truthful dreams were often associated by the Greeks with a sense of clarity. In contrast, confusing or disjointed dreams passed through the Gates of Horn—the realm of mortals rather than of deities—and were not trustworthy. Recognizing truthful dreams depended on special faculties: purity of the soul, second sight, and other avenues for discernment. However, message dreams, such as those we find in ancient Mesopotamia and Greece, depended primarily on the dreamer's social station; only shamans, chiefs, prophets, and members of the royalty and clergy could obtain direct communication from deities. Ordinary humans could not obtain these badges of political and religious power.

When I was working in Morocco, for instance, my field assistants pointed out to me repeatedly that *ruya* (truthful dreams) were the manifestations of inner purity and required leading a saintly life. They were conceived as the rewards of a good person; Allah would not send them to the heathen.[24] There is a certain circularity about these beliefs: powerful men and women have true dreams because they are favored by Allah, and Allah's grace and favor is in turn demonstrated by their political or religious prominence. Having true dreams is a sign of election. However, some other traditions held that high station sufficed to qualify for knowledge from the other world.

Anthropologists and sociologists writing in the nineteenth century assumed that native (or so-called primitive) religion arose through dreams and visions and, further, that dreams provided the concepts on whch ideas about the soul were based. Psychologist Wilhelm Wundt went so far as to propose that dream images produced the notion of an eternal soul.

SEX, DREAMS, AND DEMONS

Even though the rationalist tradition shies away from using the soul concept, cultural mythology is laden with stories of dreamed sexual unions with deities and other superhuman beings. Merlin supposedly was born from the union of Charlemagne's daughter (a nun) and an incubus, or demon. Other people supposedly born from such unions were Alexander the Great, Plato, Scipio Africanus, William the Conqueror, and the entire population of Cyprus![25]

Western tradition holds that sexual intercourse with demons disguised to make themselves seductive is a cause of possession. Initially these demonic spirits appear to be friendly, desirable, and seductive; then they turn into monstrous beings whose lasciviousness knows no bounds and who thoroughly ravish the unsuspecting dreamers. Among the Dyaks, infants who die are believed to have been carried off by incubi who have had intercourse with their mothers in dreams. The shaman must pursue these unseen creatures and do battle with them in a public ritual.

Demonic possession is common throughout Africa, the Mediterranean, and many other areas. When the dreamer awakens dramatically out of sorts, or when an individual engages in uncharacteristically negative behavior, a diagnosis of possession is often given. Therapy consists of persuading the demon to leave, or in forcibly expelling, or exorcising, it.

In Morocco, thousands of people make yearly pilgrimages to sanctuaries in search of cures for these dream illnesses. Here, as in the temples once dedicated to the healing deity Asklepios in the Greek world, dreamers await the dream that is to cure them, either by indicating that the patron saint (or other holy person) of the sanctuary has evicted the demon or by directing a course of action that will be therapeutic. The acting out of commands believed to be provided in these dreams resembles the acting out of dreams by such past and present tribes as those in Siberia, North America, and the Pacific.

INNER AND OUTER WORLDS

As we have seen, all cultures have their own notions of inside and outside, ideas about orientation with respect to dreams in which superhuman beings play important roles. In other words, dreams are equally necessary in the formation of concepts and experiences of both self and society.

Often, dreams are thought to be conditions in which the soul goes outside the body, or in which a spirit ventures inside the dreamer. Dreams passing through the Gates of Ivory and the dreams sent by God or Allah are all communications from divinities who respond to the wishes of mortals. These dreams validate political or religious power, provide instructions for healing, or answer questions posed by individuals or by groups. In Christian belief, there is a dichotomy between rationally clear, God-sent dreams and those that are demonic or Satan-sent. In Islam, however, this dichotomy is somewhat mitigated by the cult of saints who can send dreams and by the far greater variety of powerful demons.

What the natural state of the dream may be is hard to determine, just as we cannot really know the status of our natural body—our physical state stripped of decoration, garb, and social concept. It is obvious that unadorned nakedness does not mean the same thing in the Nubian desert as it does on the London or New York stage. There is always a cultural context for nudity; therefore there can never be any such thing as a natural category of nudity, which is no more a natural category than a dream.

We necessarily assign meanings to perceptions of this illusively natural state. As a result, neither our perceptions of dreams nor our perceptions of nudity can ever be purely natural. Both are influenced by our cultural values. As Shakespeare wrote (in *The Tempest,* IV:i), we are indeed such stuff as dreams are made on, and our little life is rounded with sleep. Reclaimed and recreated as illusions from the inchoate world of forgotten impressions, dream stories are fleeting and evanescent. Yet they do complete our lives, a third of which is spent in sleep.

Experiences in dreams are "re-membered," assembled again just as arms and legs—members—might be put back on a body. This dream experience is, furthermore, so private as to be impossible for anyone but the dreamer to remember. Once remembered, however, it can be brought into the social world, reborn (somewhat like the Siberian shaman), and told as a story—a story of feeling states, of wishes, and of relationships. Dreams bear the marks of the dreamer's personality: his or her age, gender, social class, education, priorities, and lifestyle. As Freud observed, dreams reflect "the events and experiences of [one's] whole previous life." We dream of what we have sensed, seen, said, wished, and done. Especially in dreams "do the remnants of our waking thoughts and deeds move and stir within the soul."[26] And since this is so, dreams are no less dependent upon cultural values, patterns, and processes than are the activities of human experience that are carried out in waking consciousness.

VI

Frontiers in Dreamwork

Myths are public dreams, dreams are private myths.
JOSEPH CAMPBELL

The first frontier to be explored in this section is that of the dreaming human brain. The findings of neurobiology have sparked a lively debate about the inherent meaning or randomness of dream content.

There are many physiological theories about how dreams are evoked in the brain, but I consider neuropsychiatrist J. Allan Hobson's model an elegant description that is firmly rooted in laboratory data. His book *The Dreaming Brain* is a monumental work that is carefully crafted and skillfully argued.[1] Simply put, Hobson contends that dreams are tales told by the brain to make sense of the random neural firings that accompany sleep cycles. Even though few visual or motor messages from the outside world enter during REM sleep, the higher-level neurons (in the cortex's visual-motor area) are stimulated by messages sent by the brain stem and act as if they are getting those messages from the external environment. The eyes are closed and the muscles are virtually paralyzed during REM sleep; thus, the ensuing activity must be internally rather than externally generated. The brain stem also activates the limbic system, the brain's emotional center, so dreams often are marked by strong feeling tones. The brain's pain, taste, and smell centers are rarely activated, so few dreams are characterized by these sensations.

Hobson's chapter summarizing his theory is somewhat technical for this book, but it is quite articulate considering the ground he must cover. As Robert C. Smith points out in his chapter, despite his rigorous scientific approach Hobson is not opposed to the search for meaning in dreams; in fact, he maintains that dream metaphors represent high-level associations that "pack lots of material into an economical unit."[2] But Hobson doubts that dreams focus on *hidden* meanings, because the dream begins when signals from the lower brain hit the higher brain, which then tries to produce a more-or-less continual narrative. His model suggests that dreams *create* meaning, pulling it from the dreamer's experiences, memories, and life issues. This stance is reminiscent of that of the existential philosophers; like them, Hobson mandates the necessity of making sense of experience and creating meaning. It is as if the dreamer takes a lump of clay (the random signals) and creates something from it.

On the other hand, psychologist Gordon G. Globus takes an existential stance that differs from Hobson in his superlative book *Dream Life, Wake Life,* a classic in its decade. Globus sees dreaming and wakefulness as equally viable ways of being. Human existence is, at heart, a creative movement that is pretty much the same across its dreaming and waking phases.[3] Globus' book pays special homage to psychiatrist Medard Boss, a leading existential thinker who once made a wry comment on laboratory sleep research:

> The findings from sleep research are certainly highly interesting in their way, and even necessary. But they tell us almost nothing about what they are supposed to represent. Not one of them brings us a single step nearer to an explanation of dreaming as a unique mode of human existence.[4]

Boss suggests that dream images and dream experiences should be accepted in their own right, on their own terms, with respect for their unique feeling tone and with a minimum of translation. He treats dreams as texts or narratives that make dreamers aware of their possible life choices.

Globus also notes the contributions of David Foulkes, who sees dream texts as cognitive plans for dealing with more-or-less randomly activated memories.[5] Dreams can be meaningful and symbolic, but they are not preplanned, encoded messages that need to be "translated" the way a linguist would work with a foreign language. Foulkes believes that the dream is knowledge-based and "bound to reflect some of the ways in which the dreamer mentally represents his or her world."[6] Where Globus takes issue with Foulkes is the extent to which bizarre intrusions in the dream are random or meaningful. Foulkes holds that they are often random, the result of neurologically evoked memories stimulating a planned scenario; Globus contends that the dream's bizarre shifts and changes are usually meaningful, a case of the planned scenario reaching for the most easily obtainable memories to continue the story.

Hobson and Globus share many points of view, and I also find these positions congenial with my own viewpoint. Globus sees the dream process as the fundamental creative action inherent in the human condition; Hobson views the brain as so determined to find meaning that it creates dreams out of random signals. Both take most dreams primarily on their own terms, rather than looking for hidden meanings that represent censored desires that have been festering for years or even decades. However, Globus takes exception to Hobson's assertion that an REM-sleepy dreamer simply "makes the best of a bad job," finding those memories that "best match" the sensations evoked by random neural firing and using these images as a giant inkblot into which meaning is injected. Hobson observes that dreams even can be induced by stimulating the neurons chemically. Once again, the dreamer would insert a meaningful story into the resulting images.

Globus agrees with Hobson on certain points, such as that dream images are neurologically based. Random neural firing turns on a switch and activates a mechanism. However, unconscious wishes and fears could well take advantage of this random stimulation and emerge fullblown once the appropriate memory is initiated. Simply because neural firing *initiates* a dream does not mean that it is necessarily responsible for its *continuation*.[7]

From my vantage point, there is a critical difference between these two dreamworkers. For Globus, the essence of dreams is not random but meaningful. There is a whole that enfolds all meanings, and the meaningful dream is unfolded from it in a formative creative act. The debate, then, is basically between randomness and fullness. Hobson and Globus' differences result, in part, from their working from different levels of the brain/mind system. As a laboratory researcher, Hobson focuses on the mind's brain; as a clinical researcher, Globus focuses on the brain's mind. Both agree that dreams have meaning, but Hobson's meaning is more immediate, whereas Globus' has deeper roots.

Additional research studies will help us to decide which emphasis is justified. In the meantime, we can gain satisfaction that dreams are being taken seriously by scientists and that models of great ingenuity are being advanced to explain their function, a quest originally begun by Freud, which has become increasingly sophisticated and scientific.

According to Globus, Freud's great achievement was his realization that dreams are the meaningful expressions of an individual's unconscious mind. Jung identified the healing dimensions of dreams, and Boss the existential stance. A biological correction was added by Aserinsky and Kleitman, who discovered the association between REM sleep and dreaming. A cognitive dimension was added by Foulkes; LaBerge added lucid dreaming and its implications for creativity.[8]

I believe that Hobson's research provides factual support to the innately creative nature of the dream process and that Globus gives dreaming a unique philosophical dimension. Thanks to these two dreamworkers, it is apparent that, in addition to everything else, dreams are a royal road to the human condition. As Globus observes, once we make our existential choice and decide to remain in the world (rather than releasing ourselves from it), we face a challenge to develop the possibilities of our being alive.[9] One of our greatest resources in this task is our potential for imagination and creativity—our ability to see what we are and what we can become and our capacity to make wise decisions that will leave our world a better place than it was when we arrived. The role of dream life in articulating these visions and anchoring them in waking life is assuming greater recognition by both scientists and laypeople.

This recognition was a long time in coming. The Society for Psychical Research, founded in Great Britain in 1882, was the first major organization to attempt the scientific study of experiences that were not easily explained by existing models of the human being. Among the topics investigated were hypnosis, multiple personalities, out-of-body experiences, near-death experiences, lucid dreaming, and parapsychological phenomena.

One by one, most of these topics have passed into the scientific mainstream. In 1913, psychiatrist F. W. Van Eeden published a lecture on lucid dreaming that he had delivered to the Society for Psychical Research. Not only did Van Eeden coin the term, but he described some of his own experiences.[10] Many years ago I read a reprint of his work, as well as the book *Lucid Dreams* by British psychophysiologist Celia Green,[11] but was told by sleep "experts" that it was impossible for dreamers to be aware that they are dreaming. Nevertheless, I ran across descriptions of lucid dreaming in Tibetan Buddhist texts and even began having lucid dreams myself. In the 1970s, another British investigator, Keith Hearne, and an American psychophysiologist, Stephen LaBerge, independently discovered that lucid dreamers could communicate with the outside world by moving their eyes in a predetermined pattern while in the middle of a lucid dream, and thus a new frontier was crossed.

The second chapter in Part Six contains psychiatrist Robert C. Smith's insightful portrayal of dreams that can be used as an "early warning system" for dreamers, providing them with information about impending health problems. Franklin Galvin and Ernest Hartmann propose some creative therapeutic strategies using lucid dreaming to deal with nightmares. Next, Jayne Gackenbach presents provocative evidence concerning the capacity to

dream lucidly. Linda Magallón and Barbara Shor contribute a fascinating account of shared dreaming. Most shared dreams can be explained on the basis
of the proximity of the two (or more) dreamers who have similar dream content, but not all. Nor can some dreams about future events be casually attributed to coincidence, previous information, or faulty dream recall. Jon
Tolaas' chapter on psychic dreams is a brilliant characterization of a puzzling
topic that some timid dreamworkers disregard, despite its potential capacity
to expand our knowledge of human consciousness. Tolaas provides sensible
guidelines for dreamers who suspect that their dreams are telepathic, clairvoyant, or precognitive.

The experiments that Montague Ullman and I conducted at Maimonides Medical Center attempted to put these claims to the test. For example, Malcolm Bessent, a British sensitive, was well known for his purported
dreams about the future. In 1969 we attempted to explore whether or not he
could dream about a waking life experience that we would arrange for him
after his night of dreaming was over. When Bessent was awakened after his final REM period, a different experimenter selected a random number that directed him to a list of dream images appearing in a book written by Calvin
Hall and Robert Van de Castle.[12] An experience was created around the randomly selected image.

One morning, the image "parka hood" was randomly chosen by a toss of
dice, and the experimenters had an hour to prepare a post-sleep experience
based on the image. When Bessent left the soundproof sleep room, he was
taken to an office draped with sheets (to resemble snow). As he inspected a
photograph of an Eskimo wearing a parka hood, an ice cube was dropped
down his back. Several hours earlier, Bessent had dreamed about ice, a room
in which everything was white, and a man with white hair. His dreams on
each of the eight nights of the study were congruent with the following morning's experience, and outside judges were able to match the correct dream
with the correct post-sleep experience with an accuracy that was statistically
significant.[13]

Bessent returned the following summer for a similar experiment, but
one in which the controls were even tighter. For example, a dozen experiences
were "packaged" by an experimenter who left for Europe shortly after he
selected the props and wrote the instructions. Again, a team of EEG specialists put Bessent to bed and collected the dreams. Another experimenter
selected a number randomly and picked the sealed container to which it cor-
responded. Outside judges (without knowing the correct match) were able to
detect traces of the post-sleep experiences in Bessent's pre-experience dreams,

and their judgments again yielded statistically significant results, indicating that coincidence was highly unlikely.[14]

One night Bessent had several dreams about birds, one of which he reported as

> just water. . . . A few ducks and things. It's fairly misty, but there are quite a lot of mandrake geese and various birds of some kind swimming around in rushes or reeds. . . . I just have a feeling that the next target material will be about birds.

The following day, in a darkened room, Bessent sat before a screen and watched several dozen slides of birds—in the water, in the air, and on the land—while an accompanying tape played bird calls.

What was the reaction of mainstream science to these two experiments? A book titled *Anomalous Psychology* dismissed them, stating that Bessent had been "primed" *before* going to sleep with pictures and music. It concluded, "The receiver was an English 'sensitive,' but it is obvious that no psychic sensitivity was required to figure out the general content of the picture and to produce an appropriate report."[15] Psychologist Irvin Child remarked, "The correct sequence of events was quite clearly stated in the . . . original research report. . . . This erroneous reading . . . could easily have been corrected by a more careful rereading."[16] The authors in question never apologized for their mistake, nor was it mentioned in the reviews of their book written by mainstream psychologists.

Some skeptics criticize the study of anomalous dreams, stating that these accounts support magical thinking and irrationality. However, our group at Maimonides, as well as most parapsychologists with whom I am acquainted, fully support the scientific method. I consider these dreams natural, not supernatural, and normal, not paranormal. So little rigorous work has been conducted with anomalous dreams that the mechanisms of their operation are currently unknown. At least a dozen possible explanations have been proposed, ranging from models based on quantum physics to those evoking geomagnetic fields.[17]

Montague Ullman, for example, believes that REM sleep is a natural arena in which creativity is at play. Dreams tend to arrange information in unique and emotionally related ways. They depart from rational thought, grouping images together in bizarre associations and making liberal use of metaphor in constructing the dream story. As a consequence, new relationships emerge that sometimes provide a breakthrough for a waiting and observant mind. Dreams serve a vigilance function, like a sentry alerting the dreamer to whatever may intrude into dream consciousness.[18]

Ullman's vigilance theory of dreaming posits that during REM sleep, the dreamer scans not only the internal environment but also those aspects of the external environment that he or she can perceive by anomalous means. During sleep, hunters and gatherers were vulnerable to attack. Contemporary human beings respond to symbolic threats, rather than to physical dangers. Yet vigilance still operates, and REM sleep, perhaps because of its linkage to a primordial-danger-sensing mechanism, provides a favorable state for anomalous communication.[19]

Ullman's theory is not incompatible with Hobson's proposal that, during REM sleep, the brain is activated internally by random neural firing from lower brain centers that stimulate higher brain centers. For Hobson, the dream results from a knitting together of these neurologically evoked memories and images.[20] I would propose that the random nature of this neurological firing provides an opportunity for parapsychological effects to operate, influencing either the portions of the cortex that are stimulated or the images that are evoked.

In Ullman's vigilance theory, however, the consciousness that produces the dream narrative reflects recent emotional residues and explores these residues from an historical perspective, connecting them to the past and projecting them into the future. Ullman implies that there is a collection of dream stories waiting to be told, while Hobson suggests that dream narratives are created "on the spot." But psychic anomalies could enter both types of dream production, either finding their niche in a carefully constructed metaphorical tale that contains an emotional linkage to the anomalous element or filling a gap in a story that is creatively but haphazardly composed to make sense of a barrage of randomly evoked images.

While research results slowly accumulate and while theoretical propositions are tested, the database on anomalous human experiences slowly grows. The founders of the Society for Psychical Research would be pleased to observe that most of the phenomena they studied finally have been taken seriously by social and behavioral scientists. Someday the study of psychic dreams will be granted respect and recognition as well.

J. Allan Hobson

Dreams and the Brain

To the extent that psychoanalytic dream theory is derived from an outmoded neurobiology, it is in need of revision on historical grounds alone. Our new theory challenges the psychoanalytic idea that the many meaningless aspects of dream mentation are the result of an active effort to disguise the meaning of unconscious wishes, which are in turn postulated to be the driving force of dreaming. Many new and important findings in neurobiology allow us to account for exactly the same processes that Freud studied, but in more accurate and economical ways. Our exploration of the neurobiological basis of dreaming constitutes a key aspect of mind/brain interaction and a model approach to the study of mental illness. In addition, it has yielded important clues to a better understanding of the brain's role as the basis of consciousness.

FREUD'S CONCEPTS

Freud's ideas about the nervous system, and the mind that it allegedly supported, were dependent upon external energy and information. Such a system was highly vulnerable, because it was subject to invasion (by energy from the outside world) and the constant threat of disruption (by the internally stored energy that could only be discharged in motor action).

These ideas became crystallized in Freud's concept of the dynamically repressed unconscious and were carried into his dream theory as the tendency for unconscious wishes to erupt during sleep, when the repressive forces of the ego were relaxed. For Freud, the nervous system was constantly in need of checks and balances to deal with the threat of disruption from within and without; his whole concept of psychic defense is related to this erroneous view of how the nervous system actually operates.

I am not saying that the concept of defense is in itself erroneous, only that the weight that is placed upon it is excessive. If the nervous system has its own means of producing energy, it is very likely to have its own means of regulating this energy. Accordingly, if it has its own means of creating information, it is likely to have its own means of regulating information. And if it is protected at every sensory-input gateway by transforming mechanisms, it is intrinsically immune to overload from the outside world. This property is particularly evident in newborn human infants, who simply "tune out" when they are either overloaded or not ready to process external information.

Modern sleep research has clearly demonstrated the elaborate, intrinsic mechanisms of "state" control. In other words, a change in the brain's state while asleep causes a change in the dreamer's mental state. We now know that sensory input can be internally controlled so that even the transforming mechanisms do not operate alone to protect the system from overload. Three features of the modern conception of the nervous system—its intrinsic plasticity, auto-regulation, and creativity—give us a very different set of operating principles upon which to construct a scientific psychology, including a modern theory of dreaming. This model depicts a nervous system that can turn itself on and off, regulate the flow of internal information in diverse ways, and control external information's access to the system.

THE ACTIVATION-SYNTHESIS HYPOTHESIS

There are several principles that my colleagues and I have put to use in constructing what we call the *activation-synthesis hypothesis* of dreaming. In contrast to viewing dreaming as the result of an uprush of normally repressed energy, our model sees dreaming as the preprogrammed running of an internal system. All energy and information are intrinsic to this system. There is no need for the system to discharge information or downgrade information (although it *could* do both). Thus, the bizarre features of the dream are seen as naturally associated with the mode of operation of the system during dreaming sleep, *and there is no need for a mechanism that would transform information.* Since the system is capable of selecting what computer scientists call the "store" or "no-store" modes, there is no need to postulate an active energy-consuming mechanism for the re-storing of dream material in the unconscious. It can simply be the "no-store" mode that is "unremembered."

Freud held that wishes and repressed desires caused dreaming; our view is that brain-stem mechanisms during sleep cause dreaming. Once these mechanisms trigger REM sleep (and dreaming), wishes may be expressed and may even shape dream plots, but they are in no sense causative of the dream process. Our reciprocal-interaction hypothesis proposes that REM sleep occurs when "REM-off" neurological activity in the brain stem has reached a low enough level to allow the inhibited "REM-on" neurological system to escape from its control. At this point, our activation-synthesis hypothesis takes over, proposing that dream elements derive from a synthesis of information produced by activation of the brain's motor-pattern generators and sensory systems. This internal information is linked and compared with information about the organism's past experiences, making the best possible fit of intrinsically chaotic data produced by the automatically activated mind/brain.

Like other subjective experience, dream material tends to be organized by the linguistic faculty of our mind/brains. Thus, we conclude that dreams are not the result of an attempt to disguise wishes but are a direct expression of a synthetic effort—that is to say, the brain is first internally activated and then synthesizes this information to form the physiological patterns of the dream experience. One's memories are scanned for images that will match these internally generated patterns.

CHARACTERISTICS OF DREAMS

The activation-synthesis hypothesis holds that stimuli are generated within the central nervous system and are processed as if they came from the outside world. The waking function of the neurons involved is sensory-motor integration; their expression during sleep provides the signals from which dreaming takes its form. During REM sleep (the state from which most dream reports are obtained), brain-stem neurons activate the brain and generate rapid eye movements, as well as various sensory-motor activities and aspects of the affective system that regulates emotions.

Therefore, dreaming is a distinctive mental state that occurs periodically in normal human sleep. Typical dream reports include such psychological features as:

1. formed sensory perceptions (akin to hallucinations);

2. cognitive abnormalities (akin to the cognitive inconsistencies and uncertainties that characterize delirium and dementia);

3. uncritical acceptance of all such unlikely phenomena as real (akin to delusions);

4. emotional intensifications (akin to those seen in panic anxiety); and

5. amnesia (akin to that seen in organic syndromes).

These five remarkable features of dreaming have invited a comparison to psychotic states of mind occurring during waking in certain clinical conditions, especially the schizophrenic, manic-depressive, and organic psychoses. In this respect, a scientifically sound dream theory could form a solid base for psychiatry as it attempts to develop a specific pathophysiology. It might also supply the current missing link between its phenomenology and the new psychopharmacology.

Dreams are characterized by vivid and fully formed hallucinatory imagery, with the visual sensory domain predominant. Auditory, tactile, and movement sensations are also prominent in most dream reports. Compared with the intense involvement of these sensorimotor domains, taste and smell are underrepresented, and reports of pain are exceedingly rare despite the involvement of dreamers in frightening and even physically mutilating scenarios. This sensory profile suggests that specific physiological systems are activated (or inactivated) in specific ways during REM sleep.

The simplest and most direct approach to the correlation of dream mentation with the physiological state of the brain in REM sleep is to assume a formal isomorphism between the subjective and objective levels of investigation. By isomorphism I mean a similarity of form in the psychological and physiological domains, often referred to as the "mind/brain isomorphism." For example, it may reasonably be assumed that subjective experience of visually formed imagery implicates activation of the central visual system in a manner similar (if not identical) to that of the waking state.

Other details of psychophysiological correlation are assumed to obey the same general law. For example, the vivid sensation of movement is assumed to be related to patterned activation of the motor systems and those central brain structures subserving the perception of position of the body in space. When we look at the psychological level, it is found that powerful, highly coordinated excitatory processes are recordable in the oculomotor, vestibular, and visual sensory centers.

Once so activated, the mind/brain synthesizes or constructs a unified conscious experience (the dream) by comparing the internally generated signals to perceptions, actions, and emotions in its memory bank. The rules of synthesis are as yet poorly worked out but involve such complex organizational processes as language (given the narrative structure of reports) and nonverbal symbolic operations (given the dream's elaborate scenarios), which are presumably a function of "higher" brain centers. The state of the art in cortical psychophysiology is so primitive even in the waking state that one must remain at least as vague and promissory in discussing dreaming. This is due to the fact that during REM sleep the mind/brain is off-line (input independent), movement free (output independent), and hence operating on its own terms. For once, we can safely agree with Freud's assertion that dreams are the "royal road" to a scientific understanding of consciousness.

MECHANISMS OF ACTIVATION AND SYNTHESIS

To be fully adequate, a psychophysiological hypothesis of dreaming has to account for several processes.

Activation. The brain has to be turned on and kept internally activated to support dream mentation throughout the REM sleep episode. Our hypothesis holds that a possible mechanism could be the activation of a set of sensorimotor circuits that ordinarily serve an inhibitory function.

Input blockade. Input from the outside world to an internally activated brain has to be prevented in order for sleep and the illusion of dreaming to be maintained. According to our hypothesis, this could be accomplished in two ways. One would be the inhibition of neurons that, during wakefulness, relay information throughout the brain stem and thalamus. The second mechanism for excluding sensory input would be occupying the higher levels of sensory circuits with internally generated messages.

Output blockade. The internally activated brain also must quell motor outputs so as to prevent the disruption of sleep by the enactment of dreamed motor commands. This could be accomplished by the inhibition of a set of motor neurons in the spinal cord and brain stem. By these processes, the brain would thus be made ready to process information arising from within, to exclude data coming from without, and to refrain from acting upon the internally generated information.

Internal signal generation. It remains to provide the activated but disconnected brain with internal signals, which it then processes as if they came from the outside world. This could occur, at least in part, by a mechanism intrinsic to brain activation: the reciprocal interaction of certain sets of neurons in the brain stem. In most mammals, including the human being, the so-called PGO waves (*P* for pons, *G* for lateral geniculate, and *O* for occipital cortex) present themselves as candidates for an internally generated information signal arising at the level of the pontine brain stem. In association with eye-movement activity, strong pulses of excitation are conducted by reticular pathways to the thalamus and radiated via independent pathways to the visual and association areas of the cortex.

It is now known that these PGO waves are generated by cellular activity, which faithfully replicates the directional aspects of generated eye movements at the level of the brain stem. Thus not only is internal information generated, but this information has a high degree of spatial specificity. According to our hypothesis, the auto-activated and auto-stimulated brain processes these signals and interprets them in terms of information stored in its memory.

Synthesis: the weak link in the logical chain. The major shortcomings of this theory are related to state-of-the-art limitations in knowledge regarding so-called higher brain functions. One way to proceed may be to identify important state-to-state differences in cognitive function and look to the brain for working hypotheses about the basis of the differences.

For example, although the basis of the cognitive disturbances occurring in dreaming is not understood, it is tempting to see these failures as perhaps related to the cessation of activity in various sets of neurons. An arrest of certain types of neuronal activity would affect the entire brain, including the cerebral cortex, by depriving it of a tonic modulatory influence normally present in waking. I speculate that this influence may be essential to attentional processes, including the capacity to organize information in a logical and coherent manner and to achieve the full self-awareness that gives waking consciousness perspective and insight.

A final caution. I must remind the reader that this activation-synthesis model of dreaming, and the reciprocal interaction theory of sleep-cycle control on which it is based, are both incomplete and controversial. They represent linked working hypotheses about the fundamental physiology of sleep and the way in which that physiology may help us to understand unique features of the dream process. The attribution of automaticity to the control system and the features of randomness in the information-generation model should not be taken to exclude the constructive nature of the synthetic process carried out by the dreaming brain. By definition, the mind/brain of each dreamer is obliged to make as much sense as possible of its internally generated signals as the adverse working conditions of REM sleep permit.

Thus, the dream product of each individual may reveal both important concerns and unique stylistic psychological features. As a result, dreams may be worthy of scrutiny when one reviews life strategies. However, our theory ascribes these cognitive properties of dreaming to unusual operating features of the internally activated, auto-stimulated brain during REM sleep. This is the heart of the theory, and I hope to have convinced readers of at least the investigative value of the new approach—even if I may have failed to convert them to all of the specific claims of the activation-synthesis hypothesis of dreaming.

MIND/BRAIN ISOMORPHISM

Freud was convinced that the scientific explanation of mental phenomena must ultimately involve physiology and biochemistry. Even in abandoning his earlier "bottom-up" approach for the "top-down" approach of psychoanalysis, he never gave up this ideal. I would like to propose some concepts that might serve to support a more supple and versatile mode of inquiry—one that could be both bottom-up and top-down. This mode of inquiry, which is called *mind/ brain isomorphism,* assumes the same similarity of form across the domains of mind and brain that Freud anticipated in his work. A strategic emphasis is placed on the investigation of states of mind and brain, particularly the mind state of dreaming and the brain state of REM sleep.[1]

I believe that the current state of knowledge limits the isomorphist approach to the most approximate, global, and statistical correlations of variables from the several levels at which states are assessed. If we take dreams as our starting point, we must then focus on the formal level of analysis, leaving to the indefinite future the analysis of content (in all its narrative and syntactical richness). We thus aim at an interpretation of *dreaming* (as a universal mental process) rather than an interpretation of *dreams* (as individual mental experiences).

A single example may help make the point. It is necessary and sufficient for the isomorphist to know that well-remembered dream reports describe color and that the common supposition that dreaming is colorless (*i.e.,* "black and white") is an incorrect inference related to the problems of recall (an after-the-fact memory defect). This means that no state-specific change in higher-order visual processing need be evoked—or sought—in developing a physiological state correlate for dreaming. Rather, a state-dependent change in memory is to be postulated and its neuronal correlate sought.

By contrast, it is neither necessary (nor even helpful) for the brain/mind isomorphist to know the incidence, in reports, of the words *red, yellow,* or *chartreuse,* since the higher-order physiological correlates of such specific details are unlikely to be state-dependent (or discovered in the near future). Of course, if all color reports were chartreuse, or if a primary color were absent, we would sit up and take notice; thus this type of content analysis is not always useless.

The choice of level that is likely to be fruitful in a state-to-state correlation is thus governed by the scientific maturity of work in one or both of the states under consideration. This limitation is severe in the case of all mental states, including dreaming, and for most physiological states, except perhaps REM sleep, which may now be the most completely defined mammalian state at the behavioral and neuronal level. In this case, it is thus the level of knowledge of the neuronal state of REM sleep that directs the contemporary-state isomorphist to the appropriate psychological level in the study of dreaming. That level is the *formal* level, and it involves a qualitative and quantitative assessment of the distinctive information-processing characteristics of the state.

Having observed certain formal features of the brain state in REM sleep, the mind/brain isomorphist then moves from the bottom-up to ask if there is an isomorphic set of formal features of the mind state in dreaming. Conversely, the presence of distinctive formal features of the mind state in dreaming directs a top-down quest for isomorphic features in the brain state of REM sleep. Such an approach already has proven useful in several studies of dream form.

Studies of dream movement. These investigations have revealed the ubiquity of movement in dream reports and its possibly distinctive character. Dream reports from subjects in REM sleep never seem to be static, but they often are static in waking life, as they almost always are when in non-REM sleep.[2] There is a superabundance of curved, circular, or spiral trajectories in dream reports.[3] The former data appear to reflect the physiological finding of intense central-motor-system activation during REM sleep, and the latter resemble the stereotyped motor patterns that issue from certain natural and experimental changes in the brain's motor system.

Studies of dream sensation. These data reveal a graded representation of sensory modalities ranging from 100 percent (vision) to 0 percent (pain) in laboratory reports.[4] While we do not know how to quantify exactly the isomorphic brain-state function, we would expect system activation to be very high in the case of vision and very low in the case of pain, both of which are the case.

Studies of dream bizarreness. These data have revealed that this distinctive psychological attribute is composed of incongruities, discontinuities, and uncertainties in the domains of dream plot, dream character, and dream action. Further, an analysis of the underlying cognitive processes reveals major defects in orientation, attention, and memory similar to those seen in organic syndromes.[5] External input differentiation, parallel channel activation, and disenablement of memory systems are candidate isomorphic brain dysfunctions. The psychological data thus confirm many of the predictions of physiology and advance the isomorphist argument to a new plane.

These studies illustrate the utility of the mind/brain isomorphist approach and demonstrate the value of the activation-synthesis model of dreaming, whose experimental development utilizes both bottom-up and top-down approaches. While the data cannot be said to disprove the Freudian hypothesis, they offer a simpler, more straightforward explanation of dream phenomena.

Therefore, the activation-synthesis hypothesis proposes that dreams result from attempts by the higher brain centers to make sense of cortical stimulation by lower brain centers. Dreams take the stimuli produced by these dream generators and use the images as story material. Any number of psychological functions can be superimposed upon the process—integrating daytime experiences with those memories already stored away, allowing the dreamer to deal with upsetting ideas and events, addressing one's unsolved problems, and coming up with tentative solutions. Dreaming in relation to REM sleep provides us with a remarkable mirror of our inner selves, but it is basically a neurobiological process. And the nature of this process must be honestly faced by those who attempt to work with dreams and the information they provide.[6]

Robert C. Smith

Traumatic Dreams as an Early Warning of Health Problems

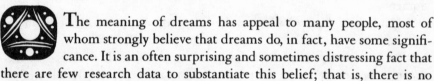 The meaning of dreams has appeal to many people, most of whom strongly believe that dreams do, in fact, have some significance. It is an often surprising and sometimes distressing fact that there are few research data to substantiate this belief; that is, there is no known technique to determine specific meanings of dreams from a scientific standpoint.[1]

With Freud's seminal work, highlighted by publication of *The Interpretation of Dreams* at the turn of the century,[2] the subject of dreams became a major issue for science. His wish-fulfillment theory was only the first of many well-formulated theories of meaning to be subjected to scientific scrutiny.[3] The various, often competing theories seemed to hold promise that one of them would answer the age-old question of meaning, and previously inaccessible recesses of the mind were postulated to harbor important information.

Then came the let-down. These rich, far-reaching theories were never tested for their accuracy,[4] and as untested theories accumulated over the years, other scientists became concerned about the lack of data to support them. This culminated in the general perception that there was no scientifically verifiable meaning of dreams and, unfortunately, that the discipline itself lacked scientific rigor.[5] It was not until the middle of the century that a small group of scientists, heralded by the work of Calvin Hall,[6] began to systematically study dreams. A core of investigators, some contributors to this book among them, gradually formed and developed as their overriding aim the scientific understanding of dreams.

The first goal of this chapter is to address some general research considerations for a scientific understanding of the meaning of dreams. For present purposes, the meaning of actual dream content (such as references to separation or sex) will be our only focus. Next, my own research will be reviewed briefly. It provides some initial experimental evidence that allows us some hope that dream content may, after all, have meaning. This work has, in addition, led to a theory of the meaning of one type of dream content, dreams with references to death and separation. The theory, its implications, and its potential practical application will then be addressed.

CONSIDERATIONS FOR STUDYING THE MEANING OF DREAM CONTENT

Science dictates that theories be supported by research data.[7] In designing research about the meaning of dream content to the dreamer, there are two important but sometimes confusing issues. First, the research must focus on dream content itself. If a theory proposes a meaning of human dream content, the research will not be effective with a focus on other dimensions of dreams. For instance, although rapid-eye-movement (REM) states are associated with dreaming, specific dream content is rarely a concern in these studies. Accordingly, despite extensive research productivity in this area, studies of REM physiology have not produced an understanding of the meaning of human dream content.[8]

Secondly, when an investigator focuses on the content of the dream, the study design must next evaluate a relationship of the content to some important overall dimension of the dreamer as a person. That is, to show that content has meaning, the research must necessarily relate it to meaningful aspects of a person's life, typically at a behavioral or holistic level, such as life, death, joy, interpersonal relationships, problem solving, or personal growth. Conversely, the investigator also must recognize that how the dream content was formed is not germane to the research question of what meaning it may have.[9] Although how the content is formed is an important question, this research does not consider the relationship of the content to the whole person in his or her life context; rather, it often considers only how isolated, fragmentary dimensions of experience, such as day residue, might be related to production of the content. Thus, in a like fashion, studies on dream formation have not answered what the content of dreams means to the dreamer.[10]

Both distinctions are important, because failure to find the meaning of dream content by studying REM physiology[11] or in studies of dream formation is predictable.[12] They are addressing questions different from the meaning of content. Although considerable careful work has been done in each of these areas, relatively little systematic work has been done in evaluating the interest of this chapter, the meaning of dream content itself.[13]

This discussion leads us to explore what a satisfactory study might look like. It would first identify some type of content that a scientist theorized to have meaning. The investigator would then predict that this content would be related to a carefully selected measure important in human affairs.[14] For instance, if the investigator wanted to test Jung's compensatory theory (that dreams contain information not recognized consciously),[15] he or she might predict that dream content of orderliness would be associated with disorderliness in the conscious, waking state as shown, for example, through a careful interview. Thus, the dream content would be used to predict an important later-determined nondream event.[16]

BIOLOGICAL MEANING OF DEATH/SEPARATION DREAMS

In a group of hospitalized medical patients, many had death and separation (traumatic) dreams. When the patients were followed up after hospitalization, men with death dreams and women with separation dreams had a worse prognosis; they had more deaths, rehospitalizations, and complications than their hospital mates, who, nevertheless, appeared to have been as sick while in the hospital.[17] Two examples follow.

A sixty-two-year-old man was hospitalized with weight loss, indigestion, and jaundice. He was found to have cancer of the pancreas and was readmitted several times during the next year. The following excerpt is from a dream with many death references that occurred one week before the first admission.

My brother and I visited our old house . . . , and mother was there in her casket. It was all black except for a weird glowing red stripe end-around. She tried to get out, but then fell back and seemed to disappear; she was a goner for sure now. We took her to the cemetery and almost got killed ourselves in a flood on the way. There weren't many people there. Dad was dead for years. . . .

A forty-five-year-old woman was admitted because of recurrence and spread of breast cancer. She died six months later, after several readmissions. Excerpts of a dream of separation ten days before the first hospitalization follow:

I can't find my husband. He's never gone this long. I keep searching. I miss him.

Then a strange dog comes in. I worry about Betsy, our cat, but can't find her. I'm more lonely and call my daughter, but she's not there. She lives in California and I never get to see her anymore. . . .

This was the first evidence in the research that traumatic dreams might be markers or warnings of severe underlying medical disease. These studies were flawed, however, because they were retrospective; that is, they started with the prognosis and looked backward in time to see what the earlier dream content of the patients had been. If there had been such a warning in dream content, a more rigorous test would have been to start with death/separation references, make a prediction about severity, and then obtain measures of severity to determine whether the prediction was correct.

Such a study was conducted,[18] using a different population of patients: a group undergoing cardiac catheterization for potential but not yet determined heart disease. Cardiac catheterization is a commonly performed diagnostic test in which tiny catheters are inserted into the heart to learn about its structure and function. We predicted that the more traumatic dreams there were, the more severe would be the patients' heart disease at catheterization. These patients were selected because a more objective measure of disease severity than prognosis was available during catheterization: a measure of the amount of blood pumped from the heart with each beat, the so-called ejection fraction, which falls as heart function declines. Although this measure is non-behavioral and less than optimally holistic, it is nevertheless the most sensitive measure of severity of heart disease and, therefore, of great importance to survival for the patients. Patients in the study ranged from having normal to severe heart disease by this measure. In brief, the prediction was confirmed: the greater the number of death (for men) and separation (for women) dream references, the more severe the heart disease; in other words, the more references, the lower the ejection fraction.

Thus, the original observation that traumatic dreams were associated with more severe biological disease was supported. This time, however, it was predicted in advance, and a more objective measure of severity was used to show the accuracy of the prediction. Because these dreams were associated with severe underlying disease, it can be said also that traumatic dreams served as a marker or warning of this dysfunctional state.

PSYCHOLOGICIAL MEANING OF DEATH/SEPARATION DREAMS

In a seemingly unrelated area, there was not only a plethora of traumatic dreams, but also support for the proposal that these dreams were markers of serious underlying dysfunction. It had been observed by many researchers that some unharmed survivors of war catastrophes had similar traumatic dreams. In contrast to survivors without these dreams, these patients with "shell-shock," post-traumatic stress disorder,[19] or traumatic war neurosis[20] have serious psychological abnormalities, as shown by careful psychiatric interviews and well-constructed questionnaires.[21] In addition to traumatic dreams, they exhibit severe anxiety and depression, constant replaying of the catastrophic event, and often severe disability. It thus can be said, as with the cardiac patients, that traumatic dreams mark or signal significant underlying disturbance but, in this instance, of psychological rather than biological origin.

Therefore, a similar circumstance of severe underlying dysfunction occurs in conjunction with traumatic dreams. Is there any way to relate these seemingly disparate areas? Scientists and others often have divided the human being into component parts, such as mind and body, for the sake of simplifying a complex subject. Although helpful in some circumstances, when considering the whole person, this artifical distortion can obscure and mask reality.[22] Our concerns about the meaning of dream content fall into this category. However, by reuniting the mind with the body, we find that these previously dissociated areas can be joined into one statement—the proposed warning theory.

A WARNING THEORY OF MEANING FOR DEATH/SEPARATION DREAMS

The warning theory indicates that traumatic dreams are associated with more severe underlying dysfunctions of the dreamer, whether biological, psychological, or both.[23] These dreams, by definition, serve also as markers of this state of serious general, or organismic, distress. Conversely, dreams without traumatic references may reveal a better, more highly integrated function of the human organism.[24] The data indicate that death/separation references and their corresponding levels of underlying disease severity exist on a continuum. Thus, the more traumatic the references, the more severe the dysfunction.[25]

The persistence of traumatic dreams indicates a continued threat as well as a failure to heal or resolve the offending problem (severe biological or psychological insult). Conversely, the disappearance of traumatic references from an otherwise active dream life indicates healing, restitution of bodily or psychological integrity, and resolution or removal of the stressful precipitant.[26]

For a theory to be useful, it must lead to logical predictions with which to test its scientific credibility. It is proposed for the next stage of research that, if traumatic dreams warn of serious underlying disruption of any type, there will be some response to the warning, such as telling someone else about the dream, going to see someone about it, or changing something in one's life as a result of it. These are testable predictions, and the occurrence of a response, whether ultimately useful or not, would help confirm the theory. Moreover, if the response proved useful for example, if the action it prompted led to resolution of the stressful precipitant—the theory would be expanded from a purely warning theory to a warning/adaptive one.[27]

Why death references are more common among men and separation references among women can only be speculated upon. There is some evidence that men as a group respond in more individualistic, aggressive ways than women, who, as a group, respond in more interpersonal, other-directed ways.[28] Such data are compatible with death and separation as markers of serious distress in men and women, respectively. Moreover, death and separation are not dissimilar concepts, one often implying the other and each used frequently to define the other.[29]

Also we can only conjecture why death/separation references serve as warnings in the first place. Perhaps the child learns early to associate death/separation themes with severe distress. These anxieties occur at very early phases of development,[30] and they also are regularly reinforced through powerful sociocultural influences at an early age. It is suggested that, with this rich heritage, themes of death/separation are called forth at subsequent times of severe distress and that, as this is done, they come to signal newly occurring stress to the organism.[31]

Once again, we can only guess how the severity of distress is communicated to as-yet unknown mechanisms of dream formation[32] and how it results in the proposed warning dreams of death/separation. It is intriguing to postulate that some neurological or chemical mediator could be involved. Such potential changes are not only obvious in those with severe heart disease, but distinctive physiological changes also have been shown in patients with post-traumatic stress disorder.[33]

OTHER THEORETICAL CONSIDERATIONS

As emphasized already, the study of the meaning of dream content should concern the whole person under some meaningful life circumstance. This approach is consistent with systems theory and other holistic and phenomenological approaches.[34] It is further consistent with the rich dream theories of the past[35] insofar as they were derived from work with individual patients and their real-life problems. This holistic approach to dreams has been particularly apparent in those psychotherapeutic circles where the dream has been central to understanding the patient.[36]

In addition to the monumental work of Freud, there are other influences from the psychoanalytical movement on the proposed warning theory. Abraham Kardiner noted long ago, when others favored working with a patient's more common neurotic dreams, that traumatic dreams also were important.[37] He clearly recognized that traumatic dreams were associated with severe dysfunction of the dreamer, at biological as well as psychological levels. The proposed warning theory, in reality, is scarcely more than a systematic rendition of what Kardiner said over fifty years ago with the benefit of more systematically obtained data to support it.

The warning theory of death/separation dreams also is consistent with the work of Hans Kohut and his revolutionary ideas of "self-psychology," a recent, more holistic theory of understanding the psyche.[38] Kohut was another product of the psychoanalytical movement who found traumatic dreams of interest. His understanding of traumatic dreams as indicating a fear of dissolution of the self, which he called "self-state," is consistent with the holistic concept of organismic dysfunction developed here.

How does the warning theory relate to other theories of meaning of dream content? In addition to having a research data base, it differs in that it addresses traumatic dreams rather than typical neurotic dreams that have been the focus of most theorists. Thus, because it concerns a different type of dream, it is not incompatible wth other theories. That is, the various theories—such as wish fulfillment, compensatory, and problem solving— concerning psychoneurotic dreams could still apply in less severely ill populations, while traumatic dreams would represent an additional meaning when patients experienced serious distress.[39] For instance, someone with neurotically based erotic dreams would be understood by wish-fulfillment theory to have unmet erotic desires; if this patient also exhibited traumatic dreams, it would indicate additional severe psychological distress. Thus, in addressing different dream material, the warning theory is not incompatible with existing theories of meaning in dreams.

As emphasized at the outset, the warning theory addresses different, more holistic subject material than most psychophysiological theories and cognitive psychological theories about dreams and dreaming. In addressing the meaning of dream content to the whole person of the dreamer, we are not concerned with the more reductionistic questions about how the dream is formed, how information is processed, or what the physiological correlates to the dream content are.[40] It is essential to emphasize that these topics, although not germane to the meaning of dream content per se, are equally important to fully understanding dreams and sleep.[41] Thus, the seminal ideas of Foulkes about the processes of dream formation,[42] of Hobson and McCarley about the activation-synthesis hypothesis,[43] and of Crick and Mitchison about "reverse learning,"[44] for example, are not incompatible with the warning theory. Once again, they address different questions.

PRACTICAL APPLICATIONS OF THE WARNING THEORY

It is important to emphasize, in considering how we might use this information, that dreams of death/separation do not predict death or separation literally. Rather, these references should be considered as danger signals, as a red flag for the dreamer's potential benefit. They almost exclusively will be danger signals of underlying psychological distress, which is far more frequent than serious physical disease. Moreover, when traumatic dreams reflect serious physical states, there is almost always other evidence of severe disease. Thus traumatic dreams should not provoke concern about underlying medical or surgical problems in otherwise healthy people. The emphasis here on physical disease (as with hospitalized medical patients) was largely for tactical reasons. It was already known that severe psychological dysfunction was attended by traumatic dreams, but it had not been prospectively established that they also were associated with severe physical disease states. To support the theory, evidence in the latter area was required, leading to the research.

We can now consider briefly the implications for someone experiencing traumatic dreams due to psychological distress. These dreams probably indicate that the person is under severe stress from some cause that may include psychiatric disease. Although the source of the stress may be evident, this is not always the case. The dreamer is advised to attempt to correct this source if it can be identified. If the dreamer is successful, as is sometimes the case, the warning signal will disappear from the dream and the dreamer will usually be happier and healthier. The persistence of traumatic dreams suggests either misidentification of the precipitating stress or, more likely, failure to satisfactorily resolve it.

In the latter circumstances or when the stress that is producing the traumatic dreams cannot be identified initially, these dreamers often can benefit from discussing both the dream and other aspects of their lives with a psychotherapist, sympathetic friends or groups, or members of the clergy. It is doubt-ful, in my mind, that working on the traumatic dream directly, to interpret the traumatic references or to somehow try to make them go away, is of any value. Interpreting and working with other dreams, however, can be attempted. To be most successful, though, the work should focus on two nondream dimensions of the dreamer's waking life: recognizing its stressful aspects, and acting to correct the stress.

In this manner, traumatic dreams could have a very adaptive, growth-promoting effect on the dreamer. When successful, dreamers and their coun-selors should expect some apprehension in the dreamer, but usually this will reflect that the dreamer is enthusiastic, engaging in new activities and behav-ing in improved ways. Traumatic dreams can thus promote self-awareness and the process of adult growth and development. There should, however, be no expectation of deterioration or dysfunctional developments in the dreamer during this process. Along with persistence of traumatic dreams, deteriora-tion in the dreamer's original state is an indication for professional help. Moreover, evidence of depression, severe anxiety, disordered thinking, sub-stance abuse, prominent psychosomatic symptoms, or other emotional diffi-culties at any time, before or after work on the dream, is an indication for im-mediate professional attention.

This chapter has reviewed research data and a theory that indicates that dreams with traumatic references warn of the presence of severe dysfunction in the dreamer, which is usually psychological but occasionally biological (physical) in origin. This is not in conflict with prior theories of the meaning of dreams, because it concerns a different type of dream. Because it addresses different questions from the ones asked by dream physiologists and cog-nitively oriented dream psychologists, it does not conflict with their findings.

The warning theory is based on a systems approach to science, relies on the contributions of psychoanalysis for its conceptual support, and derives from empirical data. In addition to the implications for its clinical use as a growth-promoting warning signal, it is important because it reflects some of the first experimental data that dream content itself may have meaning.

Franklin Galvin and Ernest Hartmann

Nightmares: Terrors of the Night

To Sigmund Freud, the nightmare was an annoyance, a stumbling block to his development of a theory of dreams as wish fulfill-ments. He first tried to include nightmares in his general view by suggesting that they represent the fulfillment of superego wishes—wishes for punishment.[1] Freud was not satisfied with this view, however, and he later suggested that certain nightmares, especially traumatic nightmares, represent a repetition compulsion—a primitive tendency of the mind to repeat what has been experienced.[2] Theodore Lidz, when studying traumatic nightmares, proposed that these dreams could be understood as a wish for punishment, as Freud first suggested, but also as an "ambivalent wish for death": both the wish for death and the wish to escape it.[3]

The manifest fear of death figured prominently in a childhood dream of Freud's. It is the first of three dreams we present to illustrate how the night-mare has heralded momentous change in the lives of three noted dream-workers.

In his discussion of anxiety dreams near the end of *The Interpretation of Dreams,* Freud presented us with the only dream from his childhood to be found in his published works and letters.[4] "A true anxiety-dream," he called it, "from my seventh or eighth year." This dating is of special import in Freud's life because it "starts—spiritually—the gestation period of a new and original thought."[5] Of this dream, Freud wrote:

> It was a very vivid one, and in it I saw my beloved mother, with a peculiarly peaceful, sleeping expression on her features, being carried into the room by two (or three) people with birds' beaks and laid upon the bed. I awoke in tears

and screaming, and interrupted my parents' sleep. . . . I remember that I suddenly grew calm when I saw my mother's face, as though I had needed to be reassured that she was not dead. . . . I was not anxious because I had dreamt that my mother was dying. . . . The anxiety can be traced back, when repression is taken into account, to an obscure and evidently sexual craving that had found appropriate expression in the visual content of the dream.[6]

Some thirty years after he dreamed this, Freud submitted the dream to interpretation. Through the associations he presented, it appears that he revealed both his incestuous wishes toward his mother and his fear of castration as a consequence of sexual excitement aroused by witnessing the primal scene. A related fear was that his mother would bleed and die as a result of sexual relations.[7] The "obscure and evidently sexual craving" giving rise to this dream was, it seems the essence of Freud's own Oedipus complex. The dream heralded a startlingly new psychological theory.

The second dream is from the first chapter of Carl Jung's autobiography, *Memories, Dreams, Reflections.* The earliest dream that Jung remembered was one from between ages three and four, "a dream which was to preoccupy me all my life," he recorded. In the dream, he "was paralyzed with terror" and "awoke sweating and scared to death." It was a dream of encountering a huge phallus standing on a magnificent throne in an underground chamber of hewn stone and hearing his mother's voice call out: "Yes, just look at him. That is the man-eater!" For many nights afterwards the young Jung was afraid to go to sleep. The dream haunted him for years, and in old age he wrote:

> Through this childhood dream I was initiated into the secrets of the earth. What happened then was a kind of burial in the earth, and many years were to pass before I came out again. Today I know that it happened in order to bring the greatest possible amount of light into the darkness. It was an initiation into the realm of darkness. My intellectual life had its unconscious beginnings at that time.[8]

The third terrifying dream was recorded in a modern sleep laboratory, and it heralded scientific change in the entire community of dreamworkers. This dream helped to establish the link between rapid eye movements and dreaming—a link that launched the scientific investigation of dreams in the early 1950s. As a graduate student in Nathaniel Kleitman's laboratory at the University of Chicago, Eugene Aserinsky observed the rapid eye movements made by infants during sleep. In pursuing this phenomenon, he attempted to find correlations between these movements and both physiological and psychological functions. He spoke years later about this early period in a follow-up discussion on somnambulism and stated:

> For a long time I was not sure whether those eye movements were associated with dreaming. Finally, one night when the polygraph pens showed deflections indicating either eye movements or instrument generated artifacts, I decided that the time was proper to make a direct visual observation of the subject's eyes. However, all of a sudden the pens practically went wild and almost went off the carriage. Well, I dashed into the sleeping chamber to see what had happened, turned on the lights, and saw the subject, a medical student, lying there, making some mumbling noises while his eyes, although closed, were moving vigorously, violently in all directions. I awakened him and he told me that he had a nightmare from which he felt he couldn't awaken. . . . Well now, this episode more or less convinced me that dreaming, or at least this nightmare, was associated with rapid eye movements.[9]

DISTINGUISHING NIGHTMARES FROM NIGHT TERRORS

Based on the pioneering work of Kleitman, Aserinsky, and William Dement, other researchers[10] have established that there are two important and very different phenomena that can wake us in a fright during the night: the *night terror* and the *nightmare*.

The night terror is an abrupt awakening early in the night, most often within the first hour or two of sleep, and usually occurring during stage three or four (deep, slow-wave) sleep. This awakening is most often accompanied by sweating, body movements, and a sudden scream or cry for help as the sleeper wakes in terror. Particularly with children, the physical movements may become intense and even continue into a sleepwalking episode. When night terrors were observed in the sleep laboratory, pulse and respiratory rates sometimes doubled during the thirty seconds or so involved in these awakenings. The night terror has been called a *disorder of arousal* and can be considered a minor abnormality in the brain's sleep-wake mechanisms.[11]

When asked about the experience, the sleeper either does not remember the night terror or simply recalls waking in fright, heart pounding, and not knowing what to make of it. Occasionally the person will be aware of a single frightening image—"Something was crushing me and I couldn't breathe." The night terror also has been called *pavor nocturnus* or an "incubus attack" because of this sensation of suffocation, as if an incubus—a kind of demon or goblin that was supposed to produce nightmares—was actually sitting on the sleeper's chest. Yet the terrifying episode is generally not described as a dream.[12]

The nightmare—sometimes called *REM-nightmare* or *dream anxiety attack*—is a quite different experience from the night terror. Usually occurring late during the night in the last three hours of sleep, the nightmare is a long, frightening dream that awakens the sleeper. Laboratory recordings show that it occurs during REM sleep, often during a long REM period of twenty to thirty minutes. Pulse and blood pressure may show some increase but not as much as in a night terror, and there are neither gross body movements nor sleepwalking, because during REM sleep the arms, legs, and trunk are temporarily paralyzed.

The person awakened by a nightmare almost always remembers very distinctly a long, intense, and vivid dream, ending with a frightening sequence. The nightmare is a very detailed, colorful, lifelike dream experience involving some of the earliest, most profound anxieties and the most thoroughly terrifying fears to which we are all subject.[13] The nightmare often includes sensations and perceptions other than vision—even including pain, which is very rarely felt in dreams. For example: "It was a wartime scene. I could *hear* awful noises: bombs bursting around me, screams. Something hit me in the shoulder; I could *feel the pain* and the blood flowing down my arm."

When a person reports having frightening sleep interruptions, the answer to one simple question—"Are these experiences dreams?"—usually will indicate whether the events are night terrors or nightmares. The nightmare sufferers will answer, "Yes, of course," whereas those who have night terrors will reply, "Definitely not." They know what they experience is something other than a dream. The two are very different events physiologically and psychologically and seldom occur in the same individual.[14]

An occasional person suffers from what are called hypnagogic nightmares—terrifying nightmarish fantasies experienced upon just falling asleep.[15] Also, some persons have a condition called nocturnal myoclonus—many jerking muscle movements during the night. Sometimes these persons will report a nightmarelike occurrence when awakened by muscle jerks.

Lastly, people troubled with chronic post-traumatic stress disorder experience repetitive nightmares depicting the traumatic episode long after the event. These repeated experiences share characteristics of both nightmares and night terrors and may occur in various stages of sleep.[16] Prominent in this group are combat veterans and victims of exceptionally violent accidents or crimes.

It is evident from the above descriptions that the experiences of the medical student observed by Eugene Aserinsky in the laboratory, that of the young Carl Jung, and that of the young Sigmund Freud were all true nightmares and not night terrors or other nightmarelike events.

NIGHTMARE INCIDENCE

Nightmares are far more common than night terrors. Almost everyone has had a nightmare on occasion, most likely in childhood. Although people tend to forget their childhood nightmares, some have had particularly frequent or especially vivid ones that are remembered clearly throughout their lives.

Nightmares are definitely more frequent in children than in adults and are particularly common at ages three through six. Evidence suggests that they probably occur as early as age one.[17] While they become less frequent after age six, their incidence may increase again in adolescence between ages thirteen to eighteen. The incidence of nightmares generally decreases with age and in healthy adults is relatively low.

Based on many survey studies, sleep researchers estimate that approximately 50 percent of the adult population have no nightmares at all, though they may have had them as children. Most others remember an occasional nightmare, and the average is perhaps one or two per year. Between 5 and 10 percent of the population report nightmares once a month or more.[18] Only a small percentage have nightmares that are frequent enough or severe enough to be significantly disturbing to their lives. Men are probably as likely to have nightmares as often as women, but they tend to be much more reluctant to mention them.[19]

WHAT PRODUCES NIGHTMARES?

For centuries the word *nightmare* has been used loosely to mean anything that wakes one up in fright, a creature that produces such terror, the frightening dream itself, or the actual awakening. Most scholars now agree that the root *mare* derives from the Old English and Old German root *mara,* meaning "an incubus or succubus," and not from *myre,* meaning "a female horse." The folklore of peoples' experiences during the night inspired the eighteenth-century Swiss artist Henry Fuseli to depict both images in his well-known painting *The Nightmare.* (See illustration on page 115.)

We no longer believe that demons or evil spirits produce nightmares, nor is there any solid evidence that eating something disagreeable will cause them. Recent evidence also contradicts another widely held view that a lack of oxygen gives rise to nightmares. Obstructive sleep apnea is a disorder in which air does not get through the throat to the lungs of the sleeper because of some obstruction at the back of the throat. This may happen 100 or more times in one night. The chest and abdomen of the sleeper heave but no air gets through, and after ten to twenty seconds there is a brief awakening, allowing normal breathing to resume. Sleep-apnea sufferers very rarely report nightmares, indicating that a lack of oxygen is not causally related to nightmares.[20]

One factor that does appear to precipitate nightmares is physical illness, although it is unclear whether illness itself or the stress that accompanies it is more important. Children who do not otherwise have nightmares report them during times of illness, particularly febrile illness. Adults, too, seem to have more nightmares during high fever or around the time of an operation. In addition, certain neurological disorders sometimes have been associated with nightmares—notably epilepsy[21] and postencephalitic parkinsonism.[22]

Mental illness is often associated with nightmares. In certain individuals nightmares occur at the onset of psychosis, especially schizophrenic episodes.[23] Depression can also be associated with an increase of nightmares.

Stressful events seem to be causally related to frequent and severe nightmares in susceptible persons. Stressful periods in adulthood, such as times of examinations, job changes, moves, or the loss of significant persons, may produce or increase nightmares.

The one generalization that seems to hold true for nightmare sufferers is that their nightmares almost always involve feelings of helplessness, most often helplessness dating from childhood. The most frequent situations in their nightmares involve being chased, attacked, thrown off a cliff, or generally feeling at the mercy of others. Almost invariably it is the dreamer who is in danger and utterly powerless—not someone else. A decrease or sometimes a cessation of adult nightmares usually occurs as the dreamer feels more confident, more mature, and thus less close to the helpless feelings of childhood.

PROFILE OF THE NIGHTMARE SUFFERER

Recent in-depth studies carried out at Ernest Hartmann's sleep laboratory at the Shattuck Hospital in Boston have provided information about the personalities of people clearly reporting nightmares rather than night terrors. Using newspaper ads, subjects were recruited who had frequent nightmares as a long-term condition. One study examined thirty-eight adults reporting nightmares at least once per week for at least one year and beginning in childhood.[24] A second study compared another twelve frequent nightmare sufferers with twelve people who reported vivid dreams but no nightmares and twelve others who reported neither nightmares nor vivid dreams.[25] All the subjects were interviewed and given a battery of psychological tests including the Rorschach Inkblot Technique and several personality inventories; some were also monitored in the sleep laboratory.[26]

Individuals in the nightmare groups from both of these studies were no different in intelligence from those in the comparison groups, and likewise there were no clearcut physical differences in appearance distinguishing the groups. The nightmare subjects were different in having jobs or lifestyles related to the arts or other creative pursuits; they ranged from painters, poets, and musicians to craftspersons, teachers, and nontraditional therapists. No blue-collar workers or white-collar executives or office personnel were found who had frequent nightmares, but there were many such workers in the comparison groups.

The artistic and creative interest of the nightmare subjects was a lifelong characteristic. These subjects felt themselves to be in some way unusual for as long as they could remember and often described themselves as sensitive in various ways. Some were sensitive to bright light or loud sound, most could be easily hurt emotionally, and some were quite empathic or sensitive to others' feelings. However, no extreme trauma could be discerned in their histories.

More commonly than in the comparison groups, those with nightmares described their adolescence as stormy and difficult, often with bouts of depression and thoughts of suicide. They tended to rebel by using drugs and alcohol, fighting with parents, or running away. From adolescence on, the nightmare sufferers appeared to be extremely open and trusting people—perhaps too trusting, making them defenseless and vulnerable. They often became quickly involved in difficult, entangling friendships and love relationships from which they could not easily escape.

However, these nightmare sufferers were *not* especially anxious, angry, or depressed people. Some were vulnerable to mental illness: 70 percent of them had been in psychotherapy, and 15 percent had previously been admitted to mental hospitals; but at the time of the interviews, as a group they were functioning quite well in life.

Hartmann and his associates described the creative, sensitive, and vulnerable nightmare subjects as having "thin boundaries" in many different senses. They had thin interpersonal boundaries—that is, they became involved with others very quickly; thin ego boundaries, being extremely aware of their inner wishes and fears; and thin sexual boundaries—they easily imagined being of the opposite sex, and many fantasized or engaged in bisexual activity. They also had thin group boundaries, for they did not strongly identify themselves with a single community or ethnic group. Their sleep-wakefulness boundaries were thin, for they often experienced in-between states of consciousness, unsure whether they were awake, asleep, or dreaming. Some would awaken from one dream only to find themselves in another.[27]

TREATMENT OF NIGHTMARES

Treatment is not usually required for nightmares. Parents of children ages three through six, when nightmares are most common, should be aware that the occurrence of nightmares is not abnormal. Talking with these children and allowing them to express any fearful feelings may be helpful, as is checking the children's environment at home and school for any potential sources of fear or anxiety.

Most of the adult subjects with frequent nightmares in the above-mentioned studies had never sought treatment specifically for their nightmares, though many had sought it for other conditions, such as stress or depression. The majority had accepted their terrifying dreams as part of themselves and sometimes made use of them in their creative endeavors. However, some sufferers wanted treatment specifically for their nightmares. Judging from published accounts of case reports and a few controlled studies, a variety of therapeutic techniques have been used with success.

In a recent review of psychological therapies for nightmares,[28] psychologist Gordon Halliday suggested four distress-producing features of the nightmare and proposed that treatment may reduce the distress by altering any of these features: the nightmare's uncontrollability, its perceived sense of reality, the dreadful and anxiety-producing story line, and the nightmare's believed importance. He categorized treatment techniques into these classes: desensitization and related behavioral procedures, psychoanalytic and cathartic techniques, story-line alteration procedures, and "face [the danger] and conquer [it]" approaches.

Desensitization and related behavioral procedures first identify the fear-generating components of the nightmares and then desensitize the dreamer to those elements through relaxation procedures, invoking pleasant imagery, or repeated exposure of those elements to the dreamer in a therapeutic setting. Psychoanalytic and cathartic techniques attempt to convey to dreamers an understanding of their nightmares in the context of their life situations and developmental histories, to allow suppressed or repressed emotion to be appropriately released, and to strengthen their adaptive mechanisms. Story-line alteration procedures try to change the nightmares through imagination or hypnotic suggestion by rehearsing different endings, confronting the nightmare figures, or modifying some detail. The "face and conquer" approaches consist of instructions to the dreamer to face and confront the nightmare figures when the dreamer is next experiencing an actual nightmare dream state. Several other methods that have been used clinically but not yet reported in the case literature include teaching dreamers, especially children, to call upon a "dream friend" for help[29] and restaging the nightmares in collages or drawings.[30]

We are currently investigating a "face and conquer" treatment procedure that attempts to teach frequent nightmare subjects to attain a lucid dream state in order to reduce the frequency and severity of their terrifying dreams. A lucid dream is one in which the sleeper is aware *during the dream* that he or she is dreaming and feels to be in full possession of mental functions as if awake. This awareness permits the dreamer to make choices as the dream occurs. For example, the dreamer may be walking through an unusual landscape, realize that the experience is a dream, and decide to fly into the air to see the dream landscape from a new perspective.

In nonlucid dreams, which are more common, there is generally a sense of the dream experience happening *to* the dreamer with little feeling of choice about what occurs. Thus, when confronted by a threatening figure in a nightmare, the dreamer usually tries to run away from it. By becoming lucid in the nightmare, the dreamer could then choose to turn and face the threatening figure and possibly master what is feared.

In nearly all of the published reports,[31] clinical accounts,[32] and first-person descriptions[33] of utilizing the lucid dream state to deal with nightmares, the actual dreamers perceived and felt their encounters to be positive, enriching, and empowering experiences both during and after their dreams. However, given that most of these persons are from a normal population, it is possible that these observations may not generalize to a population of frequent nightmare sufferers. Also, though such a treatment has therapeutic potential, it does involve some risk, because there are isolated accounts of negative lucid dream experience.[34]

The lucid-dream treatment approach has the potential to alter three of the four distress-producing aspects of the nightmare suggested by Halliday. Once one achieves lucidity within a nightmare, the nightmare's uncontrolability can be altered, because the dreamer can choose and act to change his or her response to the threatening images; the nightmare's perceived sense of reality can be altered, because the dreamer understands that the experience is a dream rather than part of everyday physical external reality; and the nightmare's dreadful and anxiety-producing story line can be altered as a result of the changed response of the dreamer. Other dreamworkers, such as Stephen LaBerge, may contend that the fourth distress-producing aspect, the believed importance of the nightmare, also may be altered, because lucid dreamers "realize that they themselves contain, and thus transcend, the entire dream world and all of its contents, because they know that their imaginations have created the dream."[35]

The major limitation cited by Halliday in utilizing the lucid dream state as a treatment modality for nightmares is that it is not yet known how to reliably induce this experience. Psychologist Joseph Dane has developed a posthypnotic suggestion technique for inducing the lucid dream state in hypnotically susceptible women. Using this technique, seven of the eight women in one group of his study succeeded in having verified lucid dreams.[36] This is a promising approach for frequent nightmare sufferers, because there is evidence that they have higher hypnotizability scores than others.[37]

Two recent studies indicate that learning lucid dreaming could be a viable treatment method for frequent nightmare sufferers. The first is a study of boundary characteristics by Franklin Galvin,[38] which matched forty spontaneous lucid dreamers with forty frequent nightmare dreamers and forty nonlucid and relatively nightmare-free dreamers (ordinary dreamers). In comparison to the ordinary dreamers, both the lucid dreamers and the nightmare dreamers were shown to have "thin boundaries." In addition, a number of the spontaneous lucid dreamers stated that they had first developed lucidity during frightening dreams.

The second is a case study by Andrew Brylowski,[39] which related the treatment of a thirty-five-year-old woman, Ms. D., with a history of major depression and a diagnosis of borderline personality disorder. She reported one to four nightmares per week and had a history of recurrent nightmares of variable frequency and intensity since age ten. The treatment focused on alleviating her nightmares using lucid dreaming. Within the first four weekly sessions, the introduction of lucidity into the patient's dream life coincided with a decrease in the frequency and intensity of her nightmares.

The report of a dream by Ms. D. seven weeks into the treatment illustrates her ability to avert a potential nightmare by using lucidity to convert a threat into a learning experience.

> Ms. D. was walking up huge grey stone stairs leading to a fortress or castle. Looking down she saw a colleague and felt thrilled. The stairs then extended over a moat. She stopped to look at the water and a vicious grey shark with big white teeth surfaced. It propelled itself along the stairs toward her. Ms. D. was frozen with fear and couldn't move. She then realized that she had been having a good dream until the shark appeared; then she thought: "It is a dream!" She was unable to do anything but stare at the shark. The shark changed into a huge whale that smiled and was no longer terrorizing. She awakened in peace.[40]

Though she had previously thought of things she might do when she became lucid in a frightening dream, at the moment of fear she could only stare and not run. When she stood her ground and faced the terror rather than attempting to flee, the threatening image was transformed into an acceptable figure positively acknowledging her. Facing the fear in her dream enabled her to wake in peace. Altering her nightmares also facilitated Ms. D. in making positive changes to deal with her waking emotions.

The skills Ms. D. learned in lucid dreaming extended into areas of her waking life. After another nine weeks of treatment, she reported a dream in which she was working on a painting with two colors, each scintillating. Upon realizing it was a dream, she created a third color by blending the first two. With this new color she added depth and dimension to the painting. This accomplishment in her dream prompted Ms. D. to complete other art projects in her waking life that she had left unfinished.

As Sigmund Freud's nightmare was able to retain "its imperishable value . . . by becoming a driving force in the making of a genius,"[41] and as Carl Jung was initiated into the secrets of the earth by a nightmare and later brought light into this realm of darkness, so too have the nightmares of others heralded some meaningful change in their lives. For those with frequent nightmares, the use of the lucid dream state could offer a unique opportunity to begin such a change.

Jayne I. Gackenbach

Women and Meditators as Gifted Lucid Dreamers

I would like to explore a set of interesting relationships that have convinced me that in females there is a propensity to dream lucidly. This capacity appears to be "hard-wired" in the physical makeup of female brains. Specifically, I will propose that the female brain has a neuroelectrical organization that predisposes it under certain waking conditions (such as the practice of meditation) to recall dreams and to be conscious during dreaming.

PARALLELS BETWEEN LUCIDITY AND MEDITATION

Electroencephalographic (EEG) research on the electrical activity of the brain during meditation and sleep supports H. T. Hunt's idea that lucid dreaming is a form of spontaneously emerging meditation.[1] There are several lines of converging evidence that support the lucidity—meditation link, most of it carried out with practitioners of Transcendental Meditation (TM). I am going to summarize this evidence before considering my hypothesis that lucidity is naturally female.

Hunt originally based this idea on his observations that lucid dreamers and TM meditators had similar experiences. However, there are now several studies of meditators and lucid dreamers that reveal important psychological and physiological parallels as well. For example, both lucid dreamers and meditators exhibit fewer stress-related personality characteristics than people who do not meditate[2] and people who do not have lucid dreams.[3] In comparison with other people tested, both meditators and lucid dreamers are able to become highly focused on one activity, are able to become "caught up" in an experience, and are aware of their inner thoughts and internal processes. In addition, meditators and lucid dreamers find it easier to recall their dreams and tend to be "field independent" (that is, they could find their way out of a forest more easily than "field-dependent" people, because they are not as easily influenced by the people or objects in their environment). Meditators find it easier to remember their dreams and may even be able to use their rapid-eye-movement (REM) periods more efficiently—that is, they may recall just as many dreams as do other people, even though their total percentage of REM might decrease once they start meditating.[4]

When the dreams of meditators are compared to those of people who do not meditate, the former tend to have more lucid dreams. And these dreams are more likely to be *transpersonal* in nature, containing images of white light, experiences of flying or floating, and encounters with spiritual and mythological beings. Even when researchers allow that meditators remember their dreams more often than nonmeditators, the relationship between meditative practice and lucid dreaming remains.[5] Furthermore, claims of breath suspension and profound experiences of clarity or transcendence during meditation are related to claims of being aware during non-REM sleep.[6]

The physiological parallels between lucidity and meditation may be of particular interest. These parallels will lead directly to my hypothesis that lucid dreaming is a natural female capacity. Although there appears to be more neuroelectrical activity in the brain and other parts of the nervous system during lucidity, some research indicates that the body's muscles actually are "more asleep" than they are during nonlucid REM dreaming. For example, one investigator measured a spinal reflex that is stimulated at the knee in a subject in REM sleep and, again, after the subject indicated (by eye-movement signals) that a lucid dream was occurring. This spinal reflex, which shows the degree to which the body is awake or asleep, is measured by electrodes that chart the electrical activity in the knee. This reflex was even more asleep (or suppressed) during lucid dreaming than during ordinary REM sleep, indicating that the lucid dreamer's body is even more paralyzed than it normally is during REM.[7] In other words, when you are experiencing REM sleep, you are essentially paralyzed from the neck down; but when you are lucid in REM sleep, you will be even more profoundly paralyzed.

Think of a time when your arm fell asleep. At its worst and deepest paralysis, you could not move it at all. That is what your body is like during lucid dreaming. As you begin to have some sensations in your arm but still cannot move it, your bodily condition resembles that of nonlucid REM sleep.

The dampening of this physical reaction during lucidity may support Hunt's idea that lucidity is a state of consciousness resembling Transcendental Meditation. Three TM researchers have reported that advanced meditators who have just finished meditation recover the full functioning of the spinal reflex in question more quickly than other people do.[8] Perhaps lucid dreamers suppress their reflexes more than usual because it helps them maintain lucidity. TM meditators may do the same, but once they come out of meditation, they can reactivate their reflexes quickly.

It is possible that these phenomena are two sides of the same coin. Both abilities suggest that lucid dreamers and TM meditators develop an adaptation to the state they are in and can move quickly and easily to another state, adapting more efficiently to the body's changing needs than can other people. At this point, of course, such an idea is speculative at best; much more research needs to be carried out to test this conjecture.

The EEG work with dream lucidity is fairly limited at this time, the bulk having been reported by Hunt and his associates. In their studies, they explored the lucidity–meditation link by examining alpha waves in lucid and nonlucid REM sleep. (Alpha activity was explored because it generally increases during TM meditation.) Hunt's group found that there was increased alpha in prelucid and early lucid REM periods; they have compared this to the first phases of waking meditation.[9] One researcher has conducted a pilot study with a long-term TM meditator who reported lucid dreams frequently, observing that bursts of alpha and theta brain waves seemed to be "riding on" the normal EEG record, both in REM and non-REM sleep. Indeed, the EEG record was described as resembling that of a TM meditator experiencing breath suspension and transcendence during waking meditation.[10] Some other researchers have not been able to confirm this observation, but they had requested that dreamers make eye signals when lucidity begins—an attempt that might have disrupted their alpha and theta activity, both of which have been associated with a suspension of voluntary effort.

M. A. West points out that a more sophisticated examination of EEG changes in meditation would include the investigation of EEG "coherence"— the constancy of EEG relationships.[11] Deepak Chopra remarks that coherence "is really a measure of the integration of neurons everywhere in the central nervous system. A good analogy would be when you go to hear the Boston Symphony, and you arrive before the performance while players are still practicing on their own as they tune up. Each performer is playing his [or her] instrument on the right notes, the right frequency, but the overall result is chaotic. There is no constancy in the relationship between the performers, and therefore what you get is noise. Once the performance starts, they are still playing the same notes on the same instruments, but there is a constancy of relationship—there is music. This constancy of relationship is coherence."[12]

Once we better understand the relationship of coherence to meditation, we will have the means to more thoroughly explore the subtle types of consciousness that occur during sleep. For example, some investigators have been studying reports of especially profound meditative experience that TM meditators refer to as *transcending*. In one study, transcendence was related to alpha, theta, and beta coherence on the EEG;[13] in another, it was related to EEG alpha coherence.[14] I have taken the position that REM sleep is associated with a greater degree of theta coherence across the two halves of the brain than non-REM sleep. Because lucidity generally occurs in REM sleep, it is likely that meditativelike experiences would take place there as well.

Coherence is especially apparent in times of transition between states, as in the movement to waking from sleeping. In one study, people who recalled their dreams frequently showed a greater continuity of rhythmic EEG in transition from sleep to wakefulness. This effect was especially pronounced among the female subjects in the study.[15] In other words, individuals who often remember their dreams are accessing information from a coherent state of brain functioning by remaining, in some sense, in the sleeping state. One of the strongest findings in the research literature on both individual differences and dream content is the association between lucidity and high dream recall. Lucid dreamers are generally high dream recallers and, in general, lucid dreams are easily recalled. Therefore, it would be logical to propose that lucid dreamers would show more coherence than nonlucid dreamers when they make the transition from sleep to wakefulness.

In a pilot study of one lucid dreamer, Stephen LaBerge (who has found no gender differences among lucid dreamers) compared a five-minute lucid dream during REM sleep to the fifteen minutes of REM that preceded it, finding an increase of EEG alpha coherence during lucidity.[16] Although these results are highly preliminary, it is of interest to observe that LaBerge measured coherence at the brain's parietal lobes, the site of visual-spatial functioning. In addition, the parietal lobes were the location of EEG alpha coherence among field-independent individuals, a personality style that characterizes high dream recallers, lucid dreamers, and meditators.[17]

I hope that I have adequately demonstrated that it is quite fair to characterize lucid dreaming as a state of consciousness similar to that sought in the practice of meditation, at least of Transcendental Meditation (the technique practiced by most of the subjects in these studies). But what of the gender differences? I needed to demonstrate the lucidity–meditation connection first because my argument of a natural female propensity to lucidity is grounded in the work on EEG coherence and its relationship to both meditation and REM sleep.

GENDER DIFFERENCES IN EEG COHERENCE

Although there is no unanimity on the topic, there are any number of studies that have found EEG coherence (both between hemispheres and within each hemisphere) to be greater in women than in men. For example, there are fewer differences between the left and right hemispheres of women's brains when both genders undertaking a variety of problem-solving tasks during wakefulness are compared.[18] It is quite possible that women have more abundant fibers in the corpus callosum, that part of the brain that connects the hemispheres. However, neurologist Richard Restak claims that even though gender differences in brain makeup are strongly suspected, there is no scientist who has "convincingly demonstrated an anatomic difference between the brain structures of males and females," and suggests that the observed gender dissimilarities may be the result of "chemical changes in brain function resulting from the influence of sex hormones in early prenatal development."[19] Another team of researchers concluded that women's "overall increase in general coherence . . . [demonstrates] a more synchronized and less lateralized pattern of neuroelectrical neurological organization."[20]

To recap the major points of my thesis: (1) Females show more EEG coherence during wakefulness; (2) EEG coherence is associated with periods of lucid dreaming as well as "transcendence" during meditation; and (3) people who recall their dreams frequently, especially females, show more coherence upon awakening than do low recallers; hence, (4) females should report more dream recall, more lucid dreaming, and more "transcending" meditative experiences than males.

I am going to briefly point out some evidence that further supports the linkage between lucidity and meditation among females. Enhanced parasympathetic nervous-system function and biological relaxation in TM meditators has been reported, supporting the claim that TM reduces stress.[21] However, only in the case of female subjects is there an association between parasympathetic functioning (nervous-system activity related to biological relaxation) and frequent lucid dreaming.[22] In a mail survey on lucid dreaming, a pattern of gender differences consistent with the meditation literature emerged. Intelligence, creativity, and low anxiety were positively associated with the practice of meditation and with frequent lucid dreaming; however, these associations to lucidity were found only with women.[23]

Many writers have commented on the association between regular meditation and improved physical health. Claims range from the enhancement of relaxation to a slowing down of the aging process. In my doctoral dissertation, I examined health variables as a function of lucid-dreaming frequency, finding that female lucid dreamers tended to be physically healthy but that there was no such relationship in the case of males. I also found, in most of my later studies, that women report more lucid dreams than men (although female subjects also tend to recall more dreams in general than male subjects).[24]

These relationships were examined in a study conducted in 1988 in which I looked directly at the effects of meditation and gender on the frequency of lucid dreaming. Working with Robert Cranson and Charles Alexander at Maharishi International University, I collected self-reports on lucid dreaming frequency from eighty nonmeditators of both genders who also differed in level of dream recall. When we controlled for the fact that women recall more dreams than men, we did not find significant gender differences in lucid dreaming. However, when we further divided the groups into meditators and nonmeditators, we found that meditating women showed an especially high incidence of lucidity relative to nonmeditating female subjects. Meditation enhances coherence; perhaps this contributed to the difference between the two groups. In any event, the difference was not found among meditating and nonmeditating male subjects, supporting my idea that their neuroelectrical "hard-wiring" is different from women's.

Exploration of coherence of the brain's hemispheres offers considerable promise for further research. I have touched on the relationships among three areas—gender, meditation, and lucidity during REM sleep—and have suggested that the naturally occurring brain coherence in women gives them an advantage in having the experiences that result from meditation practice, which enhances this type of integration. Regular meditation practice appears to increase both dream recall and dream frequency for both sexes, but especially for women.

NEUROELECTRICAL ANDROGYNY: THE MALE SIDE OF THE PICTURE

It would not be fair to ignore the male brain. Relative to the female brain, the left hemisphere of the male brain (for most right-handed men and some left-handed men) is more highly specialized for verbal, logical tasks, whereas the right is more specialized for artistic, emotional activities. Although solid evidence is lacking, some researchers suspect this is due to brain-chemical differences between the genders, others claim that there are more fibers that connect the two hemispheres in female brains, and still others attribute the differences to cultural practices.

In any event, a similar situation emerges from the studies of lucidity and meditation. Relative to nonmeditators and nonlucid dreamers, the left hemisphere of meditators and lucid dreamers is more highly specialized for verbal, logical tasks, whereas the right is more specialized for artistic, emotional activities. We might ask whether the greater brain lateralization function found in males might be related to the meditation–lucidity effect.

This may seem contradictory. On the one hand, I am saying that during meditation and lucid dreaming the brain works all at once, showing greater coherence; on the other, that those who have had experiences with meditation and lucidity have brains that are more specialized in their functioning. An attempt has been made to explain this paradox by a team of researchers from Maharishi International University. They explain that any part of the brain can engage in specialized or general functions. When a part is involved in a special function (as with, for example, the left hemisphere's activation while someone is reading), that hemisphere is low in coherence. At the same time, the other hemisphere would be high in coherence, serving to help integrate the left hemisphere's specific activity (for example, by providing an emotional context for a story being read). These researchers argue that an individual probably would prefer to engage in activities that increase coherence, both between and within hemispheres, because this integration would imply an enhanced cognitive or thinking ability as well as an increased emotional stability.[25]

Thus, although a key sign of depth in meditation is the degree to which parts of the brain are working in rhythm (high EEG coherence), the result of such brain experiences is that outside the practice of meditation (and lucid dreaming), meditators' brains are more specialized for function. In this case, high coherence occurs in the part of the brain that functions *less* in a task relative to the low coherence of the part that functions *more* during a task. As a result, scientists observe a lateralization that differentiates brain hemispheres for certain specific functions, such as writing, singing, or evoking a mental image.

Are these reported gender differences more advantageous to men or to women? This depends on the context of the activity. Males who start out being more lateralized will have a lead in the lateralization effect of meditation or lucid dreaming; females who start out being less lateralized and with higher EEG coherence will have a lead in obtaining the high EEG coherence states found with profound transcending meditative experiences or in experiencing frequent lucidity while dreaming.

Further, each gender moves toward the specialty of the other. Women who frequently report spontaneous lucid dreams have been found to show a higher degree of interhemispheric specialization than those who had never dreamed lucidly.[26] Although these women who have frequent lucid dreams are relatively well lateralized for specific functions (such as reading music or solving arithmetic problems), it is unlikely that they are as lateralized as most male lucid dreamers.

As an illustration, let's examine the kinesthetic abilities that are related to the use of touch and to cues about the body's position in space. While women who are exceptionally lucid while dreaming report more vivid kinesthetic imagery than nonlucid women, no such difference was found among men.[27] However, when asked to perform a kinesthetic task—placing an arm in a certain position on a table, with eyes blindfolded—male lucid dreamers did better than nonlucid men. There were no such differences between the two groups of women.[28]

These findings suggest that when primarily engaged with the *external* environment (the outside world), the male brain's natural organization is enhanced by the experience of meditation or lucidity; whereas when primarily engaged with the *internal* environment (imagination, and mental imagery), the female brain's natural organization is brought into play and is enhanced by meditation or lucidity. The experience of meditation (while awake) and lucidity (while asleep) enhances the brain's differentiation, or specialization, in women while enhancing the coherence, or integration, of its parts in men.

These techniques move us toward the neuroelectrical equivalent of androgyny—a holistic level of functioning. This androgyny (a reconciliation of male and female attributes) may be based in the nervous system, but it extends its influence to the psychological, social, and spiritual levels of life.

Linda Lane Magallón and Barbara Shor

Shared Dreaming: Joining Together in Dreamtime

 In January of 1987, Kay dreamed: "I reexperienced [school], feeling really confident. Everyone liked me and I was aware of it and I really felt good. There was a flag in class and I started singing 'America The Beautiful,' getting everyone to join in."

That same night, Mitchell dreamed: "A good number of the people in the restaurant (maybe everyone) stand up and sing in a 'cheer' fashion. I'm 'eating' some special national pride . . . it is very good. I stand and proudly acknowledge this."

Kay and Mitchell lived several hundred miles away from each other and had never met, except through written correspondence. Both were members of a dream team that regularly incubated dreams on prearranged target nights for specific purposes. The goal for this dream-in was to "investigate your dream location." While Kay saw her dreamspace as a classroom and Mitchell envisioned his as a restaurant, there were striking similarities in the content and emotional correspondences between their two dreams.

SAME TIME, SAME PLACE, SAME DREAM

Shared dreaming has a very simple premise: A group of people agree to try to meet in the same dream at the same time in the same dreamspace and to remember the same details when they wake. An underlying part of this premise is that shared dreaming is a learned skill that requires, above all, a joyous sense of play and a large supply of patience and perseverance.

Once dreamers believe they have begun to share the same dreamspace and similar conversations, they also begin a searching examination of what this all means. Shared dreamers quickly realize that they've been launched into a mutual exploration of boundaries—personal and societal—as well as an examination of the nature of consciousness itself, which often impels them to discard old, limiting belief systems. Shared dreaming seems to be a first step toward mutually accessing a deep level of emotional response that is a true reflection of each participant's inner concerns. This state of awareness can be used to create a forum in which a group of any size can hold conferences, create new projects and ideas, resolve conflicts, enhance cooperative efforts, and tap into the kind of information that appears to be available only in dreams shared with others.

Defining Our Terms

Mutual dreaming is the umbrella term for dreams that appear to contain correspondences with the dreams of one or more other dreamers. These can range from the "hits" (extremely close correspondences) in telepathic or group dreaming to the pooled experiences of a shared dream.

There are many factors that influence mutual correspondences in dream content. Among these are telepathic or other anomalous connections between dreamers; shared or similar events in the dreamer's waking lives that are incorporated into their dreams; and the joint symbolic vocabulary many people develop through knowing each other over time.

What is critically important here is the degree of purposefulness on the dreamer's part—from passively experiencing content, correspondences, and synchronous dream events to actively incubating dreams to meet the target night goals of the project. However, whether the dreamers' intentions are passive or active, the correspondences in the content of dreams from one dreamer to another will range from startling clarity to considerable opaqueness.

Since all of these factors may influence mutual dreaming, some of the following classifications may overlap.

Group dreaming is the developmental step that precedes shared dreaming. Participants are simply trying to dream together in simultaneously separate and joint dream realities. The evidence for success lies in "hits," in which two or more dreamers have a similar experience; witness a similar person, thing or event; or share a symbol, a color, an emotion, or an underlying theme or idea.

Examples of group dreaming include Robert Van de Castle and Henry Reed's "Dream Helper Ceremony,"[1] in which people purposely incubate dreams around a particular person's waking-life issue. This process might also employ Montague Ullman's dream-sharing techniques[2] in which the members of the dream group meet to compare their individual dream reports.

Synchronous dreaming entails no active intent to dream together: the hits between dream reports or between dreams and outer events are purely serendipitous.

Telepathic dreaming concerns at least two people, a sleeping *receiver* and a *sender* who remains awake. The sender attempts to transmit randomly selected target material—an image from a photo or picture, a sound, or a word or phrase—to the receiver, who attempts to incorporate it in his or her dreams. This was the approach pioneered in the Maimonides Medical Center dream-laboratory experiments, which attempted to rule out any possibility of dream or target correspondences being due to shared pre-sleep experiences, fraud, or chance.[3] When telepathic dream experiments involve more than one receiver, mutual correspondences between dreamers may bounce from one receiver's dream to another, as well as between the dreamers and the sender.[4]

Parallel dreaming refers to correspondences between dreams of people who are actively engaged in a cooperative dream project. No distinction is made between the sender and the receiver. In others words, A may dream of B, and B may dream of A, but A and B won't meet in the same dream.

Shared dreaming involves two or more dreamers apparently meeting in the same dreamscape and experiencing similar events. Although the dreamers are attempting to dream together on the same night, because of their geographical distance from each other, as well as differences in each individual's cycles of sleeping and dreaming, their corresponding shared dreams don't have to occur on exactly the same date or at the same hour.

MUTUAL-DREAMING PROJECTS

Some notable group-dreaming projects aimed specifically at inducing mutual dreams included Dreams 10, sponsored by the Poseidia Institute in Virginia Beach in 1983 and 1984;[5] the International Lucidity Project, facilitated by

Linda Magallón from 1984 to 1987;[6] and the Group Dreaming Project, conducted by Barbara Shor in conjunction with Dr. Mary Schmitt's "Living Systems Approach to Creativity" seminars in 1986.[7]

Along with the ongoing Bicoastal Shared Dreaming Project, the authors are facilitating several additional shared-dreaming projects. Also, Charles Upton is running Gate of Horn, an ongoing shared dreaming activity, which includes the U.S.–U.S.S.R. "Dream Bridge"[8] that appeared to link Soviet and U.S. dreamers across vast physical and ideological distances.

Because shared dreaming is the cutting edge of dream experimentation, there hasn't been a great deal written about it yet. Notable exceptions include Campbell,[9] Castaneda,[10] Fox,[11] Roberts,[12] and Watkins.[13] In addition, Hart[14] collected a small group of spontaneous mutual dreams, which he called "reciprocal dreams," and Donahoe[15] provided his own case examples. Descriptive models for mutual dreaming include Faraday's "psychic radar,"[16] Taub-Bynam's "family unconscious,"[17] and Shor's "holographic dream machine."[18]

Old Skills and New

Just as shared dreamers don't have to dream together at exactly the same time or place, neither do they need to share the same repertoire of dream skills, such as lucidity, out-of-body (OBE) travel, or precognition. Over time, the dreamers discover what their particular specialities are and they begin pooling their skills to enhance the group's chances of actually participating in the same dream. However, shared dreamers sometimes acquire each other's skills by osmosis and evolve new techniques as they explore altered states of consciousness from within the dreamstate. Separately and together, the dreamers create a composite view of the whole event. Each dreamer's version of the shared dream expands and enriches the collective dreamscape.

One of the new skills dreamers often develop is the creation of a shared language. The process is like creating a work of *découpage*—cutting, pasting, and laminating together bits of information from the dreamers' separate visual, verbal, and metaphorical dream vocabularies into a new, coherent pattern of communication. For example, at one point, the color red—on cars, carpets, scaffolding, and flames—was skipping from dreamer to dreamer, night to night, and group to group until we realized that it was our mutual signal that some form of shared dream communication was taking place.

Another of our new skills is the ability to jointly create a meeting place.[19] In addition, we're learning to recognize each other in the dreamstate no matter what our outward appearance might be.[20] And, best of all, we've discovered that we don't have to wait until the group has learned to share the same dream to tackle mutually important projects; the skills and results develop simultaneously.

A Question of Boundaries

In group dreaming, after the initial euphoria begins to wear off, dreamers often start to encounter a layer of fear and conflict within themselves and within the group as a whole. As the dreamers begin to reach across personal and societal boundaries, they may discover their individual limits of approach or aversion. As a result, they find themselves facing many of the basic problems that beset humankind: issues of trust, fear, anger, disappointment, challenges to self-esteem, competitiveness, jealousy, unmet expectations, false assumptions, and the narrow horizons of cultural blinders. Some participants will drop out at this stage. However, others will persevere and help create a new level of balance and acceptance within themselves and within the group as well, using the mutual dreaming experience to transform initial anxiety into an adventure.

Shared dreamers sometimes build on their experiences with mutual dreaming to push boundaries even further. Some of them claim that not only are they in intimate dream communication with their own and each other's friends and family members, but that they have occasional contacts with a number of apparent strangers. This is when questions may begin to arise about whether our consensus reality and our notion of privacy is simply an illusion. Do we have rigid boundaries at all?

Decoding the Messages

The hits that indicate the success of telepathic dream experiments and group-dreaming projects appear to be a developmental phase in shared dreaming, where the ultimate goal is to appear in the same dream with one's partners. There, the evidence of success is clear: you either experience the same events or you don't. It is the interfaces, where shared dreamers are shifting from hits to "being there," that are the most fascinating—and difficult—to evaluate. We've found that content analysis is a very effective approach for comparing and evaluating mutual dreams.[21] For example, the following results emerged from an examination of shared-dream reports for January 2, 1988, from a team of seven participants who had no specific goal for that target night.

Common themes included business and finances (four out of the seven dreams). Two of the men reported athletic feats: David practiced with heavy weights, while Bill readied himself for a weight-lifting display.

Synchronous symbology occurs when the same symbol appears in more than one person's dream. In this case, three people dreamed of fish and another three dreamed about windows; squares and rectangles also showed up in four dreams. Some dream events were nearly identical. Rina dreamed of a sudden heavy rain; David of a flooding rain. Among these dreamers, too, red vehicles kept appearing. In addition, it's interesting that four out of five vehicles were not enclosed.

Parallel phraseology indicates similar descriptive word patterns. Rina reported, "I'm sitting on an oddly shaped bridge or seat or passage over water and can slide along to change my position." Edward dreamed of men sitting on a long canoe that slid down the street. His dream report also mentioned, "The wind comes into the apartment through the closed windows and blows me about"; while Elsie dreamed, "Inside a white octagonal room with large windows the wind increases. I know it's coming to lift me off the ground."

Aggregate emotional content is more subtle and sometimes more difficult to detect, but similar images and parallel phraseology provide clues. David dreamed of being trapped behind a retractable accordion gate, but his emotional state was not the expected one: "There's no big deal," he wrote. "I appear calm all the way through." Edward's dream contained many beautiful spider webs. Although he was concerned because he didn't want to become entangled in them, he said; "I feel fairly detached and able to see the absurdity of the situation." Both dreams reported potential conflict or entrapment, and yet the dreamers' emotional responses were alike.

USEFUL TIPS FOR SHARED DREAMERS

Here are some suggestions for organizing and participating in a shared-dreaming group:

Agree to try meeting in a jointly chosen or co-created dreamspace on a specific night of the week or month. Do this for a minimum of six sessions, setting firm target nights and deadlines. Don't get discouraged if you don't actually make it to the chosen place, or if you don't all manage to get there together; you haven't failed. Shared dreamers are only beginning to learn how to do this. Think of sharing the same dream as the final port of call on a voyage of discovery.

Try to meet in the waking state at least once beforehand if you live in the same area. Observe your companions with care so you'll be able to recognize them—or their characteristic feeling tones—when you meet in dreams. Eye contact, hugging, or holding hands helps everyone connect at the feeling level.

If you don't live in the same area, you might want to incubate shared dreams in which you meet in some well-known spot, such as the top of the Eiffel Tower, or in the King's Chamber in the Great Pyramid. It doesn't matter if you've never been there yourself; the dream discussion of differing views and viewpoints and imagined details can be fascinating.

If you choose a natural area, select something specific and detailed, such as "Meet you in front of Old Faithful during an eruption," rather than "Let's meet outside in a natural setting." It's hard enough to meet in a specific spot; it's nearly impossible without a well-defined and specific setting. For example, a group that met awake on a certain museum's steps, and then attempted to meet there again asleep, dreamed of every sort of staircase imaginable, although not always in that museum—or in any museum, for that matter. It's very helpful for each shared dreamer to have a photocopied image or two of the proposed meeting site as an aid in incubating the shared dream.

Decide whether you want to set specific target-night goals in addition to the basic one of actually getting to the appointed place and seeing everyone. For example, you might want to "have a party," "discuss the dreamstate," or "create a ritual or ceremony." If you do decide to add specific goals, decide whether you want to list them in advance or to allow them to evolve out of the previous target night's shared-dream themes.

Incubating Shared Dreams. Send black-and-white photos (or photocopies) of each team member to all participants. For the fun of it, you might want to postpone this for the first target night or two. That way, when you finally look at everyone's picture, you can determine whether you actually may have seen your unknown team members in your dreams.

Sharing personal objects can help focus everyone's attention, but it should be kept simple. Some groups have traded seashells or pebbles picked up on walks, favorite poems, small gourds, cut out felt, fabric moons, crystals, sachets, or bags of herbal tea.

Before bedtime, relax and clear your mind of everything except your intention to have a shared dream and to attempt to meet your fellow dreamers in the appointed dreamspace. You may want to reread the previous target night's dreams and commentary. As you fall asleep, look at the pictures of your meeting place and of your team members, then tuck them and any dream-enhancing objects under your pillow or mattress. Ask your highest guidance for assistance during the night's adventures.

Choose one person as commentary editor or take turns writing the commentary. Commentary editors will search the dream reports for group themes, hits, conversational subjects, signs of progress or blockage, and clues to the next target night's subject, assuming you've decided to use the approach.

Upon waking, write down your dreams. Title and/or number each dream for easy reference. Date them using the night of dreaming as well as the day of recall, for example, "May 10–11, 1989." Type, word process, or print dreams neatly, adding brief personal comments if you choose, and send them off immediately to the commentary editor for that session. Keep your dream report short. However, little surprises such as cartoons, drawings, jokes, or poems are always treasured.

Editors will mail out commentaries, along with copies of everyone's dream reports, to each team member early enough for them to arrive before the next target night.

FUTURE FORWARD

The more we begin to share dreams intentionally and compare our waking dream reports on a regular basis, the more we may come to realize the vast scale of dreaming interconnectedness that exists between all beings. Carl Jung labeled this *the collective unconscious*; however, we believe shared dreamers are pushing beyond this level of mythic awareness to forge a *collective consciousness*.

Having other dreamers recognize us in the dreamstate—even when we don't resemble our waking selves—forces us to reassess who we think we are and to begin removing any limitations we've placed on our human capabilities. The reward for this work is the flowering of newer and deeper levels of trust and information sharing.

Shared dreaming is a complex phenomenon. It may arise from a number of sources, such as telepathy, synchronous events, or shared waking experiences on a personal, national, or even global level. However, those of us who feel a growing ease with this level of intimacy often find that shared dreaming awakens our capacities for compassionate understanding and clear communication. This awakening may well be a necessity if we are going to evolve beyond divisive fears and mistrust, as well as illness, pollution, and other challenges that threaten not only our personal survival but the Earth's.

The prospects for shared dreaming are rich and varied. They range from helping to heal troubled families and developing creative business projects to dealing with global issues and stimulating research on the nature of consciousness by studying what happens when individuals come together in altered states to learn and interact in new and different ways.[22]

An enjoyable and exciting adventure awaits anyone who gathers a group of dreamers with similar affinities to create and share with others in the dreamstate some innovative approaches to resolving specific problems. Shared dreaming may well be a key to creating the possible future. Doris Lessing was prophetic in *The Making of the Representative for Planet Eight* when she asked us, "Do you imagine you dream for yourself alone?"[23]

Jon Tolaas

The Puzzle of
Psychic Dreams

 In a *psychic dream,* the dreamer supposedly obtains information about another person's mental processes (*telepathy*), the physical environment (*clairvoyance*), or a future event (*precognition*) in ways that appear to transcend Western science's current understanding of time, space, and energy. These dreams are also referred to as *anomalous dreams* because of their puzzling nature.

If a person lives to the age of seventy, he or she may spend as much as six years in REM or dreaming sleep,[1] and most of these dreams—psychic as well as ordinary—will be forgotten. Therefore, it is important to study purportedly psychic dreams under rigorous laboratory conditions in order to rule out such explanations as coincidence, deception, sensory cues, and faulty memory. However, most psychic dreams occur not in the laboratory but spontaneously while we are asleep. This does not mean that spontaneous dreams are worthless as research material. On the contrary, increasing knowledge about dreams may help us avoid some common pitfalls in labeling these dreams *psychic* or *anomalous.* In this chapter, we will explore some common sources of error people make when they decide that a dream is psychic.

RECENT REALITY EVENTS AND PSYCHIC DREAMS

The fact that recent events are reflected in our dreams has been apparent for ages, but it was Freud who categorized several types of so-called day residues,[2] all of which were assigned the role of mediating unconscious wishes. In contrast, Jung and Alder gave primary attention to the manifest content of

261

dreams. Adler claimed that dreams typically contain an exogenous factor—a current provocative event for which the dreamer seeks a solution.[3]

Recent events also have been explored by Montague Ullman, who says that an event that is likely to be incorporated in dreams has the quality of novelty in the sense that it catches the person off guard. At the time it is encountered in waking life, there are no immediately available ways of coping with it. According to Ullman, the event is intrusive to the extent that it is linked to earlier unsolved issues from the past, or it may be experienced as novel on the basis of being truly new and outside the range of past experience.[4] This view is in keeping with experimental findings. Kramer studied seven subjects for ten nights under laboratory conditions and found that "daily activities which judges rated as being most prevalent in the night's dreams were the same activities to which the subject had given the highest emotional rating."[5]

In dealing with psychic dreams, unexpected elements are worthy of special attention. For example, at the beginning of February a woman told me she dreamed that the blue anemones were blooming in her garden. In her dream, she was delighted to find a whole bed of vivid blue flowers and bent down to look more closely at them. In reality, it was at least two months too early for blue anemones to sprout. But the morning following her dream, the woman's brother telephoned her quite unexpectedly, saying, "Do you know what I found behind the garage yesterday? The first blue anemones!"

This correspondence may seem at first glance either precognitive (involving the correct prediction of a forthcoming event—her brother's comment), clairvoyant (the correct perception of a distant event—the blooming of the anemones), or telepathic (the correct identification of another person's thought processes—her brother's delight in his discovery). On closer inspection, however, I discovered an alternative explanation. The day before, while the woman was cleaning the windows of her home, she kept looking down at a bed of blue anemone roots, wondering whether or not they were alive. In her brother's part of the country, the climate is extremely mild, allowing anemones to bloom much earlier.

In Ullman's conceptualization, the recent intrusive event (in this case, the woman's gaze at the anemone roots) may have functioned as a polarizing instrument, pulling related past events from memory storage and arranging them into metaphoric statements about significant relationships (in this case, the woman's relationship with her brother). Or the intrusive event could have played its polarizing role by obtaining pertinent information distant in time or space, providing the dream content with a psychic element.

Long experience with dreams has taught me to be particularly attentive to seasonal variations, birthdays, anniversaries, traditional holidays, and festivals. These may be powerful polarizing instruments in our waking lives as well as in our dreams. For example, a young student told me her dream about a female friend. In the dream, the friend was deeply depressed and was walking down to a dark lake to take her life. On awakening, the dreamer felt a strong urge to contact her friend, although she thought her fear was irrational. Nevertheless, the urge was irresistible and she called her friend, who she discovered was in the middle of a deep depression, relying on antidepressive drugs to keep her going.

On the face of it, the dreamer thought that this dream was telepathic. The last time the two students had seen each other, the friend was happy and fit. However, the dreamer recalled that her friend had experienced an intense depression a few years earlier. It was the end of November, it had been raining for several weeks, and the sky was overcast and gray. The present dream occurred at the end of November during a period of very similar weather. There was no way of proving that the dream was precipitated by "meteorological memory," yet we both found it quite likely that it had sprung from an unconscious link between "depressive weather" and her friend's state of mind.

When the link between dream content and waking reality is especially striking, and when a reasonably skeptical dreamer is unable to identify any recent precipitating event around which the dream revolves, the likelihood of the dream being anomalous increases. For example, a sixty-year-old woman dreamed that the flag on the neighboring farm was at half mast. The dream impressed her and she shared it with her husband in the morning. Then, while they were still at the breakfast table, the flag at the adjacent farm was run up at half mast, signifying that someone was dead.

Many such dreams can be explained in terms of sensory cues; the dreamer may pick up signs of a neighbor's illness, and the unconscious interpretation of these cues as signifying a terminal illness shows up in a dream. However; in this case the person who died was a young man who did not live at the nearby farm. He apparently had been in good health but collapsed suddenly of a cerebral hemorrhage. The neighbors received the news early in the morning and sadly ran up their flag at half mast. According to the dreamer, there was no possible way in which she could have obtained the news; nor in reviewing the previous day could she recall anything she had seen, heard, read, or experienced that might have precipitated a dream about flags, death, and the neighbor's farm. Could the dream have been coincidental? The dreamer recalled no other dream that had featured flags.

We could speculate that the dream was clairvoyant (the dreamer having perceived the distant event), telepathic (the dreamer having perceived the neighbor's thought processes), or precognitive (the dreamer having predicted the running up of the flag). But none of these possibilities indicates that the dream or the dreamer is pathological; they simply suggest that some unknown, anomalous process is at work.

Crisis cases are overrepresented in collections of spontaneous psychic dreams.[6] The reason may be simply that dreams involving death, accidents, and illness are more impressive than trivial ones and are more easily remembered. In time, by chance alone, some of these dreams could be linked to waking events. On the other hand, the high incidence might reflect the possible biological function of telepathy as a preverbal emergency channel that may have been lost when, in the course of evolution, verbal language developed.[7]

The fact that women's dreams are overrepresented in collections of psychic dreams[8] may be due to the fact that emotions and dreams, in the Western world, traditionally have been considered the province of females. However, it may also reflect the possible origin and function of telepathy as a bridge between mother and child in situations that are threatening to the child, where cries and screams are useless because of distance.[9]

What is the nature of telepathy and related psychic phenomena? The popular notion of energy that leaves the sender and travels to the receiver does not seem plausible, given the amount of energy that would have to be generated by the brain to travel over distances. However, the carrier of psychic information might be conveying extremely low electromagnetic frequencies that could be modulated by a distant event or by sender–receiver interaction.[10]

DREAM SENSING AND PRECOGNITION

Far from being a passive state, REM sleep is a complex state of consciousness characterized by a high degree of brain arousal that has been described as vigilance,[11] superwakefulness,[12] wakefulness within sleep,[13] and activation-synthesis.[14] I use the term *dream sensing,* because in REM sleep we can pick up and incorporate in ongoing dreams a number of stimuli from the body and the external environment.

I believe that dream sensing of the body occurs in so-called diagnostic dreams. For example, one of my children awakened from a dream in early morning, saying: "I dreamed that my zipper had jammed itself under my chin. I felt I was choking and pulled and pulled at it. When I woke up, I discovered I was pulling the bedspread."

My son had difficulties relating the dream because of a throat irritation, even though he was fine when he went to bed. But during the night he had developed a sore throat; he suggested that the choking sensation in the dream was actually referring to his hoarseness.

Some diagnostic dreams may be precognitive in nature, because they do not appear to depend on bodily signals for their occurrence. For example, a young woman began to dream about her contact lenses shattering. In one dream they shattered in her eyes, causing severe injuries; in another, they projected out of her eyes and were crushed. Some time later, her eyes began to secrete a mucuslike substance that spread over her lenses, making it impossible for her to see.[15] At first consideration, this dream could be considered precognitive, because contact lenses do not emit body signals. However, the bodily reactions that were associated with the mucus secretion could have found their way into her dreams before they were manifested externally.

While we are dreaming, we turn from a public to a private way of existence. The usual bombardment of external stimuli is strongly dampened in REM sleep, while nature draws our attention to the "inner theater." Even though the ratio of internal to external stimuli rises in REM sleep, the dreamer is far from being "dead to the world." On the contrary, the brain can admit important material from the outside world when necessary. In addition, middle-ear muscle activity resembles that which occurs during the waking state. As a result, dreamers are likely to incorporate into ongoing dreams the whispered names of significant others and to shut out random noises.[16] These findings have great relevance for the identification of psychic dreams. For example, a thirty-year-old man was sleeping on the second floor of a farmhouse. During the night he dreamed that his friend, who was on a hunting trip, was dead. On awakening, he received the news that his friend, who had shown no sign of illness earlier, had suddenly dropped dead while hunting and had been brought back to the farm that night. The vicar soon arrived to console the relatives.

This dream has many characteristics of a telepathic crisis case, yet the dreamer suggested that it might have been an instance of dream sensing. He might have overheard portions of the conversations, sobs, and cries from downstairs and blended them into a dream message. Whenever the waking reality event pictured in a dream occurs within hearing range, we cannot label the dream psychic. I have conducted informal experiments in which I have entered the room of children during REM sleep, pretending to steal their belongings or scare them. The children's dreams, as recalled the following morning, often contain monsters or thieves. My results are more impressive than most of those obtained in the laboratory when indifferent or meaningless stimuli are presented during REM sleep.[17]

Could dream sensing explain some purportedly precognitive dreams that concern such natural catastrophes as earthquakes and landslides? For example, a twenty-two-year-old student living on the west coast of Norway dreamed that there had been a terrible avalanche in the region where she lived. In the morning she was very disturbed because she felt, as she remarked, that it was unavoidable. She told her family about the dream and began to listen for the news on a radio. She soon learned that indeed there had been an unusually large avalanche during the night in which several people had been killed.

It was difficult to ascertain whether the student had her dream before, during, or after the avalanche had occurred. Had the dream occurred previous to the disaster, it could have been precognitive; had it occurred during it or afterwards, it could have been clairvoyant. However, this particular student lived in a region where inhabitants are aware of the weather conditions often associated with avalanches, and such conditions were present at the time of the dream. Furthermore, weather forecasts often report whether there is a danger of avalanches. In other words, one could attribute the dream to coincidence and/or to an unconscious piecing together of information obtained through ordinary means.

Dream sensing is another alternative. Would the distance between the location of the avalanche and the dreamer's home necessarily preclude her hearing or feeling the sounds and rumbles of the avalanche? We should bear in mind that natural infrasound may contain wavelengths that come very close to audible levels. Propagation of natural infrasound is connected with volcanic eruptions, earthquakes, large landslides, and other seismic events. Human subjects in laboratory experiments who have been exposed to low frequency sounds have reported visual impressions and bodily sensations. Extremely low-frequency sounds, in laboratory experiments, have led to feelings of anxiety, dizziness, and sickness.[18] There also have been reports of depression, headaches, and fatigue associated with infrasound.

Sleep in general and REM sleep in particular (with its scanning of possible threats depicted in dramatic visual imagery) may be an ideal state for perceiving infrasound. The background of the dreamer, as well as his or her current concerns, could account for the accompanying dream content. Needless to say, this is an open question but one deserving more attention than it has received.

There is also the psychodynamic alternative. Some dreamworkers would view the student's dream as a metaphorical expression of her personal feelings and existential situation. They would propose that there had been an "avalanche" in her life that "killed" several people. In fact, I have a dream on record in which there can be little doubt that a landslide symbolizes the dreamer's recent abortion.

Arguing against all of these explanations is the dreamer's feeling (if accurately recalled and reported) that this dream was clearly different from any of her previous dreams. For example, she was convinced of the avalanche's reality and its unavoidability. She was certain that several people had been killed. She demonstrated her conviction by turning on the radio and listening to it until the tragic news was announced. It is clear that no final decision can be made concerning the anomalous nature of this type of dream, but one can consider the range of possibilities that exist and can refrain from dismissing the dreamer's concern over catastrophic dream content until a reality check is attempted.

FINE CUING AND SELF-FULFILLING PROPHECIES

By *fine cuing,* I mean the verbal and nonverbal cues in social interactions of which we are not consciously aware but that often register with us unconsciously. I would also include the weak sonic activity (such as infrasound) and the electromagnetic and chemical stimuli in our environment. I believe that many purportedly psychic dreams can be explained by fine cuing. The problem in making this determination is the unknown capacity of the human brain for making inferences. Consider the fact that the brain contains about 20 billion neurons, each of which is in constant communication with 10,000 others at a rate of at least 100 times per second.[19] This should lead to humility among dreamworkers, as well as an openness to the possibility of anomalous events.

Cuing is closely linked to the subtleties of body language. This language both reveals and conceals, both conceives and deceives, through deliberate movements and gestures and through inadvertent ticks, jerks, voice intonations, and speech cadences. Body language is full of surprises, even to trained observers, and it sometimes has great relevance for dreams, such as this one related to me by a civil engineer.

When I was a student at the technological institute at Trondheim, I had a wonderful dream. One night in the spring before an examination, I saw the test paper we were going to receive in organic chemistry. I was left with a feeling of strong conviction and told my classmates about the dream. Most of them scoffed at me. But you should have seen their faces when the test papers were handed out. My dream had hit a bull's eye! In retrospect, however, the test items I dreamed about were those that the instructor had emphasized with his body language during our class sessions.

I view this dream from the perspective of a similar experience I had when I was a student. While attending class, I slipped into a waking reverie. Suddenly I became convinced that my Latin professor was reading a passage that we were going to be given during our examination. I noticed that he was speaking clearly and distinctly. He was slightly flushed and was even pressing the chalk more firmly against the blackboard than was his custom. Then he asked two of the weakest students to translate the passage and emphasized the importance of certain grammatical structures. At home, I studied the passage thoroughly and, of course, it appeared on the examination.

I believe that many so-called psychic examination dreams have their origins in fine cuing but may appear anomalous because the dreamer is unaware of the grammar of body language. Invariably, when I had the opportunity to question dreamers who report accurate dreams about tests and exams, I have found they have been in situations where they could have obtained a number of cues. For example, the dreamers frequently report preexamination conversations with their instructors in the classroom, in an office, or during a coffee break. Whenever such experiences precede the examination dream, fine cuing is a likely explanation.

In some cases, cuing relates to environmental stimuli rather than to human interactions. Let us consider the dreams of a hunter.

> During the hunting season, I often have similar dreams while I am camping out. I dream that a deer comes running towards me in a place I recognize and can locate after awakening. Although the location might seem improbable, experience has taught me that such dreams are messages as to where I should hide. Then the deer might come running towards me just as it had in the dream. I do not claim that this happens every time I have such a dream, but it is the general rule.

I would characterize the dreamer as sensible and reliable. He is also a very experienced hunter with a profound knowledge of deers' feeding and mating behavior, favorite hiding places, and seasonal migration patterns. I suspect that he is keenly aware of tracks, odors, winds, light, and a number of other subtle cues he would not even be able to pinpoint. While asleep, all of these fine cues develop, combine, and produce the image of a deer in a location where he unconsciously expects it to appear.

The anecdotal literature in parapsychology contains hundreds of reports of psychic dreams as well as waking reveries, intuitions, and hunches. Neuroscientist Michael Persinger analyzed three collections of these spontaneous cases of alleged psychic phenomena, correlating them with global geomagnetic activity on the day of their occurrence. His results showed that these reported events are more likely to happen on calm, quiet days more free from electrical storms or from sunspot activity than the days before or after the purported psychic experience.[20]

There were several dreams in these collections, but most had not been critically examined in regard to alternative explanations. However, Persinger and Krippner analyzed the dreams of sixty-two subjects in psychic dream experiments in a laboratory setting that attempted to rule out coincidence, sensory cues, falsification of memory, and other ordinary causal factors. The dream reports that judges had ascertained to contain the highest degree of telepathic or clairvoyant content were more likely to occur on calm nights with low geomagnetic activity.[21]

In spite of the fact that the most frequently used indices of geomagnetic activity are still rather crude and that the extent of the influence of geomagnetic activity on human behavior remains controversial, I consider these studies valid and of great interest for our topic. As I mentioned earlier, REM sleep is a state in which we attend selectively to significant impinging stimuli; thus it is potentially a state where we might expect the organism to be aware of extremely weak environmental effects. Psychic dreams in a laboratory as well as spontaneous cases dealing with psychic information about crises (death, illness, or accidents) were linked by Persinger with calm geomagnetic conditions. This finding raises the possibility that the carrier for this information is disrupted by electrical storms and sunspot activity. Of course, this research is still at a very early stage.

In regard to purportedly precognitive dreams, a self-fulfilling prophecy is a common explanation, especially of those dreams that involve unexpected meetings with people. For example, you may feel like going to a place where you happen to meet someone you dreamed of the previous night. Unconsciously, you may have chosen that location precisely because you "knew" that you were likely to meet the dream character there at that time.

However, there are more complex examples of self-fulfilling prophecies. For example, a young lawyer told me that when he was ten years of age, his uncle was diagnosed as diabetic. Together with his parents, he visited his uncle at the hospital, then he noticed that in front of his uncle's room there was a kind of balcony. The following night, the boy dreamed that he himself had diabetes and was hospitalized. Then he was on a balcony in front of his room, where he stood on his head. A dozen years later he found out that he had diabetes. In front of his apartment, there happened to be a small balcony. One day when he was on the balcony, he felt an urge to stand on his head; upon doing so, he suddenly recalled the dream.

It is not surprising that the boy's trip to see his sick uncle was reflected in a dream the night after the visit; this is just the type of unsettling experience that might find its way into a dream. The boy may have been told that juvenile diabetes is hereditary and runs in families, so it is understandable that he pictured himself as having diabetes. It is of interest to note that metaphorically speaking, standing on one's head may mean turning one's world upside down—a consequence of being struck by a serious disease. Twelve years later, the dream was fulfilled. We might ask whether the dreamer stood on his head as an enactment of his own situation. If so, the dream metaphor, far from being erased from memory, had been living its secret life in the dreamer's memory.

As for the dreamer's contracting diabetes, we may attribute it to the family disposition for the condition. More speculatively, however, we may ask whether or not he "made himself ill" to fulfill the dream, or—more likely—the family myth reflected in the dream.

We are faced with the problem that the self-fulfilling prophecy as a workable model has flimsy theoretical underpinnings. No matter whether a dream contains long-term prophecies (such as of future career choices) or short-term ones (as of the kind of car we will buy the following week), the operating mechanisms are obscure. Perhaps a self-fulfilling prophecy is made unconsciously as a result of childhood conditioning and the ensuing personal myth. It could then be reflected in a dream and, if the dream were recalled, would give the dreamer an opportunity to prevent the prophecy from taking place if the foreseen course of events were unpleasant or disagreeable.

In summary, psychic dreams present us with an opportunity to conduct imaginative research. They have a variety of potential explanations, both ordinary and anomalous. Because psychic dreams are so closely associated with the dreamer's memory system, REM sleep offers a splendid opportunity for the joint study of both areas of human capacity.

Notes

Preface

1. Cavallero, C., and Natale, V. "Was I Dreaming or Did It Really Happen? A Comparison Between Real and Artifical Dream Reports," *Imagination, Cognition and Personality* 8(1988–89):19–24.
2. Aserinsky, E., and Kleitman, N. "Regularly Occurring Periods of Eye Motility, and Concomitant Phenomena, During Sleep," *Science* 118(1953):273–74.
3. Kahn, E. et al. "Incidence of Color in Immediately Recalled Dreams," *Science* 137(1962):1054–55.
4. Krippner, S. et al. "Content Analysis of 30 Dreams from 10 Pre-operative Male Transsexuals," *Journal of the American Society of Psychosomatic Dentistry and Medicine,* Monograph Supplement 2(1974).
5. Krippner, S. et al. "An Investigation of Dream Content During Pregnancy," *Journal of the American Society of Psychosomatic Dentistry and Medicine* 21(1974):111–23.
6. Krippner, S., and Ullman, M. "Telepathy and Dreams: A Controlled Experiment with Electro-encephalogram-electro-oculogram Monitoring," *Journal of Nervous and Mental Disease* 151(1970):394–403.
7. Belvedere, E., and Foulkes, D. "Telepathy and Dreams: A Failure to Replicate," *Perceptual and Motor Skills* 33(1971):783–89. Globus, G. G. et al. "An Appraisal of Telepathic Communication in Dreams," *Psychophysiology* 4(1968):365. Hall, C. S. "Experiments with Telepathically Influenced Dreams," *Zeitschrift für Parapsychologie und Grenzgebiet der Psychologie* 10(1967):18–47. Van de Castle, R. L. "The Study of GESP in a Group Setting by Means of Dreams," *Journal of Parapsychology* 35(1971):312. Ullman, M., and Krippner, S., with Vaughan, A. *Dream Telepathy: Experiments in Nocturnal ESP,* 2nd ed. (Jefferson, NC: McFarland, 1989).
8. Persinger, M. A., and Krippner, S. "Dream ESP Experiments and Geomagnetic Activity," *Journal of the American Society for Psychical Research* 83(1989):101–16.
9. Van de Castle, R. L. *The Psychology of Dreaming* (Morristown, NJ: General Learning Press, 1971).

Part 1 Introduction

1. Ullman, M. "Dreaming and the Dream: Social and Personal Perspectives," in *Cognition and Dream Research,* ed. R. E. Haskell (New York: Institute for Mind and Behavior, 1986), pp. 299–317.

2. Caligor, L., and May, R. *Dreams and Symbols: Man's Unconscious Language* (New York: Basic Books, 1968), p. 3.

3. Feinstein, D., and Krippner, S. *Personal Mythology: The Psychology of Your Evolving Self* (Los Angeles: Jeremy P. Tarcher, 1988).

4. Krippner, S. "Dreams and the Development of a Personal Mythology," in *Cognition and Dream Research,* ed. R. E. Haskell (New York: Institute for Mind and Behavior, 1986), pp. 319–31.

5. Jung, C. G. *Symbols of Transformation* (Princeton: Princeton University Press, 1956).

6. Pieracci, M. "The Mythopoesis of Psychotherapy," *The Humanistic Psychologist* 18(1990): 208–25.

7. Krippner, S. "Shamanism, Personal Mythology and Behavior Change," *International Journal of Psychosomatics* 34(1987):22–27.

8. Caligor and May, *Dreams and Symbols,* p. 4.

Dreams for Personal and Spiritual Growth

1. Larsen, S. *The Shaman's Doorway* (Barrytown, NY: Station Hill Press, 1986), pp. 82–117.

2. Kelsey, M. *God, Dreams, and Revelation* (Minneapolis, MN: Augsburg, 1974).

3. Savary, L. M.; Berne, P. H.; and Williams, S. K. *Dreams and Spiritual Growth* (New York: Paulist Press, 1984).

4. Williams, S. K. *Jungian-Senoi Dreamwork Manual* (Berkeley: Journey Press), p. 129

The Emergence of the Grassroots Dreamwork Movement

1. Ullman, M. "The Experiential Dream Group," in *Handbook of Dreams,* ed. B. B. Wolman (New York: Van Nostrand Reinhold, 1979), pp. 406–23. Ullman, M., and Zimmerman, N. *Working with Dreams* (Los Angeles: Jeremy P. Tarcher, 1979). Ullman, M. "The Experiential Dream Group," in *The Variety of Dream Experience,* ed. M. Ullman and C. Limmer (New York: Continuum, 1987), pp. 1–26.

2. Hillman, D. J. "Dream Work and Field Work: Linking Cultural Anthropology and the Current Dream Work Movement," in *The Variety of Dream Experience,* ed. M. Ullman and C. Limmer (New York: Continuum, 1987), pp. 117–41.

3. Tedlock, B. "Dreaming and Dream Research," in *Dreaming: Anthropological and Psychological Interpretations,* ed. B. Tedlock (New York: Cambridge University Press, 1987), pp. 1–30.

4. Locke, R. G. and Kelly, E. F. "A Preliminary Model for the Cross-cultural Analysis of Altered States of Consciousness," *Ethos* 13:1(1985):3–55. Sperry, R. W. "Structure and Significance of the Consciousness Revolution," *ReVISION* 11:1(1988):39–55. Originally published in 1987.

5. Sperry, "Structure and Significance," p. 53.

6. Hillman, "Dream Work," p. 125.

7. Hillman, "Dream Work," p. 124.

8. Hillman, "Dream Work," p. 131.

9. Ibid.

10. Ullman, M. "On Relearning the Forgotten Language: Deprofessionalizing the Dream," *Contemporary Psychoanalysis* 18(1982):153–59.

11. Ullman and Zimmerman, *Working with Dreams,* p. 243.
12. Dodd, J. "A Mothers' Dream Group," in *The Variety of Dream Experience,* ed. M. Ullman and C. Limmer (New York: Continuum, 1987), pp. 29–43.
13. Hillman, "Dream Work," p. 130.
14. Ibid., pp. 128–29.
15. Ullman, "On Relearning."
16. Hillman, "Dream Work," p. 127.
17. Taylor, J. *Dream Work,* (Ramsey, NJ: Paulist Press, 1983), p. 117.
18. Randall, A. "Dream Sharing and Shared Metaphors in a Short-Term Community" (Ph.D. diss., Teacher's College, Columbia University, 1978).
19. Ibid., p. 106.
20. Tart, C. T. "The High Dream: A New State of Consciousness," in *Altered States of Consciousness,* ed. C. T. Tart (Garden City, NY: Anchor Books), pp. 171–79. Hunt, H. T. *The Multiplicity of Dreams* (New Haven, CT: Yale University Press, 1989).
21. See note 13 above.
22. Ullman, M. "Dreams and Society," in *The Variety of Dream Experience,* ed. M. Ullman and C. Limmer (New York: Continuum, 1987), pp. 194–213.
23. Wikse, J. "Night Rule: Dreams as Social Intelligence," in *The Variety of Dream Experience,* ed. M. Ullman and C. Limmer (New York: Continuum, 1987), pp. 194–213.
24. Wikse, "Night Rule," p. 201.
25. See note 13 above.
26. Feinstein, D., and Krippner, S. *Personal Mythology: The Psychology of Your Evolving Self* (Los Angeles: Jeremy P. Tarcher, 1988), p. 8.
27. Taylor, *Dream Work,* p. 17.

The Dream as a Window on Your Evolving Mythology

1. Many of the ideas in this chapter were originally set forth in Feinstein, D. "Mythmaking Activity Through the Window of the Dream," *Psychotherapy in Private Practice* 4(1986): 119–35.
2. Campbell, J. *Historical Atlas of World Mythology,* vol. 1. (San Francisco: Harper and Row, 1983).
3. Campbell, J. *The Inner Reaches of Outer Space: Metaphor as Myth and as Religion* (New York: Alfred van der Marck, 1986).
4. Feinstein D., and Krippner, S. *Personal Mythology: The Psychology of Your Evolving Self* (Los Angeles: Jeremy P. Tarcher, 1988).
5. James, W. *Varieties of Religious Experience* (1902; reprint ed., New York: Crowell-Collier, 1961), p. 332.
6. Wheelwright, P. "Poetry, Myth, and Reality," in *The Language of Poetry,* ed. A. Tate (Princeton, NJ: Princeton University Press, 1942), p. 10.
7. Stevens, A. *Archetypes: A Natural History of the Self* (New York: Quill, 1983).
8. McCarley, R. W., and Hobson, J. A. "The Form of Dreams and the Biology of Sleep," in *Handbook of Dreams: Research, Theories and Application,* ed. B. B. Wolman (New York: Van Nostrand Reinhold, 1979), pp. 76–130.

9. Rossi, E. "The Cerebral Hemispheres in Analytical Psychology," *Journal of Analytical Psychology* 22(1977):32–51.

10. Feinstein, D. "Personal Mythology as a Paradigm for a Holistic Public Psychology," *American Journal of Orthopsychiatry* 49(1979):198–217.

11. Cavendish, R. *An Illustrated Encyclopedia of Mythology* (New York: Cresent, 1980), p. 11.

12. Jung, C. G. "The Practice of Psychotherapy," *Collected Works,* vol. 16, 2nd ed., trans. R. F. C. Hull (Princeton, NJ: Princeton University Press, 1966).

13. Piaget, J. *The Development of Thought: Equilibrium of Cognitive Structures,* trans. A. Rosin (New York: Viking, 1977).

14. Cartwright, R. D. *Night Life: Explorations in Dreaming* (Englewood Cliffs, NJ: Prentice-Hall, 1977).

15. Cohen, D., and Cox, C. "Neuroticism in the Sleep Laboratory: Implications for Representational and Adaptive Properties of Dreaming," *Journal of Abnormal Psychology* 84(1973): 91–108.

16. DeKonnick, J., and Koulack, D. "Dream Content and Adaptation to a Stressful Situation, *Journal of Abnormal Psychology* 84(1975):250–60.

17. Freud, S. *The Interpretation of Dreams,* trans. J. Strachey (1900. reprint ed., London: Hogarth, 1953), p. 573.

18. Piaget, *Development of Thought,* p. 33.

19. Feinstein, D., Krippner, S., and Granger, D. "Mythmaking and Human Development," *Journal of Humanistic Psychology* 28:3(1988):23–50.

20. Epstein, S. "The Unconscious, the Preconscious, and the Self-Concept," in *Psychological Perspectives on the Self,* vol. 2, ed. J. Suls and A. Greenwald (Hillsdale, NJ: Lawrence Erlbaum, 1983), pp. 219–47.

21. Freud, *Interpretation of Dreams,* p. 573.

22. Greene, T. A. "C. G. Jung's Theory of Dreams," in *Handbook of Dreams: Research, Theories and Application,* ed. B. B. Wolman (New York: Van Nostrand Reinhold, 1979), pp. 298–318.

23. Ullman, M. "Dreaming, Life Style and Physiology: A Comment on Adler's Review of the Dream," *Journal of Individual Psychology* 18(1962):18–25.

24. Piaget, *Development of Thought,* p. 10.

25. Hillman, J. *Re-Visioning Psychology* (New York: Harper and Row, 1975), p. 146.

Part 2 Introduction

1. Erwin, E. "Holistic Psychotherapies. What Works?" in *Examining Holistic Medicine,* ed. D. Stalker and C. Glymour (Buffalo, NY: Prometheus Books, 1985), pp. 245–72.

2. Crick, F., and Mitchison, G. "The Function of Dream Sleep," *Nature* 304(1986):111–14.

3. Van de Castle, R. L. *The Psychology of Dreaming* (Morristown, NJ: General Learning Press, 1974).

4. Ibid., p. 41.

5. Monroe, R.; Nerlove, S.; and Daniels, R. "Effects of Population Density on Food Concerns in Three East African Societies," *Journal of Health and Social Behavior* 10(1969):161–71.

6. Levine, R. *Dreams and Deeds: Achievement Motivation in Nigeria* (Chicago: University of Chicago Press, 1966).

7. Cartwright, R. "Affect and Dream Work from an Information Processing Point of View," *Journal of Mind and Behavior* 7(1986):411–28.

8. Eysenck, H. J. "The Effects of Psychotherapy," In *Handbook of Abnormal Psychology*, ed. H. J. Eysenck (New York: Basic Books, 1961), pp. 697–725.

9. Smith, M. L.; Glass, G. V.; and Miller, T. I. *The Benefits of Psychotherapy* (Baltimore: Johns Hopkins University Press, 1980).

10. Adler, A. *Social Interest: Challenge to Mankind* (London: Faber and Faber, 1938).

11. Gold, L. "Adler's Theory of Dreams: An Holistic Approach to Interpretation," in *Handbook of Dreams: Research, Theories and Applications*, ed. B. B. Wolman (New York: Van Nostrand Reinhold, pp. 319–41).

12. Bonime, W. *The Clinical Use of Dreams* (New York: Basic Books, 1960).

13. Bonime, W. *Collaborative Psychoanalysis: Anxiety, Depression, Dreams, and Personality Change* (Rutherford, NJ: Fairleigh Dickinson University Press, 1989), p. 263.

14. Bonime, W., with Bonime, F. "Culturalist Approach," in *Handbook of Dreams: Research, Theories and Applications*, ed. B. B. Wolman (New York: Van Nostrand Reinhold, 1979), pp. 79–124.

15. Fantz, R. E. "Gestalt Approach," in *Dream Interpretation: A Comparative Study*, ed. J. L. Fosshage and C. A. Loew (Jamaica, NY: Spectrum, 1978), pp. 126–48.

16. Padel, J. H. "Object Relational Approach," in *Dream Interpretation: A Comparative Study*, ed. J. L. Fosshage and C. A. Loew (Jamaica, NY: Spectrum, 1978), pp. 126–48.

17. Savary, L. M.; Berne, P. H.; and Williams, S. K. *Dreams and Spiritual Growth: A Christian Approach to Dreamwork* (New York: Paulist Press, 1984). Thurston, M. *Dreams: Tonight's Answers for Tomorrow's Questions* (San Francisco: Harper and Row, 1988).

18. Ullman, M. "Image and Metaphor: Some Thoughts on Their Healing Power" (Paper presented at the annual meeting of the Interregional Society of Jungian Analysts, Salado, TX.)

The Role of Dreams in Psychotherapy

1. Eisenstein, S. O. "The Dream in Psychoanalysis," in *The Dream in Clinical Practice*, ed. J. M. Natterson (New York: Jason Aronson, 1980), pp. 319–31. Langs, R. "The role of dream in psychotherapy," in *The Dream in Clinical Practice*, ed. J. M. Natterson (New York: Jason Aronson, 1980), pp. 333–68.

2. Jung, C. G. *Dreams* (Princeton, NJ: Princeton University Press, 1974).

3. Kohut, H. *The Restoration of the Self* (New York: International Universities Press, 1971). Colodzin, B. *Trauma and Survival: A Self Help Learning Guide* (Laramie, WY: Ghost Rocks Press, 1989).

4. Weiss, L. *Dream Analysis in Psychotherapy* (New York: Pergamon, 1986).

5. Greenson, R. "The Exceptional Position of the Dream in Psychoanalytic Practice," *Psychoanalytic Quarterly* 39(1970):519–49. Levay, A. N., and Wessberg, J. "The Role of Dreams in Sex Therapy," *Journal of Sex and Marital Therapy* 5(1979):344–39.

6. Wolff, W. *The Dream—Mirror of Conscience* (New York: Grune and Stratton, 1952).

7. Mattoon, M. A. *Understanding Dreams* (Dallas, TX: Spring, 1984).

8. Delaney, G. *Living Your Dreams* (San Francisco: Harper and Row, 1981). Faraday, A. *The Dream Game* (New York: Harper and Row, 1974). Morris, J. *The Dream Notebook* (New York: Random House, 1985).

9. Baylor, G. W., and Deslauriers, D. "Dreams as Problem-solving: A Method of Study. Part I: Background and theory," *Imagination, Cognition and Personality* 6(1987):105–18. Fosshage, J. L. "New Vistas in Dream Interpretation," in *Dreams in New Perspective,* ed. M. L. Glucksman and S. L. Warner (New York: Human Sciences Press, 1987), pp. 23–43. Greenberg, R., and Pearlman, C. "The Private Language of the Dream," in *The Dream in Clinical Practice,* ed. J. M. Natterson (New York: Jason Aronson, 1980), pp.85–98.

10. Corriere, R. et al. *Dreaming and Waking: The Functional Approach to Dreams* (Culver City, CA: Peace Press, 1980).

11. Boss, M. *I Dreamt Last Night . . .* (New York: Gardner Press, 1977). Garfield, P. *Creative Dreaming* (New York: Ballantine, 1977).

12. Rossi, E. L. *Dreams and the Growth of Personality* (New York: Pergamon, 1972).

13. Caruso, I. A. *Existential Psychology* (New York: Herder and Herder, 1964).

14. Ansbacher, H., and Ansbacher, L. *The Individual Psychology of Alfred Adler* (New York: Basic Books, 1956). Bonime, W. *The Clinical Use of Dreams* (New York: Basic Books, 1962).

15. Angyal, A. *Neurosis and Treatment: A Holistic Theory* (New York: John Wiley and Sons, 1965). Hall, C. S. *The Meaning of Dreams* (New York: McGraw-Hill, 1966).

16. Guntrio, H. *Schizoid Phenomena, Object Relations, and the Self* (New York: International Universities Press, 1969).

17. Krippner, S. "Access to Hidden Reserves of the Unconscious Through Dreams in Creative Problem Solving," *Journal of Creative Behavior* 15(1980):11–23. Perls, F. S. *Gestalt Therapy Verbatim* (Moab, UT: Real People's Press, 1969).

18. Jung, C. G. *Modern Man in Search of a Soul* (New York: Harcourt Brace, 1933).

19. Mahrer, A. R. *How to Do Experiential Psychotherapy: A Manual for Practitioners* (Ottawa Press, 1989); idem, *Experiencing: A Humanistic Therapy of Psychology and Psychiatry* (1978; reprint ed., Ottawa: University of Ottawa Press, 1989); idem, *Dream Work in Psychotherapy and Self-Change* (New York: W. W. Norton, 1990).

20. Freud, S. *The Interpretation of Dreams,* trans. J. Starchey (1900; reprint ed., New York: Modern Library, 1950).

21. Piotrowski, Z. A., with Biele, A. M. *Dreams: A Key to Self-Knowledge* (Hillsdale, NJ: Lawrence Erlbaum, 1988). Kohut, *Restoration of the Self.*

22. Boss, *I Dreamt Last Night.*

23. Langs, "The role of dream . . ."

24. Perls, *Gestalt Therapy Verbatim,* p. 69.

25. Mahrer, *Dream Work in Psychotherapy,* p. 69.

A Psychoanalytic Approach to Dreamwork

1. Schwartz, W. "What Makes Something Psychoanalytic?" *Psychiatry* 51(1988):417–26.

2. Freud, S. *The Interpretation of Dreams,* trans. J. Strachey, (1900; reprint ed., London: Hogarth, 1975).

3. Freud, S. *Beyond the Pleasure Principle,* trans. J. Strachey, (1920; reprint ed., London: Hogarth, 1976).

4. Stein, M. "How Dreams Are Told: Secondary Revision—the Critic, the Editor, and the Plagiarist," *Journal of the American Psychoanalytic Association* 37(1989):65–88.

5. Greenberg, R. et al. "A Research Based Reconsideration of the Psychoanalytic Theory of Dreaming" (Paper presented at the fall meeting of the American Psychoanalytic Association, New York, 1989).
6. Schwartz, "What Makes Something Psychoanalytic?" idem., "The Two Concepts of Action and Responsibility in Psychoanalysis," *Journal of the American Psychoanalytic Association* 32(1984):557–72.
7. Freud, S. "The Handling of Dream-Interpretation in Psychoanalysis," in *The Standard Edition of the Complete Psychological Works of Sigmund Freud,* vol. 12, trans. J. Strachey (1911; reprint ed., London: Hogarth, 1975).
8. Schafer, R. *Language and Insight* (New Haven: Yale University Press, 1978), p. 72.
9. Freud, *Interpretation of Dreams,* p. 460.
10. Freud, S. *Introductory Lectures on Psychoanalysis,* trans. J. Strachey (1916; reprint ed., London: Hogarth Press, 1975).

A Jungian Approach to Dreamwork

1. Jung, C. G. *The Structure and Dynamics of the Psyche, Collected Works,* vol. 8 (Princeton, NJ: Princeton University Press, 1969), para. 509.
2. Welwood, J. "Meditation and the Unconscious; A New Perspective," *Journal of Transpersonal Psychology* 1(1977): 1–26.
3. Jung, C. G. *Modern Man in Search of a Soul* (New York: Harcourt Brace, 1933), p. 185.
4. Welwood, "Meditation and the Unconscious," p. 4.
5. Ibid., p. 15.
6. Gendlin, E. T. "A Phenomenology of Emotions. Anger," in *Explorations in Phenomenology,* ed. D. Carr and E. Casey (The Hague: Martinus Nijhoff, 1973), p. 370.
7. Welwood, "Meditation and the Unconscious," pp. 8–19.
8. Ibid., p. 1.
9. Jung, C. G. *Mysterium Coniunctionis, Collected Works* 14 (Princeton, NJ: Princeton University Press, 1969), para. 759.

An Existential Approach to Dreamwork

1. Heidegger, M. *Being and Time* (New York: Basic Books, 1962), pp. 49–63.
2. Binswanger, L. "Dream and Existence," in *Being-in-the-World* (New York: Basic Books, 1963), pp. 222–248. Boss, M. *The Analysis of Dreams* (New York: Philosophical Library, 1958). Boss, M. *I Dreamt Last Night* . . . (New York: Gardner Press, 1977). Craig, E. "The Realness of Dreams," in *Dreams Are Wiser than Men,* ed. R. Russo (Berkeley, CA: North Atlantic Books, 1987), pp. 34–57. Craig, E. "Dreaming, Reality and Allusion," in *Advances in Qualitative Psychology,* ed. F. Van Zurren, F. Wertz, and B. Mook (Berwyn, PA: Swets North America, 1987), pp. 115–36.
3. Stern, P. "Dreams: The Radiant Children of the Night," in *In Praise of Madness* (New York: W. W. Norton, 1972).

4. Boss, M. *Existential Foundations of Medicine and Psychology,* (New York: Jason Aronson, 1978), p. XIII.

5. Auden, W. H. *The Collected Poetry of W. H. Auden* (New York: Random House, 1945), p. 167.

A Body-Oriented Approach to Dreamwork

1. Coxhead, D., and Hiller, S. *Dreams: Visions of the Night* (Netherlands: Thames and Hudson, 1976), p. 6.

2. Krippner, S., and Dillard, J. *Dreamworking: How to Use Your Dreams for Creative Problem Solving* (Buffalo, NY: Bearly, 1987), pp. 12–13. Huang Ti Nei and Ching Su Wen. *The Yellow Emperor's Classic of Internal Medicine,* trans. I. Veith (Berkeley: University of California Press, 1966). Kakar, S. *Shamans, Mystics and Doctors* (New York: Alfred A. Knopf, 1982).

3. Sigerist, H. *A History of Medicine: Primitive and Archaic Medicine,* vol. 1 (Oxford: Oxford University Press, 1951), pp. 458–59.

4. Huang Ti Nei and Ching Su Wen, *Yellow Emporer's Classic,* p. 163.

5. Siegel, B. *Love, Medicine, and Miracles* (New York: Harper and Row, 1986), pp. 157–58.

6. Freud, S. *The Interpretation of Dreams,* trans. J. Strachey (1900; reprint ed., New York: Random House, 1938). Adler, A. *The Practice and Theory of Individual Psychology* (Paterson, NJ: Littlefield, Adams, 1963).

7. Reich, W. *The Function of the Orgasm* (New York: Noonday Press, 1971). Lowen, A. *Bioenergetics* (New York: Coward, McCann, and Geoghegan, 1975).

8. Mindell, A. *Dreambody: The Body's Role in Revealing the Self* (Los Angeles: Sigo Press, 1982).

9. Perls, F. *Gestalt Therapy Verbatim* (Moab, UT: Real People Press, 1969).

10. Personal communication from "Nancy," 1988.

11. Gendlin, E. *Focusing* (Toronto: Bantam Books, 1978).

12. Gendlin, E. *Let Your Body Interpret Your Dreams* (Wilmette, IL: Chiron Publications, 1986).

13. Personal communication from "Jim," 1988.

14. Bernstein, P., ed., *Eight Theoretical Approaches in Dance-Movement Therapy* (Dubuque, IA: Kendall/Hunt, 1979).

15. Ibid.

16. Personal communication from "Kay," 1988.

17. Mindell, A. *River's Way: The Process Science of the Dreambody* (London: Routledge and Kegan Paul, 1985).

18. Ibid.

19. Mindell, A. *The Dreambody in Relationships* (London: Routledge and Kegan Paul, 1987); idem, *The Year I: Global Process Work* (New York: Penguin Books, 1990).

20. Mindell, *River's Way,* pp. 34–36.

21. Mindell, A. *Working with the Dreaming Body* (London: Routledge and Kegan Paul, 1985).

22. Ibid.

23. See note 17 above.

24. Mindell, *River's Way,* ch. 2.

25. Mindell, *Working with the Dreaming Body,* ch. 1.

Part 3 Introduction

1. Ansbacher, H. L., and Ansbacher, R. R. *The Individual Psychology of Alfred Adler* (New York: Basic Books, 1956).
2. Gold, L. "Adler's Theory of Dreams: An Holistic Approach to Interpretation," in *Handbook of Dreams: Research, Theories and Applications,* ed. B. B. Wolman (New York: Van Nostrand Reinhold, 1959), pp. 319–41.
3. Wood, J. M.; Sebba, D.; and Domino, G. "Do creative people have more bizarre dreams? A reconsideration," *Imagination, Cognition and Personality* 9(1989–90):3–16.
4. Hobson, J. A. *The Dreaming Brain* (New York: Basic Books, 1988), p. 297.
5. Davé, R. "Effects of Hypnotically Induced Dreams on Creative Problem Solving," *Journal of Abnormal Psychology* 88(1979):293–302.
6. Barrios, M. V., and Singer, J. L. *Imagination, Cognition and Personality* 1:89–109.
7. Hughes, J. D. "The Dreams of Alexander the Great," *Journal of Psychohistory* 12(1984): 168–92.
8. Kaempffert, W. A. *A Popular History of American Invention* (New York: Scribners, 1924).
9. de Becker, R. *The Understanding of Dreams and Their Influence on the History of Man,* trans. M. Heron (New York: Hawthorn, 1968), p. 26.
10. Krippner, S., and Dillard, J. *Dreamworking: How to Use Your Dreams for Creative Problem Solving* (Buffalo, NY: Bearly, 1988), pp. 4–5.
11. Fagin, H. "Creativity and Dreams," in *The Variety of Dream Experience,* ed. M. Ullman and C. Limmer (New York: Continuum 1987), pp. 59–81.
12. Storm, E. F. "Dreaming and Learning: The Dream in a College Classroom," in *The Variety of Dream Experience,* ed. M. Ullman and C. Limmer (New York: Continuum, 1987), pp. 171–93.

Personal and Professional Problem Solving in Dreams

1. Pearlman, C. "Rat Models of the Adaptive Function of REM Sleep," in *Sleep, Dreams, and Memory,* ed. W. Fishbein (New York: Spectrum Publications, 1981) pp. 37–45. Horne, James. "Sleep Loss and Divergent Thinking Ability," *Sleep,* 6(1988):528–36. Glaubman, H., et al. "REM Deprivation and Divergent Thinking," *Psychophysiology* 15(1978):75–9. Greenberg, R.; Pillard, R.; and Pearlman, C. "The Effect of REM Deprivation on the Adaptation to Stress," *Psychosomatic Medicine* 34(1972):257–62. Greenberg, R., and Pearlman, C. "An Integrated Approach to Dream Theory and Clinical Practice," in *Contemporary Methods of Dream Interpretation,* ed. G. Delaney, 1990.
2. De Konnick, J., et al. "Intensive Language Learning and REM Sleep: Further Results," *Sleep Research* 7(1977):146.
3. Greenberg, R., and Pearlman, C. "A Psychoanalytic Dream Continuum: The Source and Function of Dreams," *International Review of Psychoanalysis* 2(1975):441–48.
4. Kedrof, B. M. "On the Question of Scientific Creativity," *Voprosy Psikhologie,* 3(1957): 105–106.
5. Loewi, Otto. "An Autobiographic Sketch," *Perspectives in Biology and Medicine,* 4:(1960):18.
6. Kaempffert, W. B. *A Popular History of American Invention,* vol. 2 (New York: Scribners, 1924).

7. Cannon, W. B. *The Way of an Investigator: A Scientist's Experiences in Medical Research* (New York: W. W. Norton, 1945), p. 61.

8. Ibid., pp. 57–58.

9. Tory to Delaney, 7 November 1985.

10. Newman, J. R. "Srinivasa Ramanujan," *Scientific American,* 178:6(1948):57.

11. Delaney, G. *Living Your Dreams,* rev. ed., (San Francisco: Harper and Row, 1988), pp. 139–155.

12. D. H. Lawrence to Edward Garnett, 29 January 1912.

13. For a discussion of the history of dream incubation, *see* Delaney, G., *The Hidden Language of the Heart* (New York: Bantam Books, 1990) and de Becker, R. *The Understanding of Dreams and Their Influence on the History of Man,* trans. M. Heron (New York: Hawthorn, 1968).

Dreams, Literature, and the Arts

1. de la Barca, Pedro Calderón. *La Vida es Sueño,* in *Obras Completas,* ed. L. A. Marin and trans. K. Atchity (Madrid: M. Aguilar, 1932), p. 302.

2. Homer *The Iliad,* trans. R. Lattimore (Chicago: University of Chicago Press, 1957), book 2.36.

3. Some of the material in this chapter has been adapted from K. Atchity, "Dream and Poetry: The Cave of Imagination," *Dreamworks* 1:2 (1980):pp. 169–80.

4. Amory, A. R., "Omens and Dreams in the *Odyssey*" (Ph.D. diss., Radcliffe College, 1957). Amory associates horn with "unmistakable truth," ivory with "unrecognized truth."

5. Vergil *The Aeneid,* ed. R. Sabbadini and trans. K. Atchity (Chicago: University of Chicago Press, 1960), 6.893–98.

6. Dante *Inferno* 1.10. Dante uses the uncertainty about the boundary between dreams and reality to good effect when the narrator establishes his own uncertainty about the wakeful or sleeping nature of what he experienced, thereby allowing us to suspend our disbelief.

7. Chaucer, G. *Booke of the Duchesse,* ed. F. N. Robinson (Chicago: University of Chicago Press, 1951), pp. 291–97.

8. Borges, J. L. *Dreamtigers,* trans. M. Boyer and H. Morland (Austin: University of Texas Press, 1970), p. 46.

9. de Cervantes, Miguel *Don Quijote,* ed. F. R. Martin and trans. K. Atchity (Chicago: University of Chicago Press, 1959).

10. Borges, *Dreamtigers,* p. 44.

11. García Márquez, G. *One Hundred Years of Solitude,* trans. B. Rabassa (New York: Harper and Row, 1970), pp. 143, 46, respectively.

12. Ibid.

13. Aristotle *De Poetica,* trans. I. Bywater, in *The Basic Works of Aristotle,* ed. R. McKeon (New York: Random House, 1941), p. 1464.

Painting Dream Images

1. Powell, N. *The Nightmare* (New York: Viking, 1973), pp. 68–69.

2. Janson, H. W. *History of Art* (Englewood Cliffs, NJ: Prentice Hall, New York: Abrams, 1966), p. 467.

3. Frye, N. *Fearful Symmetry: A Study of William Blake* (Boston: Beacon, 1947), p. 3.
4. De la Croix, H., and Tansey, R. *Art Through the Ages,* 3rd ed. (New York: Harcourt Brace Jovanovich, 1980), pp. 828–29.
5. Sandrow, N. *Surrealism* (New York: Harper and Row, 1972).
6. Onslow-Ford, G. *Yves Tanguy and Automatism* (California: Bishop Pine, 1938), pp. 1, 2.
7. Onslow-Ford, G. *Creation* (Basel: Galerie Schreinerag, 1978), p. 63.
8. Bogzaran, F. "The Message from the Inner World," *Dream Network Bulletin* 5:1 (1986):10–11.
9. Rossi, D. "The Gift of the Dolphin," *Dream Network Bulletin* 5:5(1987):9.
10. Onslow-Ford, *Creation,* p. 75.
11. Ibid.

Guidelines for Teaching Dreamwork

1. Ullman, M. "The Experiential Dream Group," in *Handbook of Dreams: Research, Theories and Applications,* ed. B. B. Wolman (New York: Van Nostrand Reinhold), 1979, pp. 406–23.

Part 4 Introduction

1. Freud, S. "Introductory Lectures on Psycho-analysis," in *Standard Edition of the Complete Psychological Works of Sigmund Freud,* vol. 15 (London: Hogarth, 1916–17), p. 153.
2. Begley, S. "The Stuff That Dreams Are Made Of," *Newsweek,* 14 August 1989, pp. 41–42.
3. Hall, C., and Van de Castle, R. L. *The Content Analysis of Dreams* (New York: Appleton Century Crofts, 1966).
4. Krippner, S. et al. "Content Analysis of 30 Dreams from 10 Pre-operative Male Transsexuals," *Journal of the American Society of Psychosomatic Dentistry and Medicine,* Monograph Supplement 2 (1974).
5. Benjamin, H. *The Transsexual Phenomenon* (New York: Julian, 1966).
6. Benjamin, H., and Ihlenfeld, C. L. "The Nature and Treatment of Transsexualism," *Medical Opinion and Review* 6(1970):20–26.
7. Fleming, M. et al. "A Study of Pre- and Postsurgical Transsexuals: MMPI Characteristics," *Archives of Sexual Behavior* 9(1981):161–70.

How Men and Women Dream Differently

1. Winget, C., and Kramer, M. *Dimensions of Dreams* (Gainesville, FL: University Presses of Florida, 1979).
2. Jersild, A.; Markey, F.; and Jersild, C. "Children's Fears, Wishes, Daydreams, Likes, Dislikes, Pleasant and Unpleasant Memories," *Child Development Monograph,* no. 12 (1933).
3. Witty, P. A., and Kopel, D. "The Dreams and Wishes of Elementary School Children." *Journal of Educational Psychology* 30(1939):199–205.

4. Gahagan, L. "Sex Differences in Recall of Stereotyped Dreams, Sleep-talking, and Sleep-walking," *Journal of General Psychology* 48(1936):227–36. Demartino, M. "Sex Differences in the Dreams of Southern College Students," *Journal of Clinical Psychology* 9(1953): 199–201.

5. Hall, C., and Van de Castle, R. L. *The Content Analysis of Dreams* (New York: Appleton-Century Crofts, 1966).

6. DeMartino, M. "Some Characteristics of the Manifest Dream Content of Mental Defectives," *Journal of Clinical Psychology* 10(1954):175–78. Paolino, A. "Dreams: Sex Differences in Aggressive Content," *Journal of Projective Techniques* 28(1964):219–26.

7. Griffith, R.; Miyagi, O.; and Tago, A. "The Universality of Typical Dreams: Japanese vs. Americans," *American Anthropologist* 60(1958):1173–79.

8. Hall, C. "A Modest Confirmation of Freud's Theory of a Distinction Between the Super-ego of Men and Women," *Journal of Abnormal and Social Psychology* 69(1964):440–42.

9. Hall, C. "A Ubiquitous Sex Difference in Dreams' Revisited," *Journal of Personality and Social Psychology* 46(1984):1109–17.

10. Freud, S. *The Interpretation of Dreams,* trans. J. Strachey, (1900; reprint ed., New York: Basic Books, 1955).

11. Urbina, S., and Grey, A. "Cultural and Sex Differences in the Sex Distribution of Dream Characters," *Journal of Cross-Cultural Psychology* 6(1975):358–64.

12. Grey, A., and Kalsched, D. "Oedipus East and West: An Exploration via Manifest Dream Content," *Journal of Cross-Cultural Psychology* 2(1971):337–52.

13. Wood, J.; Sebba, D.; and Griswold, R. "Stereotyped Masculine Interests as Related to the Sex of Dream Characters," *Sleep Research* 18(1989):133.

14. Feingold, A. "Cognitive Gender Differences Are Disappearing," *American Psychologist* 43(1988):95–103.

15. Hall, C. et al. "The Dreams of College Men and Women in 1950 and 1980: A Comparison of Dream Contents and Sex Differences," *Sleep* 5(1982):188–94.

16. Kramer, M.; Kinney, L.; and Scharf, M. "Sex Differences in Dreams," *Psychiatric Journal of the University of Ottawa* 8(1983):1–4.

17. Cramer, P. "Fantasies of College Men: Then and Now," *Psychoanalytic Review* 73(1986):163–74.

18. Lortie-Lussier, M.; Schwab, C.; and DeKonnick, J. "Working Mothers vs. Homemakers: Do Dreams Reflect the Changing Roles of Women?" *Sex Roles* 12(1985):1009–21.

19. Krippner, S., and Rubinstein, K., "Gender Differences in Dream Content," *A. S. D. Newsletter,* 7:3(1990):4.

20. Gregor, T. "A Content Analysis of Mehinaku Dreams," *Ethos* 9(1981):352–90.

21. Munroe, R. L. et al. "Sex Differences in East African Dreams," *Journal of Social Psychology* 125(1985):405–06.

22. Freud, *Interpretation of Dreams.*

23. Hendricks, M., and Cartwright, P. "Experience Level in Dreams: An Individual Difference Variable," *Psychotherapy: Theory Research and Practice* 15(1978):3.

24. Foulkes, D. *Children's Dreams* (New York: Wiley, 1981).

25. McHugh, M.; Koeske, R.; and Frieze, I. "Issues to Consider in Conducting Non-Sexist Psychological Research: A Guide for Researchers," *American Psychologist* 41(1986):879–90.

26. Eagly, A. "Reporting Sex Differences," *American Psychologist* 42(1987):756.

27. Baumeister, R. "Should We Stop Studying Sex Differences Altogether? *American Psychologist* 43(1988):1092–95.

Pregnancy and Dreams

1. Van de Castle, R. L., and Kinder, P. "Dream Content During Pregnancy," *Psychophysiology,* 4(1968):375.
2. Maybruck, P. "An Exploratory Study of the Dreams of Pregnant Women," *Dissertation Abstracts International* (University Microfilm, 1986), No. 86–05, 318.
3. Verny, T., and Kelly, J. *The Secret Life of the Unborn Child* (New York: Dell, 1981), pp. 42, 87–88.
4. Stukane, E. *The Dream Worlds of Pregnancy* (New York: Quill, 1985).
5. Garfield, P. *Women's Bodies, Women's Dreams* (New York: Ballantine, 1988), pp. 161–209.
6. Maybruck, P. *Pregnancy and Dreams* (Los Angeles: Jeremy P. Tarcher, 1989).
7. Krippner, S. et al. "An Investigation of Dream Content During Pregnancy," *Journal of the American Society of Psychosomatic Dentistry and Medicine* 21(1974):111–23.
8. Jones, C. "An Exploratory Study of Women's Manifest Dream Content During First Pregnancy," *Dissertation Abstracts International* (University Microfilms, 1978) No. 78–19, 359.
9. Bower, E. "The Pregnant Body," in *The Columbia University College of Physicians and Surgeons Complete Guide to Pregnancy,* ed. F. Talley et al. (New York: Crown, 1989), p. 128; and Margulis, E. "The Pregnant Lifestyle," op. cit., p. 180.
10. Hotchner, T. *Pregnancy and Childbirth* (New York: Avon), pp. 140–53.
11. Karacan, I. et al. "Characteristics of Sleep Patterns During Late Pregnancy and the Postpartum Periods," *American Journal of Obstetrics and Gynecology* 101(1968):579–86. Karacan, I. et al. "Some Implications of the Sleep Patterns of Pregnancy for Postpartum Emotional Disturbance," *British Journal of Psychiatry* 115(1969):929–35.
12. Hartmann, E. *The Nightmare* (New York: Basic Books, 1984), pp. 35–36, 102–109.
13. Krippner, S., and Dillard, J. *Dreamworking* (Buffalo, NY: Bearly, 1988), pp. 1–15, 58, 90, 152.
14. Van de Castle, R. L. *The Psychology of Dreaming* (Morristown, NJ: General Learning Press, 1971).
15. Hartmann, *Nightmare.*
16. Jones, "Exploratory Study . . ."
17. Ballou, J. W. *The Psychology of Pregnancy* (Lexington, MA: Lexington Books, 1978).
18. Leifer, M. *Psychological Effects of Motherhood: A Study of First Pregnancy* (New York: Praeger, 1980).
19. Winget, C., and Kapp, F. T. "The Relationship of the Manifest Content of Dreams to Duration of Childbirth in Primiparae," *Psychoanalytic Medicine* 34(1972):313–20.
20. Bassoff, E. S. "The Pregnant Client: Understanding and Counseling Her," *Personnel and Guidance Journal* 62(1983):20–23, 21.
21. Boss, M. *The Analysis of Dreams* (New York: Philosophy Library, 1958).
22. Van de Castle, *Psychology of Dreaming.*
23. Garfield, *Women's Bodies.*

24. Cheek, D. H. "Significance of Dreams in Initiating Premature Labor," *American Journal of Clinical Hypnosis* 12(1969):5–15.

Women's Body Images Revealed in Dreams

1. Garfield, P. *Women's Bodies, Women's Dreams.* (New York: Ballantine, 1988).
2. *The Random House Dictionary of the English Language,* 2nd ed., unabridged (New York: Random House, 1987).
3. Garfield, *Women's Bodies.*
4. Maderas, L., with Madaras, A. *What's Happening to My Body? A Growing Up Guide for Mothers and Daughters* (New York: Newmarket, 1983).
5. Lamberg, L. *The American Medical Association Guide to Better Sleep* (New York: Random House, 1984).
6. Shuttle, P., and Redgrave, P. *The Wise Wound: Eve's Curse and Everywoman* (New York: Richard Marek, 1978).
7. Van de Castle, R. L. Quoted in C. Winget and M. Kramer, *Dimensions of Dreams* (Gainesville, FL: University Presses of Florida, 1979).
8. Van de Castle, R. L. *The Psychology of Dreaming.* (Morristown, NJ: General Learning Press, 1971).
9. Kinsey, A., et al. *Sexual Behavior in the Human Female* (Philadelphia: W. B. Saunders, 1953).
10. Fisher, C.; Gross, J.; and Zuch, J. "Patterns of Female Sexual Arousal During Sleep and Waking: Vaginal Thermo-conductance Studies," *Archives of Sexual Behavior* 12(1983): 2, 98.
11. Maybruck, P. *Pregnancy and Dreams* (Los Angeles: Jeremy P. Tarcher, 1989).
12. Ibid.
13. Ibid.
14. Ibid.
15. Cutler, W. B.; Garcia, C. R.; and Edwards, D. A., *Menopause* (New York: W. W. Norton, 1983).
16. Thomson, J., and Oswald, I. "Effect of Oestrogen on the Sleep, Mood and Anxiety of Menopausal Women," *British Medical Journal* 2:(1957):317–19.
17. Mankowitz, A. *Change of Life: A Psychological Study of Dreams and the Menopause* (Toronto: Inner City Books, 1984).
18. Spiegel, R. *Sleep and Sleeplessness in Advanced Age* (New York: Spectrum, 1981).
19. Altshuler, K. et al. "A Survey of Dreams in the Aged," *Archives of General Psychiatry* 4(1963):419–24.
20. Garfield, P. "Nightmares in the Sexually Abused Female Teenager." *Psychiatric Journal of the University of Ottawa* 12:2(1987):93–97.
21. Ibid.
22. Breger, L.; Hunter, I.; and Lane, R. *The Effect of Stress on Dreams* (New York: International Universities Press, 1971).
23. Garfield, "Nightmares in the Sexually . . ."

Dreamers Do It in Their Sleep

1. Another approach to this subject was published in *Genesis,* November 1988, pp. 28–31. A second version appeared in *Men's Health,* Fall 1989. Excerpts are adapted from the book manuscript *Moments Outside of Time, the Dream Lives of Sex Addicts and Incest Survivors.*
2. Foulkes, D. *The Psychology of Sleep* (New York: Scribner's, 1966), p. 135.
3. Money, J. "Phantom Orgasms in Dreams of Paraplegic Men and Women," *Archives of General Psychiatry* 3(1960):373–83.
4. Carnes, P. *The Sexual Addiction* (Minneapolis, MN: CompCare Publications, 1983), p. 163.
5. Faraday, A. *The Dream Game* (New York: Harper and Row, 1974), p. 85.
6. Garfield, P. *Creative Dreaming* (New York: Ballantine, 1974), p. 115.
7. Ibid., p. 105.
8. Domhoff, G. W. *The Mystique of Dreams* (Berkeley: University of California Press, 1985), p. 62.
9. Ibid., pp. 24–25.
10. Leveton, A. "The Night Residue," *International Journal of Psychoanalysis* 42(1961):506–16.
11. McLeester, D. "Safe Sex and the Erotic Dream," *Dream Network Bulletin* 7(1988):1–16.
12. Taylor, J. *Dream Work* (New York: Paulist, 1983); p. 151.

Part 5 Introduction

1. Stewart, K. "Dream Theory in Malaya," *Complex* 6:(1951):21–3.
2. Domhoff, G. W. *The Mystique of Dreams: A Search for Utopia through Senoi Dream Theory* (Berkeley: University of California, 1985).
3. Degarrod, L. N. "Coping with Stress: Dream Interpretation in the Mapuche Family" (Paper presented at the 6th Annual Conference of the Association for the Study of Dreams, London, 1989).
4. Van de Castle, R. L. *The Psychology of Dreaming* (Morristown, NJ: General Learning Press, 1971), pp. 3–4.
5. Stevens, A. *Archetypes: A Natural History of the Self* (New York: William Morrow, 1982).
6. Jung, C. G. *The Integration of the Personality* (London: Kegan Paul, 1940).
7. Stevens, *Archetypes,* p. 296
8. Ibid., p. 23.
9. Murdock, G. P., and White, D. R. "Standard Cross Cultural Sample," *Ethnology* 8(1969):329–69.

Historical Perspectives: From Aristotle to Calvin Hall

1. Webb, W. B. "A Historical Perspective on Dreams," in *Handbook of Dreams,* ed. B. B. Wolman (New York: Van Nostrand Reinhold, 1979), pp. 3–19.

2. Aristotle "De Somniis & De Divinatione per Somnum," in *The Works of Aristotle,* vol. 3. ed. W. D. Ross (Oxford, England: Clarendon, 1931), pp. 454–58. Original work written ca. 330 B.C.

3. Ibid., p. 459.

4. Ibid., p. 460.

5. Ibid., p. 463.

6. See note 5 above.

7. Ibid., p. 464.

8. Cicero *De senectute, de amicitia, de divinatione,* trans. W. A. Falconer (Cambridge, MA: Harvard Press, 1923), p. 517. Original work written ca. 40 A.D.

9. Ibid., p. 527.

10. Ibid., pp. 533–35.

11. Dunlop, C. E. M. *Philosophical Essays on Dreaming* (Ithaca, NY: Cornell University Press, 1977).

12. Maritain, J. *The Dreams of Descartes* (New York: Philosophical Library, 1944).

13. Savary, L. M.; Berne, P. H.; and Williams, S. K. *Dreams and Spiritual Growth* (New York: Paulist Press, 1984), p. 39.

14. Kelsey, M. T. *God, Dreams and Revelations* (Minneapolis: Augsburg, 1968), p. 159.

15. Vande Kemp, H. "The Dream in Periodical Literature: 1800–1910," *Journal of the History of the Behavioral Sciences* 17(1981):88–113.

16. Ibid.

17. Freud, S. *The Interpretation of Dreams,* trans. J. Strachey (1900; reprint ed., New York: Avon, 1965).

18. Calkins, M. "Statistics of Dreams," *American Journal of Psychology* 5(1893):311–24.

19. Freud, *Interpretation of Dreams,* p. 36.

20. Hobson, J. A. *The Dreaming Brain* (New York: Basic Books, 1988), pp. 45–46.

21. Lavie, P., and Hobson, J. A. "Origin of Dreams: Anticipation of modern theories in the philosophy of the eighteenth and nineteenth centuries," *Psychological Bulletin* 100 (1986):229–40.

22. Hobson, *Dreaming Brain.*

23. Freud, *Interpretation of Dreams,* p. 128.

24. Parsi, T. "Why Freud Failed: Some Implications for Neurophysiology and Sociobiology," *American Psychologist* 42(1987):235–25.

25. Neilsen, T. "One Century of Dream Research," *Association for the Study of Dreams Newsletter* 2:3(1985):1–3.

26. Aserinsky, E., and Kleitman, N. "Regularly Occurring Periods of Eye Mobility and Concomitant Phenomena During Sleep," *Science* 118(1953):273–74.

27. Winget, C., and Kramer, M. *Dimensions of Dreams* (Gainesville, FL: University of Florida Press, 1978).

28. Hall, C. S. *The Meaning of Dreams* (New York: Harper and Row, 1953).

29. Hall, C. S. "Processes of Fantasy," *Science* 153(1966):626–27.

30. Chase, M., ed., *Sleep Research* (Los Angeles: Brain Research Institute, 1978–82).

31. The core of this historical background has appeared previously in Webb, W. B. "Sleep and Dreaming," in *Topics in the History of Psychology,* ed. G. Kimble and R. Schlesinger (Hillsdale, NJ: Lawrence Erlbaum, 1985), pp. 191–97.

Tribal Shamans and Their Travels into Dreamtime

1. Gilberg, R. "How to Recognize a Shaman Among Other Religious Specialists," in *Shamanism in Eurasia*, ed. M. Hoppal (Gottingen, West Germany: Edition Herodot, 1984), pp. 21–27. Winkelman, M. "A Cross-cultural Study of Magico-religious Practitioners," in *Proceedings of the International Conference on Shamanism*, ed. R. I. Heinze (Berkeley, CA: Independent Scholars of Asia, 1984), pp. 27–28.

2. Halifax, J. *Shaman: The Wounded Healer* (New York: Crossroad, 1982), p. 72.

3. Halifax, *Shaman*.

4. Vastokas, J. M. "The Shamanic Tree of Life," in *Stones, Bones and Skin: Ritual and Shamanic Art*, ed. A. T. Brodzky, R. Danesewich, and N. Johnson (Toronto: Society for Art Publications, 1977), pp. 93–117.

5. Eliade, M. *Shamanism: Archaic Techniques of Ecstasy*, trans. W. Trask (1951; reprint ed., Princeton, NJ: Princeton University Press, 1964).

6. Halifax, *Shaman*, pp. 76–77.

7. Villoldo, A., and Krippner, S. *Healing States* (New York: Fireside, 1987), pp. XI–XIII.

8. Benedict, R. *The Concept of the Guardian Spirit in North America* (Menasha, WI: American Anthropological Association, 1923).

9. Rouget, G. *Music and Trance: A Theory of the Relations between Music and Possession* (Chicago: University of Chicago Press, 1985), p. 126.

10. Peters, L. G., and Price-Williams, D. "Towards an Experiential Analysis of Shamanism," *American Ethnologist* 7(1981):398–418.

11. Topper, M. D. "The Traditional Navajo Medicine Man: Therapist, Counselor, and Community Leader," *Journal of Psychoanalytic Anthropology* 10(1987):217–49.

12. Wallace, A. F. C. "Dreams and the Wishes of the Soul: A Type of Psychoanalytic Theory among the Seventeenth Century Iroquois," *American Anthropologist* 60(1958):234–48.

13. Roheim, G. *The Gates of the Dream* (New York: International Universities Press, 1952), p. 193.

14. Tedlock, B., ed., *Dreaming: Anthropological and Psychological Interpretations* (Cambridge, England: Cambridge University Press, 1987).

15. Duerr, H. P. *Dreamtime: Concerning the Boundary between Wilderness and Civilization* (New York: Basil Blackwell, 1985), p. 67.

16. Devereux, G. *Essai d'Ethnopsychiatrie Generale* (Paris: Gallimard, 1970).

17. Boyer, L. B. et al. "Comparisons of the Shamans and Pseudo-shamans of the Apaches of the Mescalero Indian Reservation: A Rorschach Study," *Journal of Projective Techniques* 28 (1964):173–80.

18. *Diagnostic and Statistical Manual*, 3rd ed. (Washington, DC: American Psychiatric Association, 1980).

19. Noll, R. "Mental Imagery Cultivation as a Cultural Phenomenon: The Role of Visions in Shamanism," *Current Anthropology* 26(1985):443–52.

20. Wilson, S. C. and Barber, T. X. "The Fantasy-prone Personality: Implications for Understanding Imagery, Hypnosis, and Parapsychological Phenomena," in *Imagery: Current Theory, Research, and Application*, ed. A. A. Scheik (New York: John Wiley, 1983), pp. 340–87.

21. Harner, M. "The Way of the Shaman: *The Laughing Man* Interviews Anthropologist and Shaman Michael Harner," *The Laughing Man* 3:4(1981):24–29.

22. Rogers, S. L. *The Shaman: His Symbols and His Healing Power* (Springfield, IL: Thomas, 1982), p. 14.

23. An earlier version of this paper appeared in Krippner, S. "Dreams and Shamanism," in *Shamanism: An Expanded View of Reality,* ed. S. Nicholson (Wheaton, IL: Theosophical Publishing House, 1987), pp. 125–32.

Ancient and Native Peoples' Dreams

1. Lincoln, J. S. *The Dream in Primitive Cultures* (London: Cressett, 1935). Caillois, R., and Von Grunebaum, G. E., eds. *The Dream and Human Societies* (Berkeley: University of California, 1966). Kilborne, B. *Interpretations du reve au Maroc* (Claix, France: La Pensee Sauvage, 1978). Tedlock, B., ed. *Dreaming: Anthropological and Psychological Interpretations* (Cambridge, MA: Cambridge University Press, 1987). These are the four principle works on culture, dreams, and dream interpretation.

2. Hallowell, A. I. *Culture and Experience* (Philadelphia: University of Pennsylvania Press, 1955).

3. Devereux, G. *From Anxiety to Method in the Behavioral Sciences* (The Hague, Netherlands: Mouton, 1967).

4. Kenton, E., ed. *The Indians of North America* (New York: Harper, 1927).

5. Levy-Bruhl, L. *How Natives Think* (1910; reprint ed., Princeton: Princeton University Press, 1985), pp. 56–57.

6. Kenton, *Indians of North America,* p. 57.

7. Mooney, J. *The Ghost Dance Religion and Wounded Knee* (1896; reprint ed., New York: Dover, 1973).

8. Benedict, R. "The Vision in Plains Indian Culture," *American Anthropologist* 24(1922).

9. Durkheim, E. *The Elementary Forms of the Religious Life* (Glencoe, IL: The Free Press, 1947).

10. Lincoln, J. S. *The Dream in Primitive Cultures* (London: Cressett, 1935).

11. Ibid., pp. 24–25.

12. Wallace, W. J. "The Dream in Mohave Life," *Journal of American Folklore* 60(1947):252–58.

13. Devereux, G. "Dream Learning and Individual Ritual Differences in Mohave Shamanism," *American Anthropologist* 59(1957):1036–45.

14. Spier, L. *Yuman Tribes of the Gila River* (Chicago: University of Chicago Press, 1933), p. 326.

15. Ibid., p. 326.

16. Eliade, M. *The Encyclopedia of Religion,* vol. 4 (New York: Macmillan, 1988), p. 202.

17. Park, W. A. *Shamanism in Western North America* (1938; reprint ed., New York: Cooper Square Publishers, 1975).

18. Eliade, M. *Shamanism: Archaic Techniques of Ecstasy,* trans. W. Trask (1951; reprint ed., Princeton: Princeton University Press, 1964).

19. Ibid.

20. Duerr, H. P. *Dreamtime: Concerning the Boundary between Wilderness and Civilization* (1978; reprint ed., New York: Basil Blackwell, 1985), p. 119.

21. Kilborne, B. "Pattern, Structure and Style in Anthropological Studies of Dreams," *Ethos* 9(1981):294–312.

22. O'Flaherty, W. *Dreams, Illusions and Other Realities* (Chicago: University of Chicago Press, 1984).

23. Kilborne, B. "On Classifying Dreams," in *Dreaming: Anthropological and Psychological Interpretations,* ed. B. Tedlock (Cambridge, England: Cambridge University Press, 1987), pp. 171–93.

24. Fahd, T. *La Divination Arabe: Etudes Religieuses, Socioloquies et Folkloriques sur le Milieu Natif de l'Islam* (Leiden, Netherlands: E. J. Brill, 1966).

25. Jones, E. *On the Nightmare* (London: Liverright, 1951), p. 60.

26. Freud, S. *The Interpretation of Dreams,* trans. J. Strachey (1900; reprint ed., London: Hogarth, 1975) p. 9.

Part 6 Introduction

1. Hobson, J. A. *The Dreaming Brain* (New York: Basic Books, 1988).

2. Begley, S. "The Stuff That Dreams Are Made Of" *Newsweek,* 14 August 1989, pp. 41–44.

3. Globus, G. G. *Dream Life, Wake Life* (Albany, NY: State University of New York Press, 1987).

4. Boss, M. *I Dreamt Last Night* . . . (New York: Gardner, 1977), p. 10.

5. Foulkes, D. *Dreaming: A Cognitive-Psychological Analysis* (Hillsdale, NJ: Lawrence Erlbaum, 1985).

6. Ibid., pp. 46–47.

7. Farrell, B. "What Dreams Are Made Of" *New York Review of Books,* 15 June 1989, pp. 28–29.

8. Globus, *Dream Life,* p. 178.

9. Ibid., p. 179

10. Van Eeden, F. W. "A Study of Dreams," in *Altered States of Consciousness: A Book of Readings,* ed. C. T. Tart (New York: John Wiley, 1969), pp. 145–58.

11. Green, C. E. *Lucid Dreams* (Oxford: Institute of Psychophysical Research, 1968).

12. Hall, C. S., and Van de Castle, R. L. *The Content Analysis of Dreams* (New York: Appleton Century Crofts, 1966).

13. Krippner, S.; Ullman, M.; and Honorton, C. "A Precognitive Dream Study with a Single Subject," *Journal of the American Society for Psychical Research* 65(1971):192–203.

14. Krippner, S.; Honorton, C.; and Ullman, M. "A Second Precognitive Dream Study with Malcolm Bessent," *Journal of the American Society for Psychical Research* 66(1974):269–79.

15. Zusne, L., and Jones, W. H. *Anomalistic Psychology: A Study of Extraordinary Phenomena of Behavior and Experience* (Hillsdale, NJ: Lawrence Erlbaum, 1982).

16. Child, I. L. "Psychology and Anomalous Observations: The Question of ESP in Dreams," *American Psychologist* 4(1985):1219–30.

17. Stokes, D. M. "Theoretical Parapsychology," in *Advances in Parapsychological Research,* ed. S. Krippner 5(1987):77–189.

18. Ullman, M. "Dreaming, Altered States of Consciousness and the Problem of Vigilance," *Journal of Nervous and Mental Disease* 133(1961):529–35.

19. Ullman, M.; and Krippner, S.; with Vaughan, A. *Dream Telepathy: Experiments in Nocturnal ESP,* 2nd ed. (Jefferson, NC: McFarland, 1989).

20. McCarley, R. W., and Hobson, J. A. "The Form of Dreams and the Biology of Sleep," in *Handbook of Dreams: Research, Theories and Applications,* ed. B. B. Wolman (New York: Van Nostrand Reinhold, 1979), pp. 76–130.

Dreams and the Brain

1. Hobson, J. A. "What Is a Behavioral State?" in *Aspects of Behavioral Neurobiology,* ed. J. A. Ferrendelli (Bethesda, MD: Society for Neuroscience, 1978), pp. 1–15.

2. McCarley, R. W., and Hoffman, E. "REM Sleep Dreams and the Activation-Synthesis Hypothesis," *American Journal of Psychiatry* 138(1981):7.

3. Hobson, J. A. *The Dreaming Brain* (New York: Basic Books, 1988), p. 255.

4. McCarley and Hoffman, "REM Sleep Dreams."

5. Hobson, J. A.; Lydic, R.; and Baghdoyan, H. A. "Evolving Concepts of Sleep Cycle Generation: From Brain Centers to Neuronal Populations," *Behavioral and Brain Sciences* 9(1986): 371–448.

6. Most of the material in this chapter appeared earlier in Hobson, J. A. "Psychoanalytic Dream Theory: A Critique Based upon Modern Neurophysiology," in *Mind, Psychoanalysis and Science,* ed. P. Clark and C. Wright (Oxford, England: Basil Blackwell, 1988), pp. 277–308. I am grateful to Basil Blackwell for permission to use this material and to Stanley Krippner for his help with editing this chapter.

Traumatic Dreams as an Early Warning of Health Problems

1. Foulkes, D. *A Grammar of Dreams* (New York: Basic Books, 1978); idem., *Dreaming: A Cognitive-Psychological Analysis* (London: Lawrence Erlbaum, 1985). Smith, R. C. "The Meaning of Dreams: A Current Warning Theory," in *Dream Images: A Call to Mental Arms,* ed. J. Gackenbach and A. Sheikh (Farmingdale, NY: Baywood Publishing, 1990).

2. Freud, S. *The Interpretation of Dreams,* trans. J. Strachey (1990; reprint ed., London: Hogarth, 1953).

3. Jones, R. M. *The New Psychology of Dreaming* (New York: Grune and Stratton, 1970).

4. Smith, "The Meaning of Dreams."

5. Smith, R. C. "Evaluating Dream Function: Emphasizing Study of Patients with Organic Disease," in *Cognition and Dream Research,* ed. R. Haskell (New York: Institute of Mind and Behavior, 1986), pp. 267–80.

6. Jones, *New Psychology.*

7. Smith, "Evaluating Dream Function."

8. Foulkes, *Grammar of Dreams* and *Dreaming;* Smith, "Meaning of Dreams."

9. Smith, "Meaning of Dreams" and "Dream Function."

10. See note 9 above.

11. Foulkes, *Grammar* and *Dreaming.*

12. See note 9 above.

13. Ibid.

14. Kramer, M. "The Function of Psychological Dreaming: A Preliminary Analysis," in *Sleep, 1980: Fifth European Congress on Sleep Research* (Basel: Karger, 1981), pp. 182–89.

15. Jones, *New Psychology.*

16. Urbina, S. P. "Methodological Issues in the Quantitative Analysis of Dream Content," *Journal of Personality Assessment* 45(1981):71–78. Webb, S. B., and Cartwright, R. D. "Sleep and Dreams," *Annual Review of Psychology* 29(1978):223–52.

17. Jones, *New Psychology*; Urbina, "Methodological Issues."

18. Smith, "Meaning" and "Evaluating"; idem, "Do Dreams Reflect a Biological State?" *Journal of Nervous and Mental Disease* 147(1987):587–604.

19. *Diagnostic and Statistical Manual of Mental Disorders,* 3rd ed. rev. (Washington, DC: American Psychiatric Association, 1987).

20. Kardiner, A. "The Bioanalysis of the Epileptic Reaction," *Psychoanalytic Quarterly* 1(1933):375–483. Fenichel, O. *The Psychoanalytic Theory of Neurosis* (New York: W. W. Norton, 1972).

21. Hartmann, E. *The Nightmare: The Psychology and Biology of Terrifying Dreams* (New York: Basic Books, 1984).

22. Mayr, E. *The Growth of Biological Thought* (Cambridge, MA: Belknap Press of Harvard University Press, 1982).

23. Jones, *New Psychology.*

24. Ibid.

25. Ibid.

26. Ibid.

27. Ibid.

28. Cohen, D. "Sex Role Orientation and Dream Recall," *Journal of Abnormal Psychology* 82(1973):246–52.

29. See note 9 above.

30. Fenichel, *Psychoanalytic Theory of Neurosis.*

31. Smith, "Meaning of Dreams."

32. See note 11 above.

33. Smith, "Meaning of Dreams."

34. Mayr, *Growth of Biological Thought.*

35. Jones, *New Psychology.*

36. See note 30 above.

37. Kardiner, "Bioanalysis." Kolb, L. C. "A Neuropsychological Hypothesis Explaining Post-traumatic Stress Disorders," *American Journal of Psychiatry* 144(1987):989–95.

38. Kohut, H. *The Restoration of the Self* (New York: International Universities Press, 1977).

39. Smith, "Meaning of Dreams."

40. Ibid.

41. Ibid.

42. See note 11 above.

43. Hobson, J. A., and McCarley, R. W. "The Brain as a Dream State Generator: An activation-synthesis Hypothesis," *American Journal of Psychiatry* 134(1977):1335–48.

44. Crick, F., and Mitchison, G. "The Function of Dream Sleep," *Nature* 304(1983):111–14.

Nightmares: Terrors of the Night

1. Freud, S. *The Interpretation of Dreams,* trans. J. Strachey (1900; revised ed., London: Hogarth, 1953).
2. Freud, S. *Beyond the Pleasure Principle.* (1920; revised ed., London: Hogarth, 1955). Original work published 1920.
3. Lidz, T. "Nightmares and the Combat Neuroses," *Psychiatry* 9(1946):37–49.
4. Anzieu, D. *Freud's Self-Analysis* (Madison, CT: International Universities Press, 1986).
5. Rosenfield, E. M. "Dreams and Vision: Some Remarks on Freud's Egyptian Bird Dream," *The International Journal of Psycho-Analysis* 37(1956):97–105.
6. Freud, *Interpretation of Dreams.*
7. Grinstein, A. *Sigmund Freud's Dreams* (New York: International Universities Press, 1980).
8. Jung, C. G. *Memories, Dreams, Reflections* (London: Random House, 1961), pp. 11–12.
9. Aserinsky, E. "Discussion of Somnambulism," *Research Publications of the Association of Nervous and Mental Disease* 45(1967):448–455.
10. Broughton, R. "Sleep Disorders: Disorders of Arousal? *Science* 159(1968):1070–78. Fisher, C. et al. "A Psychophysiological Study of Nightmares." *Journal of the American Psychoanalytic Association* 18(1970):747–82.
11. Broughton, "Sleep Disorders."
12. Fisher, C. et al. "A Psychophysiological Study of Nightmares and Night Terrors. III. Mental Content and Recall of Stage 4 Night Terrors," *The Journal of Nervous and Mental Disease* 15(1970):174–89.
13. Hartmann, E. *The Nightmare: The Psychology and Biology of Terrifying Dreams* (New York: Basic Books, 1984).
14. Hartmann, E.; Greenwald, D.; and Brune, P. "Night Terrors-Sleep Walking: Personality Characteristics," *Sleep Research* 11(1982):121. Hartmann, E. et al. "Who Has Nightmares? The Personality of the Lifelong Nightmare Sufferer," *Archives of General Psychiatry* 44(1987):49–56
15. Gastaut, H., and Broughton, R. "A Clinical and Polygraphic Study of Episodic Phenomena During Sleep." *Recent Advances in Biological Psychiatry* 7(1964):197–221.
16. Schlosberg, A., and Benjamin, M. "Sleep Patterns in Three Acute Combat Fatigue Cases," *Journal of Clinical Psychiatry* 39(1978):546–49.
17. Mack, J. E. *Nightmares and Human Conflict* (Boston: Little, Brown, 1970).
18. Feldman, M. J., and Hersen, M. "Attitudes Toward Death in Nightmare Subjects," *Journal of Abnormal Psychology* 72(1967):421–25. Bixler, E. O. et al. "Prevalence of Sleep Disorders in the Los Angeles Metropolitan Area," *American Journal of Psychiatry* 136(1979):1257–62.
19. Fischer, "Psychological Study."
20. Ibid.
21. Forster, F. M. "Comparison of Auras and Triggering Factors in Epilepsy," *Pavlovian Journal of Biological Science* 13(1978):206–10.
22. Sacks, O. W. *Awakenings* (Garden City, NY: Doubleday, 1974).
23. Mack, *Nightmares and Human Conflict.*
24. Hartmann, E. et al. "A Preliminary Study of the Personality of the Nightmare Sufferer: Relationship to Schizophrenia and Creativity?" *American Journal of Psychiatry* 138(1981): 794–97.

25. Hartmann, E. et al. "Who Has Nightmares? Persons with Lifelong Nightmares Compared with Vivid Dreamers and Non-vivid Dreamers," *Sleep Research* 10(1981):171.

26. Hartmann, E. et al. "The Biochemistry of the Nightmare: Possible Involvement of Dopamine," *Sleep Research* 7(1978):186.

27. Ibid.

28. Halliday, G. "Direct Psychological Therapies for Nightmares: A Review," *Clinical Psychology Review* 7(1987):501–23.

29. Garfield, P. *Your Child's Dream* (New York: Ballantine, 1984).

30. Wiseman, A. S. *Nightmare Help: A Guide for Parents and Teachers* (Berkeley: Ten Speed, 1989).

31. Tholey, P. "A Model for Lucidity Training as a Means of Self-Healing and Psychological Growth," in *Conscious Mind, Sleeping Brain,* ed. J. I. Gackenbach and S. La Berge (New York: Plenum, 1988), pp.263–90.

32. Dane, J. "A Comparison of Waking Instructions and Post-hypnotic Suggestion for Lucid Dream Induction," (University Microfilms International, 1985), No. 85–03, 800. Brylowski, A. "Clinical Applications of Lucid Dreaming," (Paper presented at the Annual Conference of the Association for the Study of Dreams, London, England, July 1989.)

33. Tart, C. "From Spontaneous Event to Lucidity: A Review of Attempts to Consciously Control Nocturnal Dreaming, in *Handbook of Dreams: Research, Theories, and Applications,* ed. B. B. Wolman (New York: Van Nostrand Reinhold, 1979), pp. 226–68. Garfield, P. "Banishing Nightmares." Audio cassette. (Available from Proseminar, 77 Vanderwater St., San Francisco, CA 94133). Worsley, A. "Dream Lucidity Induction and Control," *Lucidity Letter* 7:1(1988):44.

34. Gackenbach, J., and Bosveld, J. *Control Your Dreams* (New York: Harper and Row, 1989).

35. LaBerge, S. *Lucid Dreaming: The Power of Being Awake and Aware in Your Dreams* (Los Angeles: Jeremy P. Tarcher, 1985).

36. Dane, "Comparison of Waking Instructions."

37. Belicki, K. and Belicki, D. "Predisposition for Nightmares: A Study of Hypnotic Ability, Vividness of Imagery, and Absorption," *Journal of Clinical Psychology* 42(1986):714–18.

38. Galvin, F. "The Boundary Characteristics of Lucid Dreamers" (Paper presented at the Annual Conference of the Association for the Study of Dreams, London, England, July 1989.)

39. Brylowski, "Clinical Applications of Lucid Dreaming."

40. Ibid.

41. Rosenfield, "Dreams and Vision."

Women and Meditators as Gifted Lucid Dreamers

1. Hunt, H. T. *The Multiplicity of Dreams: A Cognitive Psychological Perspective* (New Haven, CT: Yale University Press, 1989).

2. Alexander, C. N.; Boyer, R.; and Alexander, V. "Higher States of Consciousness in the Vedic Psychology of Maharishi Mahesh Yogi: A Theoretical Introduction and Research Review," *Modern Science and Vedic Science* 1:1(1987):89–126.

3. Snyder, T. J., and Gackenbach. J. I. "Individual Differences Associated with Lucid Dreaming," in *Conscious Mind, Sleeping Brain: Perspectives on Lucid Dreaming,* ed. J. I. Gackenbach and S. L. LaBerge (New York: Plenum, 1988), pp. 221–59.

4. Gackenbach, J. I., and Bosveld, J. *Control Your Dreams* (New York: Harper and Row, 1989).

5. Gackenbach, J. I.; Cranson, R.; and Alexander, C. "Lucid Dreaming, Witnessing Dreaming, and the Transcendental Meditation Technique: A Developmental Relationship," *Lucidity Letter* 5:2(1986):34–40.

6. Kesterson, J. "Respiratory Control During Transcendental Meditation" Maharishi International University, Fairfield, IA, 1985.

7. Brylowski, A. "H-reflex in Lucid Dreams," *Lucidity Letter* 5:1(1986):116–18.

8. Dillbeck, M. C.; Orme-Johnson, D. W.; and Wallace, R. K. "Frontal EEG Coherence, H-Reflex Recovery, Concept Learning, and the TM-Sidhi Program," *International Journal of Neuroscience* 15(1981):151–57.

9. Hunt, H. T., and Ogilvie, R. "Lucid Dreams in Their Natural Series," in *Conscious Mind, Sleeping Brain: Perspectives on Lucid Dreaming,* ed. J. I. Gackenbach and S. L. LaBerge, (New York: Plenum Press, 1988), pp. 389–417.

10. F. Travis to J. I. Gackenbach, July 1989.

11. West. M. A. "Meditation and the EEG," *Physiological Medicine* 10(1980):369–75.

12. Chopra, D. *Return of the Rishi* (New York: Bantam, 1988), p. 103.

13. Farrow, J. T., and Herbert, J. R. "Breath Suspension During the Transcendental Meditation Technique," *Psychosomatic Medicine* 44(1982):133–53.

14. Orme-Johnson, D. W., and Haynes, C. T. "EEG Phase Coherence, Pure Consciousness, Creativity, and TM-Sidhi Experiences," *Neuroscience* 13(1981):211–17.

15. Armitage, R.; Hoffmann, R.; and Moffitt, A. "Interhemispheric EEG Activity in Sleep and Wakefulness: Individual Differences in the Basic Rest-Activity Cycle (BRAC)," in *The Mind in Sleep,* vol. 2, ed. J. Antrobus (Hilldale, NJ: Lawrence Erlbaum, 1990).

16. Snyder and Gackenbach, "Individual Differences."

17. O'Connor, K. P., and Shaw, J. C. "Comment on Zoccolotti's Field Dependence, Laterality and the EEG: A Reanalysis of O'Connor and Shaw," *Biological Psychology* 15(1982):29–13.

18. Flor-Henry, P.; Koles, Z. J.; and Reddon, J. R; "Age and Sex Related EEG Configurations in Normal Subjects," in *Individual Differences in Hemispheric Specialization,* ed. A. Glass (New York: Plenum, 1987), p. 150.

19. Restak, R. *The Brain* (New York: Bantam, 1984), p. 244.

20. Flor-Henry, Koles, and Reddon, "Age and Sex Related," p. 135.

21. Wallace, R. K. *The Maharishi Technology of the United Field: The Neurophysiology of Enlightenment* (Fairfield, IA: Maharishi International University Press, 1986).

22. Gackenbach, J. I.; Walling, J.; and LaBerge, S. "The Lucid Dreaming Ability and Parasympathetic Functioning," *Lucidity Letter* 3:4(1984):101.

23. Gackenbach, J. I. et al. "Intelligence, Creativity, and Personality Differences Between Individuals Who Vary in Self-reported Lucid Dreaming," *Lucidity Letter,* 2:2(1983):52.

24. Gackenbach, J. I. "Sex Differences in Lucid Dreaming Self-Reported Frequency: A Second Look," *Lucidity Letter* 4(1981):127.

25. Orme-Johnson, D. et al. "Activities that Promote Brain Coherence," in *Scientific Research on the Transcendental Meditation . . . Programme,* ed. R. Chalmers et al., vol. 4 (Vlodrop, Netherlands: M.I.U. Press, 1990.)

26. Hunt, *Multiplicity of Dreams*.
27. See note 16 above.
28. Gackenbach, J. I. et al. "Lucid Dreaming: Individual Differences in Perception," *Sleep Research* 10(1981):146.

Shared Dreaming: Joining Together in Dreamtime

1. Reed, H. "Dreaming for Your Neighbor," *The Omni WholeMind Newsletter* November 1988, p. 7.
2. Ullman, M. "Dream, Metaphor, and PI" *Research in Parapsychology 1983*, ed. R. A. White and R. S. Broughton (Metuchen, NJ: Scarecrow, 1984), pp. 138–52; idem, "PI Communication Through Dream Sharing," in *Communication and Parapsychology*, ed. B. Shapin and L. Coly (New York: Parapsychology Foundation, 1971) pp. 83–97.
3. Ullman, M.; Krippner, S.; and Vaughan, A. *Dream Telepathy*, 2nd ed. (Jefferson, NC: McFarand, 1989).
4. Van de Castle, R. L. "The D.N.B. Telepathy Project," in *Dream Network Bulletin* (1986):4–7.
5. Campbell, J. "Beyond Dreaming," in *Dream Network Bulletin/Dream Craft* 2(1983):1–2.
6. Magallón, L. "The Lucidity Project: An Experiment in Group Dreaming," in *Dream Network Bulletin* 4(1985):10–11.
7. Shor, B. "Shared Dreaming," in *Dream Network Bulletin* 7(1988):14–15.
8. Upton, C. "Dream Bridge Complete," in *Dream Network Bulletin* 7(1988):5.
9. Campbell, J. *Dreams Beyond Dreaming* (Virginia Beach, VA: Donning, 1980), pp. 106–20.
10. Castaneda, C. *The Eagle's Gift* (New York: Simon & Schuster, 1981).
11. Fox, O. *Astral Projection* (Secaucus, NJ: Citadel Press, 1980), p. 47.
12. Roberts, *Psychic Politics* (Englewood Cliffs, NJ: Prentice Hall, 1976), pp. 208–21.
13. Watkins, S. *Conversations With Seth, Volume Two* (Englewood Cliffs, NJ: Prentice Hall, 1981), pp. 366–407.
14. Hart, H. "Reciprocal Dreams," *Proceedings of the Society for Psychical Research* 41(1933): 234–40.
15. Donahoe, J. J. "Shared Dreams," *Dream Network Bulletin* 1(1982):1, 6.
16. Faraday, A. *The Dream Game* (New York: Harper and Row, 1974), pp. 327–36.
17. Taub-Bynum, E. B. *The Family Unconscious* (Wheaton, IL: Theosophical, 1904).
18. Shor, B. "Future Tech: Shared Dreaming." *Dream Network Bulletin* 7(1988):19.
19. Ibid.
20. Magallón, L. "Mutual Lucid Dreaming," *Lucidity Letter*, (1990).
21. Magallón, L. "Telepathic and Group Dreaming: Some Considerations of Process and Analysis" (Paper presented at 5th Annual ASD Conference, Santa Cruz, CA.)
22. For more information on mutual dream research and ongoing projects, contact Linda Magallón, 1083 Harvest Meadow Court, San Jose, CA 95136; or Barbara Shor, c/o Dreamgates, P.O. Box 20219, Cathedral Finance Station, New York, NY 10025-1511.
23. Lessing, D. *The Making of the Representative for Planet Eight* (New York: Vintage Books, 1983).

The Puzzle of Psychic Dreams

1. Hobson, J. A. *The Dreaming Brain* (New York: Basic Books, 1988).

2. Freud, S. *The Interpretation of Dreams,* trans. J. Strachey (1900; reprint ed., London: Hogarth Press, 1953), p. 563.

3. Ansbacher, H., and Ansbacher, L. *The Individual Psychology of Alfred Adler* (New York: Basic Books, 1956).

4. Ullman, M. "The Experiential Dream Group," in *Handbook of Dreams: Research, Theories and Applications,* ed. B. B. Wolman (New York: Van Nostrand Reinhold, 1979), pp. 406–23.

5. Kramer, M. "The Psychology of the Dream: Art or Science?" *Psychiatric Journal of the University of Ottawa* 7:2(1982):187–200.

6. Rhine, L. E. *Hidden Channels of the Mind* (New York: William Sloane, 1961), pp. 115–30.

7. Tolaas, J. "Vigilance Theory and Psi. Part 1. Ethnological and phylogenetic aspects," *Journal of the American Society for Psychical Research* 80(1986):357–73.

8. Rhine, *Hidden Channels,* p. 132.

9. Tolaas, "Vigilance Theory and Psi."

10. Persinger, M. A. "Psi Phenomena and Temporal Lobe Activity . . .," in *Research in Parapsychology 1988,* ed. L. A. Henkel and R. E. Berger (Metuchen, NJ: Scarecrow, 1989), pp. 121–56.

11. Ullman, "Experiential Dream Group."

12. Meddis, R. "On the Function of Sleep. *Animal Behavior* 23(1975):676–91.

13. Horne, J. *Why We Sleep* (Oxford: Oxford University Press, 1988).

14. Hobson, *Dreaming Brain.*

15. West, K. L. "Dream Incubation for Eyesight Improvement." *Sundance Community Dream Journal* 3:1(1979):91–97.

16. Berger, R. J. "Experimental Modification of Dream Content by Meaningful Verbal Stimuli." *British Journal of Psychology* 109(1963):722–40.

17. Tolaas, J. "REM Sleep and the Concept of Vigilance." *Biological Psychology* 13(1978):7–31.

18. Persinger, M. A. "Geophysical Models for Parapsychological Experiences." *Psychoenergetic Systems* 1(1975):63–74.

19. Hobson, *Dreaming Brain.*

20. Persinger, "Psi Phenomena."

21. Persinger, M. A., and Krippner, S. "Dream ESP Experiments and Geomagnetic Activity." *Journal of the American Society for Psychical Research* 83(1989):101–16.

Suggested Readings

Perhaps your appetite has been whetted and you would like to know more about dreams and dreamworking. Here are fifteen of my favorite books for the general reader, as well as twenty books that are more academic in nature. It has been difficult to make a judicious selection from the dozens of volumes in bookstores and the hundreds of books in the libraries.

I have eliminated such obvious classics as Sigmund Freud's *The Interpretation of Dreams,* originally published in 1899 (although Freud's publisher placed a 1900 publication date on the volume, being so convinced of the book's importance that he wanted to greet the new century with its explosive contents. Alas, the book sold only 351 copies during its first six years in print.) I also have left out some excellent books that are difficult to locate, such as the 1974 anthology *The New World of Dreams,* edited by J. L. Woods and H. B. Greenhouse, which presents a more comprehensive mosaic of dream life than anything published before or since.

I have listed only books published since 1979. I have not included such splendid works as *The Clinical Use of Dreams* by Walter Bonime, *Night Life* by Rosalynd Cartwright, *The Dream Game* by Ann Faraday, and *The New Psychology of Dreaming* by Richard Jones. So, within the space limitations of this appendix and leaving out my own work, I would like to introduce you to these titles.

Books for the General Reader

Bosnak, R. *A Little Course in Dreams: A Basic Handbook of Jungian Dreamwork.* Boston: Shambhala, 1988.

Constable, G., ed. *Dreams and Dreaming.* Alexandria, VA: Time–Life Books, 1990.

Delaney, G. *Living Your Dreams: Using Sleep to Solve Problems and Enrich Your Life,* rev. ed. San Francisco: Harper and Row, 1988.

Domhoff, G. W. *The Mystique of Dreams: A Search for Utopia through Senoi Dream Theory.* Berkeley: University of California Press, 1985.

Garfield, P. *Women's Bodies, Women's Dreams.* New York: Ballantine, 1988.

Gendlin, E. T. *Let Your Body Interpret Your Dreams.* Wilmette, IL: Ciron, 1986.

LeBerge, S. *Lucid Dreaming: The Power of Being Awake and Aware in Your Dreams.* Los Angeles: Jeremy P. Tarcher, 1985.

Maguire, J. *Night and Day: Use the Power of Your Dreams to Transform Your Life.* New York: Fireside/Simon and Schuster, 1989.

Maybruck, P. *Pregnancy and Dreams.* Los Angeles: Jeremy P. Tarcher, 1989.

Morris, J. *The Dream Workbook: Discover the Knowledge and Power Hidden in Your Dreams.* Boston: Little, Brown, 1985.

Reed, H. *Getting Help from Your Dreams: Understand and Enjoy Your Dreams in Creative New Ways!* Virginia Beach, VA: Inner Vision, 1985.

Savary, L. M.; Berne, P. H.; and Williams, S. K. *Dreams and Spiritual Growth: A Christian Approach to Dreamwork.* New York: Paulist Press, 1984.

Thurston, M. *Dreams: Tonight's Answers for Tomorrow's Questions.* San Francisco: Harper and Row, 1988.

Ullman, M., and Limmer, C., eds. *The Variety of Dream Experience: Expanding Our Ways of Working with Dreams.* New York: Continuum, 1987.

Ullman, M., and Zimmerman, N. *Working with Dreams: Self-Understanding, Problem-Solving, and Enriched Creativity through Dream Appreciation.* Los Angeles: Jeremy P. Tarcher, 1979.

Additional References

Almansi, G., and Begun, C. *Theatre of Sleep: An Anthology of Literary Dreams.* London: Pan Books, 1986.

Edel, L. *Stuff of Sleep and Dreams: Experiments in Literary Psychology.* New York: Harper and Row, 1982.

Foulkes, D. *Dreaming: A Cognitive-Psychological Analysis.* Hillsdale, NJ: Lawrence Erlbaum, 1985.

French, T. M., and Fromm, E. *Dream Interpretation: A New Approach.* Madison, WI: International Universities Press, 1986.

Gackenbach, J. I., and Sheikh, A. A. *Dream Images: A Call to Mental Arms.* New York: Plenum Press, 1990.

Gackenbach, J. I., and LaBerge, S., eds. *Conscious Mind, Sleeping Brain: Perspectives on Lucid Dreaming.* New York: Plenum Press, 1988.

Globus, G. *Dream Life, Wake Life: The Human Condition through Dreams.* Albany: State University of New York Press, 1987.

Haskell, R. E., ed. *Cognition and Dream Research.* New York: Journal of Mind and Behavior, 1986.

Hartmann, E. *The Nightmare: The Psychology and Biology of Terrifying Dreams.* New York: Basic Books, 1984.

Hobson, J. A. *The Dreaming Brain.* New York: Basic Books, 1988.

Hunt, H. H. *The Multiplicity of Dreams: A Cognitive Psychological Approach.* New Haven: Yale University Press, 1989.

Mahrer, A. R. *Dream Work in Psychotherapy and Self-Change.* New York: W. W. Norton, 1989.

Mavromatis, A. *Hypnagogia: The Unique State of Consciousness between Wakefulness and Sleep.* New York: Routledge and Kegan Paul, 1987.

Mindell, A. *Working with the Dreaming Body.* Boston: Routledge and Kegan Paul, 1985.

Parsifal-Jones, N. *The Dream: 4,000 Years of Theory and Practice. A Critical, Descriptive, and Encyclopedic Bibliography.* West Cornwall, CT: Locust Hill, 1986.

Piotrowski, Z. A., with Biele, A. M. *Dreams: A Key to Self-Knowledge.* Hillside, NY: Lawrence Erlbaum, 1986.

Robbins, P. R. *The Psychology of Dreams.* Jefferson, NC: McFarland, 1988.

Tedlock. B., ed. *Dreaming: Anthropological and Psychological Interpretations.* New York: Cambridge University Press, 1987.

von Franz, M.-L. *On Dreams and Death: A Jungian Interpretation.* Boston: Shambhala, 1986.

Wolman, B. B., ed. *Handbook of Dreams: Research, Theories and Applications.* New York: Van Nostrand Reinhold, 1979.

Contributors

Kenneth Atchity, Ph.D., President of Atchity Entertainment International, is former Professor of Comparative Literature at Occidental College in Los Angeles and co-editor of *Dreamwork* magazine. His books include *A Writer's Time: A Guide to the Creative Process* and *From Vision Through Revision.*

Vincent Atchity, B.A., is a doctoral student in comparative literature at the University of Southern California.

Fariba Bogzaran, M.A., is an expressive dream artist and Program Advisor for the Arts and Creativity Studies at the California Institute of Integral Studies in San Francisco. She is co-founder of Dream Creations and has created numerous drawings, paintings, and other artistic products from her dreams.

P. Erik Craig, Ed.D., directs the Center for Existential Studies and Human Services, Worcester and Cambridge, Massachusetts. He is the editor of *Psychotherapy for Freedom: The Daseinsanalytic Way in Psychology and Psychoanalysis.*

Gayle Delaney, Ph.D., Founding President of the Association for the Study of Dreams and director of the Delaney and Flowers Center for the Study of Dreams in San Francisco, is the author of *Living Your Dreams* and *The Hidden Language of the Heart.*

David Feinstein, Ph.D., a clinical psychologist and currently the Director of Innersource in Ashland, Oregon, has taught at The Johns Hopkins University School of Medicine, Antioch College, and the California School of Professional Psychology. He is co-author of *Personal Mythology: The Psychology of Your Evolving Self* and *Rituals for Living and Dying: A Guide to Spiritual Awakening.*

Jayne I. Gackenbach, Ph.D., is a former president of the Association for the Study of Dreams and Executive Director of the Lucidity Association. She is editor of *Sleep and Dreams: A Sourcebook,* co-editor of *Conscious Mind, Sleeping Brain: Perspectives on Lucid Dreaming,* co-editor of *Dream Imagery: A Call to Mental Arms,* and co-author of *Control Your Dreams.*

Franklin Galvin is a doctoral candidate in Clinical Psychology at Boston University, conducting research at the Lemuel Shattuck Hospital Sleep Laboratory. He is also an intern at Westborough State Hospital in Westborough, Massachusetts. For three years he was a Peace Corps volunteer in Iran, working as an architect and city planner.

Patricia Garfield, Ph.D., a consultant on dreams in San Francisco, is the author of *Creative Dreaming* and one of the co-founders of the Association for the Study of Dreams. She also wrote *Pathway to Ecstasy: The Way of the Dream Mandala, Your Child's Dreams,* and *Women's Bodies, Women's Dreams.*

Ernest Hartmann, M.D., is Professor of Psychiatry, Tufts University School of Medicine; Senior Psychiatrist and Director of the Sleep Research Laboratory, West-Ros-Park Mental Health Center at Lemuel Shattuck Hospital, Boston; and Director of the Sleep Disorders Center, Newton-Wellesley Hospital, Newton, Massachusetts. He is the author of, among other works, *The Biology of Dreaming, The Sleeping Pill,* and numerous scientific articles.

Deborah Jay Hillman, Ph.D., is a cultural anthropologist with a special interest in dreams. She has investigated and participated in dream groups in New York City and has contributed a chapter to the anthology *The Variety of Dream Experience.*

J. Allan Hobson, M.D., Professor of Psychiatry, Harvard Medical School, Boston, is director of the Laboratory of Neurophysiology at the Massachusetts Mental Health Center. He is the author of *The Dreaming Brain* and *Sleep.*

Benjamin Kilborne, Ph.D., is the author of *Interpretation of Dreams in Morocco,* and has contributed the article "Dreams" to the Macmillan Encyclopedia of Religion. He has taught history and anthropology at a number of universities both in France and in the U.S., and is a practicing psychoanalyst in Los Angeles.

Stanley Krippner, Ph.D., Professor of Psychology, Saybrook Institute, San Francisco, is former Director of the Dream Laboratory, Maimonides Medical Center, Brooklyn. He is co-author of *Dreamworking, Dream Telepathy, Personal Mythology,* and *Healing States.*

Linda Lane Magallón, M.B.A., is a dream educator and researcher in lucidity and anomalous dreams. A co-founder of the Bay Area Professional Dream-workers Group, she is the former publisher and editor of the *Dream Network Journal.*

Alvin R. Mahrer, Ph.D., Professor of Psychology at the University of Ottawa in Canada, is the author of ten books and over 100 articles on experiential psychotherapy, the experiential theory of human beings, and psychotherapy research. His most recent book is *Dream Work in Psychotherapy and Self-Change.*

Patricia Maybruck, Ph.D., received her doctorate in psychology from Saybrook Institute, San Francisco, for her in-depth exploratory study of more than 1,000 dreams of pregnant women. She is Director of the Neonatal Obstetrical Research of America, Inc., a nonprofit organization, and author of *Pregnancy and Dreams* and *Romantic Dreams.*

Karen Surman Paley, M.Ed., is a licensed certified social worker and a Massachusetts state-certified alcoholism counselor. Formerly in private practice, she now works as a freelance magazine writer, popularizing mental-health issues, especially those relating to addiction and recovery.

Kenneth Rubinstein, M.A., is teaching in Vermont and conducting research on the subject of dreams and gender differences. He received his master's degree in clinical psychology from the University of Michigan.

Louis M. Savary, S.T.D., Ph.D., serves on the adjunct faculty of six universities, where he teaches courses on spirituality and religious studies. An expert on the Judeo-Christian dreamwork tradition, he has co-authored *The Sleep Book* and *Dreams and Spiritual Growth.*

Wynn Schwartz, Ph.D., teaches at Harvard Medical School at The Cambridge Hospital and also at the Boston Psychoanalytic Society and Institute. He maintains a private practice in Boston.

Barbara Shor is a professional writer, dreamworker, and consulting editor for several major publishing houses. For over a decade she has directed the Dreamgates Communities, written and lectured on dreams, and given dream workshops at the New York Open Center and the annual conventions of the Association for the Study of Dreams, as well as other locations across the country.

June Singer, Ph.D., is a Jungian analyst in Palo Alto, California. She is the author of *Seeing Through the Visible World: Jung, Gnosis, and Chaos; Boundaries of the Soul; The Unholy Bible;* and *Androgyny,* and is co-author of the *Singer-Loomis Inventory of Personality.*

Robert C. Smith, M.D., is Associate Professor of Internal Medicine and Psychiatry at the Michigan State University College of Human Medicine. His interests are teaching and research in the context of a biopsychosocial model of health and disease.

Jon Tolaas, Professor at Eid vidg. skule, Nordfjordeid, Norway, is the author of several articles, book chapters, and three books in Norwegian on various aspects of dreams. His most recent work is a doctoral thesis on the Norse conception of dreaming.

Montague Ullman, M.D., is Clinical Professor Psychiatry Emeritus, Albert Einstein College of Medicine, New York City. He is the co-author of *Dream Telepathy* and *Working with Dreams,* and co-editor of the *The Variety of Dream Experience* and *Handbook of States of Consciousness.*

Wilse B. Webb, Ph.D., Graduate Research Professor Emeritus, University of Florida, Gainesville, is former director of the Sleep Laboratory at the university. He has written, edited, or co-edited eight books, thirty-five chapters, and over 200 papers on sleep research.

Adam Zwig, M.A., is a teacher, trainer, and therapist at the Center for Process-oriented Psychology in Oregon. He is a student and colleague of Arnold Mindell, founder of process-oriented psychology, and is a doctoral candidate at Saybrook Institute, San Francisco.

About the Editor

Stanley Krippner, Ph.D., is a professor of psychology at Saybrook Institute in San Francisco and former director of the Dream Laboratory at Maimonides Medical Center, Brooklyn. In a dozen volumes and more than 700 articles, he has investigated developments in consciousness research, education, and healing. Krippner has served as president of the Association for Humanistic Psychology, the Parapsychological Association, and the American Psychological Association's Division of Humanistic Psychology. He is a Fellow of the American Psychological Association, the American Psychological Society, the American Society of Clinical Hypnosis, and the Society for the Scientific Study of Sex.

New Consciousness Reader Series

Dreamtime and Dreamwork. The definitive book on the worldwide use of dreams as a special source of knowledge, dream interpretation, problem solving and healing through dreams, shared dreaming, lucid dreaming, forming dream groups, and new brain research. $12.95 Tradepaper, 272 pages

Healers on Healing. Reveals the common thread that unites healers from a wide range of approaches and techniques. Thirty-seven original essays by leading physicians, therapists, and writers in alternative and mainstream healthcare. Over 35,000 copies in print. $10.95 Tradepaper, 224 pages

Reclaiming the Inner Child. The best writing on the most current topic in psychology and recovery by the world's leading experts. Thirty-seven wide-ranging articles offer a comprehensive overview of the inner-child concept and its application to healing, creativity, and daily joy. Highlights many applications for people in all forms of recovery. $12.95 Tradepaper, 336 pages

Spiritual Emergency. Leading experts explore the relationship between spirituality, madness, and healing. Edited by Stan and Christina Grof, this ground-breaking work reveals that within the crisis of spiritual emergency lies the promise of spiritual emergence and renewal. $12.95 Tradepaper, 272 pages

To Be a Woman. A striking collection of original writing by the best-selling authorities in women's psychology. In twenty-three essays this book reveals the next stage of development in women's awareness: conscious femininity. For all women who long to feel strong, yet fully feminine. $12.95 Tradepaper, 288 pages

What Survives? This thought-provoking collection of twenty new essays examines emerging evidence and developments in the fields of parapsychology, near-death studies, consciousness research, new-paradigm biology, and physics, helping the reader to arrive at an optimistic, yet informed and rational, answer to the question "what survives the body after death?" $12.95 Tradepaper, 304 pages